D0338591

CONGREGATIONS IN AMERICA

Congregations
in America

❧ *Mark Chaves* ❧

HARVARD UNIVERSITY PRESS

Cambridge, Massachusetts
London, England

2004

Library of Congress Cataloging-in-Publication Data

Chaves, Mark.
Congregations in America / Mark Chaves.
p.   cm.
Includes bibliographical references and index.
ISBN 0-674-01284-4 (alk. paper)
1. Religious institutions—United States.
2. United States—Religion—20th century.
I. Title.

BL2525.C445 2004
206'.5'097309049—dc22   2003068817

For Christopher

Contents

Acknowledgments

In this book I draw on many kinds of evidence, from varied sources, to examine religious congregations in the United States. The most important evidence, however, comes from the National Congregations Study (NCS). The NCS progressed remarkably quickly from gleam in my eye to reality, thanks to the people and institutions who supported it from its inception. Michael Hout, who was chairing the committee charged with designing a religion module for the 1998 General Social Survey, embraced my proposal to use a few minutes of the module to generate a nationally representative sample of congregations. Chris Coble, at the Lilly Endowment, saw the project's potential and shepherded it through two major grants from the Endowment. Tom Smith, at the National Opinion Research Center (NORC), helped integrate the NCS into the 1998 General Social Survey. William Bridges, R. Stephen Warner, and the sociology faculty at the University of Illinois–Chicago provided a home for me and for the NCS in 1997–98. A five-minute conversation with Elizabeth Boris of the Urban Institute led to two additional grants, one from the Smith Richardson Foundation (expedited by Phoebe Cottingham) and one from the Nonprofit Sector Research Fund at the Aspen Institute (expedited by Alan Abramson). The Louisville Institute and the Henry Luce Foundation also supported the NCS. The former grant was expedited by Jim Lewis, the latter was facilitated by Peter Marsden. Each of these people and institutions was individually necessary, and collectively they were sufficient, to bring the NCS to life. Thank you.

One does not achieve an 80 percent response rate while remaining within budget—well, almost within budget—without the help of an expert and efficient survey research operation. The National Opinion Research Center at the University of Chicago has been called the gold standard in survey research, and deservedly so. Norman Bradburn found a place for me, as well as for the NCS, at NORC. Joan Law, Nicole Kirgis, Ann Burke, and Ann Cederlund, at NORC's Chicago office, were a pleasure to work with, and the field staff, spread across the country, took well-deserved professional pride in gathering high-quality data in a timely fashion.

Not even NORC would have been able to gather such high-quality data without the help of leaders in the more than 1,200 churches, synagogues, mosques, and temples who thoughtfully and generously told us about their congregations. By spending an hour or so talking with us, these leaders became a crucial part of the ongoing effort to enrich our understanding of American religion. I remain deeply grateful for their participation in this project, and I hope they find something in these chapters that rewards their cooperation.

Talented graduate students have served this project well. In Chicago, Emily Barman, Kraig Beyerlein, Mary Ellen Konieczny, and Grace Lee contributed to early phases of the project, beginning with developing and pretesting the questionnaire. In Arizona, Helen Giesel, Martin Hughes, Jeffrey Kroll, Nancy Martin, Rhonda Rubio, Laura Stephens, and

William Tsitsos worked on later parts of the project, up to and beyond preparing the data for public release. These students' contributions are too many and varied to detail here, but their hard work and dedication were essential both to the NCS and to this book. Indeed, as is duly noted in appropriate places throughout these chapters, parts of the book originated as collaborations with one or more of these students.

Dozens of scholars and religious leaders helped to shape the NCS questionnaire. Al Bergesen, Paul DiMaggio, Ted Gerber, Don Grant, James Montgomery, Lester Salamon, Sarah Soule, Lyn Spillman, and Ann Swidler read and commented on specific chapters—or on papers that eventually became chapters. Nancy Ammerman, Jackson Carroll, William Hutchison, Jim Lewis, and Rhys Williams read and commented on the entire manuscript; Bill Hutchison deserves special mention for reading multiple drafts of Chapter 1. Peg Fulton, at Harvard University Press, provided helpful comments on early drafts of all the chapters and supported this book before it was a book. Amanda Heller's copyediting smoothed many rough spots. I am grateful to all of these individuals. Whatever its remaining flaws, the book is better for their input.

The NCS was not the only gleam in my eye in recent years. Christopher Alan Nagle Chaves was born after Chapter 4. The subsequent chapters might have come at a somewhat slower pace than I anticipated, but this was a small price to pay for the sheer pleasure of having him around. And all of these chapters would have come more slowly still were it not for Ami Nagle's patience, love, and support—support that predates Chapter 1 and extends well beyond Chapter 8.

✥ 1 ✥

What Do Congregations Do?

People gather for many reasons and in many places, but no voluntary or cultural institution in American society gathers more people more regularly than religious congregations. Congregations vary in many ways. There is variation in their core rituals, in the types of nonritual activities sponsored or encouraged by the congregation, in internal organization, in the level of engagement with the world outside the congregation, and in the extent to which the gathered form real communities as opposed to aggregations of relatively anonymous individuals. This variation notwithstanding, virtually all churches, synagogues, mosques, and temples share a primary function: they gather people, usually every week, for collective religious activity. This is the sociological truth justifying *congregation* as the generic label for this organizational manifestation of religion.

This book is about American religious congregations and what they do. By "congregation" I mean a social institution in which individuals who are not all religious specialists gather in physical proximity to one another, frequently and at regularly scheduled intervals, for activities and events with explicitly religious content and purpose, and in which there is continuity over time in the individuals who gather, the location of the gathering, and the nature of the activities and events at each gathering.[1] This distinguishes congregations from other religious social forms such as monasteries or denominational agencies, which are constituted mainly, perhaps exclusively, by religious specialists; religious television and radio productions, whose audiences are not in physical proximity to one another; seasonal celebrations, holiday gatherings, and other religious assemblies that may occur at regular but infrequent intervals; rites of passage, corroborees, and other events that occur neither frequently nor at regular intervals; and camp meetings, post-game prayer circles, pilgrimages, religious rock concerts, passion plays, revivals, and other religious social forms that lack continuity across gatherings in participants, location, or content of activities. There are, of course, borderline cases. The lunchtime workplace prayer circle seems something less than a congregation, and the religious community in which individuals live, work, and worship together seems something more than a congregation, yet neither is clearly excluded by the definition I have offered. Fuzzy boundaries acknowledged, this definition nevertheless distinguishes congregations from other social expressions of religion.

Religion need not be organized in congregational form. In some times and places religion's most prevalent and sociologically important forms have been guilds of religious specialists, schools, state agencies, fee-for-service religious treatments for illness or other worldly ills, keepers of sacred sites to which individuals occasionally come to achieve religious goals or to achieve worldly goals by religious means, and so on. As Max Weber observed long ago, there is no simple answer to the question, Under what social and historical conditions is religion organized congregationally? Congregational religion can emerge within various religious traditions, under various social conditions, along various historical trajectories, and with various consequences for religion's influence on social life (Weber [1922] 1991:60–79).

Christianity, Judaism, and Islam, of course, promote congregational religion, but even religious traditions which elsewhere are not organized congregationally tend to take this form in the United States. This is particularly evident among immigrants to the United States, whose efforts to perpetuate cultural traditions (while simultaneously reducing the appearance of foreignness), raise money for religious and community buildings, meet the diverse social and economic needs of immigrants, compete with other organizations for individuals' time and donations, and materially support religious specialists all push religious expression in a congregational direction, not least because, in the United States, these efforts must be wholly supported with voluntary donations of time and money (Yang and Ebaugh 2001; Ebaugh and Chafetz 2000a, b; Bankston and Zhou 2000; Warner and Wittner 1998).

Whatever their historical and sociological origins, congregations clearly are the predominant way in which American religion is socially organized.[2] There are more than 300,000 religious congregations in the United States. More than 60 percent of American adults have attended a service at a religious congregation within the last year, and perhaps as many as one quarter attend services in any given week. Both religious affiliation and participation in congregational life have declined in recent decades. The number of people who answer "none" when asked about their religion has risen from 3 percent in 1957 to 14 percent in 2000, and the number attending services weekly probably dropped from about 40 percent in the 1960s to about 25 percent in the 1990s. But that still leaves a substantial amount of congregation-based religious activity in

American society, more than in any other modern industrialized society.[3]

Congregations are a common feature of the American landscape, many people are associated with them, and they obviously are central sites of religious expression in this society, so it is not surprising that congregations have attracted substantial attention from scholars in several disciplines. The systematic sociological study of congregations began in the 1920s with the remarkable work of H. Paul Douglass and his colleagues, work that combined case studies with nonrandom surveys of large numbers of congregations in a variety of denominations. Recent empirical work on congregations tends to be of two sorts. Scholars and journalists have conducted case studies of small numbers of congregations—sometimes just one—to examine fundamentalism, conflict, change over time, adaptations to changing communities, leadership, social networks, social service activities, and many other things. Sociologists have surveyed larger numbers of congregations. Until very recently, however, surveys of congregations mainly were conducted within one denomination, within a small number of denominations, within a single locale, or, in a few instances, within several locales. Many such studies, but not all, selected congregations randomly. We have learned much from these studies about subjects such as growth and decline, finances, leadership dynamics, and more.[4]

This work is valuable, and I draw on it throughout the book. It is important, however, to recognize a major gap in previous research on congregations. The study of congregations—and therefore the study of the most prevalent form of collective religious expression in American society—has been hamstrung by the absence of a nationally representative sample of congregations. Without a comprehensive national sample, many basic facts about congregations cannot be known. How many congregations are nondenominational? How many big and small congregations are there? How many congregations perform what kinds of social services? How many distribute voter guides? How common is speaking in tongues? What proportion of worship services use soloists, drums, or other sorts of music? To what extent do congregations connect with their communities, and in what ways? And so on. This list merely skims the surface of a sea of basic descriptive questions that only a survey of a nationally representative sample of congregations can answer.

In this book I draw on a nationally representative sample of congregations—the 1998 National Congregations Study (NCS)—to provide, for the first time, an accurate national picture of congregations from across the religious spectrum, one that answers the questions just posed, as well as many others.[5] In the chapters that follow I explore the nature of congregational involvement in social service, political, ritual, educational, and artistic activities, and I argue that the most significant activities and contributions of congregations to American society are cultural in a way that is not sufficiently appreciated by many observers of American religion.

Congregations' activities and contributions are cultural in two senses. On the one hand, their core activity is the broadly cultural one of expressing and transmitting religious meanings through ritual and religious education. On the other hand, largely but not only because congregations' primary ritual—the worship service—almost always uses music and frequently uses drama, dance, and other art forms, congregational activity is cultural in the narrower sense of facilitating a surprising amount of artistic activity. Worship and religious education are congregations' central pursuits, and artistic activity is the most significant by-product of these pursuits. More pointedly, public and scholarly interest in congregations' social service and political activities notwithstanding, artistic activity emerges as more significant to congregational life than either social services or political activities.

Contemporary concern with social service efforts continues a long-standing preoccupation among religious leaders and others with congregations' response to the neediest segments of the communities in which they are located. At least since Douglass surveyed urban churches in the 1920s, some observers of American religion have emphasized—and tried to encourage—the community-serving aspects of congregational life. Douglass's typology of congregations is revealing on this point. For him, "typically developed" congregations, the most common type of urban congregation in his 1920s surveys, do little more than the core activities of weekly worship and religious education classes. "Under-developed" congregations do not perform even these functions on a regular basis, while "elaborated" congregations add to the core with a set of cultural, social, and recreational programs. Only "socially adapted" congregations "definitely undertake to become agencies of social ministry to especially handicapped populations" (Douglass and Brunner 1935:143). The labels for these categories indicate that Douglass and his collaborators viewed these congregational types as stages along a progressive evolutionary scale, with only those most active in social services considered to be fully adapted to their urban environment. Indeed, Douglass saw his work as providing the foundation for "a science of ecclesiastical eugenics" (Douglass 1926:309) that would help religious leaders weed out the congregations falling below minimum standards of development. This positive valuation of congregations' social service activities, and the associated disdain for congregations that are less than fully active in this sort of work, recur in sociological and theological writing about congregations throughout the twentieth century (Marty 1994).

A recent manifestation of this concern with congregations' social service activities is a movement whose roots lie in a resurgent Evangelicalism and whose aim is to encourage new partnerships, including financial partnerships, between government and religious organizations doing antipoverty work. This movement received a major boost when the authors of the Personal Responsibility and Work Opportunity Reconciliation Act of 1996—welfare reform—included a provision known as "charitable choice." This provision requires states, if they contract with nonprofit organizations for social service delivery using funding streams established by this legislation, to include religious organizations as eligible contractees. It forbids states from requiring that a religious organization "alter its form of internal governance" or "remove religious art, icons, scripture, or other symbols" as a condition for contracting to deliver services, and it asserts that a contracting religious organization shall retain "control over the definition, development, practice, and expression of its religious beliefs" (*Guide to Charitable Choice* 1997:27–28). Similar language has since been included in legislation affecting other funding streams (Burke 2001). By 2001, more significant than these legislative developments were administrative actions and programs at both national and state levels—programs inspired by the Bush administration's "faith-based initiative"—that actively encouraged religious organizations to apply for government funding, aggressively publicized funding opportunities among religious organizations, provided technical assistance to religious applicants, and directed public funds to religious organizations.

For reasons described in Chapter 3, these efforts are unlikely to change the nature or extent of congregations' involvement in publicly funded social services. The movement has, however, renewed interest in congregations' community activities, and it has raised many questions about the nature of those activities. In Chapter 3 I examine congregations' social service activities in detail, but the core conclusion is simple: congregations are not, in general, social service organizations. The vast majority devote little of their energy or resources to social services, and they play—and will continue to play—only a small role in our society's social service system.

If congregations' social service activities are in the public eye at the turn of the twenty-first century, the 1980s rise of the religious right in American politics has drawn attention since that decade to congregations' political activities. In Chapter 4 I examine these political activities, placing them within the larger context of congregations' public and civic activities. Regarding political activities, I reach a conclusion very much like the conclusion about social services: only a minority of congregations engage in politics qua congregations, and congregations play only a small role in our society's political system. At the same time, the absolute level of political activity within congregations is not trivial; there is interesting variation across religious traditions in the types of political activity congregations typically pursue; and there is interesting religious variation of another sort in the extent to which congregations engage in public and civic activities other than explicitly political activities. I explore all this in Chapter 4.

If congregations are, in general, neither social service agencies nor political organizations, what are their core activities? My answer is that congregations mainly gather people to engage in the cultural activity of expressing and transmitting religious meanings. If neither social services nor politics constitutes a congregation's main point of contact with the outside world, what is the secular arena with which congregations most overlap? My answer again is "cultural activity," but this time in the narrower sense of artistic activity. Both of these claims need elaboration.

There is a sense in which it is obvious that congregations involve people in cultural activities. Knowledge and ritual are key aspects of culture by any definition, and congregations are centrally involved in both. They transmit religious knowledge through religious education and enact religious traditions through collective ritual. I do not mean to draw a sharp distinction here between transmitting religious knowledge and enacting religious tradition, or between religious education and collective ritual. Religious knowledge is transmitted through collective ritual as well as through didactic exposition, and religious traditions are enacted in classrooms as well as in worship and other sorts of ritual. But the basic point is that the core purpose for which congregations gather people, the purpose to which congregations devote most of their resources and involve most of their members, is producing and reproducing religious meanings through ritual and religious education. This point has been emphasized, in one way or another, by many recent observers.[6]

Most previous research about congregations and culture has used a broad notion of culture that, while usefully illuminating some aspects of congregational life, obscures certain uses of culture in congregations. Virtually all sociological analysts of congregations have approached congregational culture in what Robert Wuthnow (1987:36–50) has called "neoclassical" fashion. From this perspective, a congregation's "culture" is defined, following Clifford Geertz, in terms of "an historically transmitted pattern of meanings embodied in symbols, a system of inherited conceptions expressed in symbolic forms by means of which men communicate, perpetuate, and develop their knowledge about and attitudes towards life" (Geertz 1973:89). Congregations are characterized, in other words, as symbolic universes in which the various parts—symbols, rituals, conceptions, communications, practices—cohere into a discernible "pattern" or "system."

9

On this conception of culture, the primary analytical task is to discern the pattern created by all the specific parts of each congregation's symbolic universe. That pattern is the congregation's culture. James Hopewell (1987:5), for example, finds that "an abundant system of language and significance seems to come with any congregation . . . a deep current of narrative interpretation and representation by which people give sense and order to their lives." For Nancy Ammerman (1997a:47), congregational culture "consists of physical artifacts, patterns of activity, and the language and story that embellish those objects and activities with meaning." Lowell Livezey (2000a:12) "highlights the publicly significant cultural work of congregations by examining the symbolic images and language, narrative stories, and social identities that they generate." Penny Edgell Becker (1999:7) argues that "congregations develop distinct cultures that comprise local understandings of identity and mission and that can be understood analytically as bundles of core tasks and legitimate ways of doing things."

We have learned much from scholars employing this broad notion of culture, but here I approach congregational culture from another direction, one that points to specific sets of practices rather than to all-encompassing symbolic universes. More specifically, I emphasize three overlapping sets of practices: those involving worship, education, and the arts. Emphasizing worship and religious education will cause no controversy and surprise no one. Emphasizing congregations' facilitation of artistic activity is more unusual.

Everyone recognizes that regular worship events are a central manifestation of a congregation's culture, and the worship activities I emphasize are subsumed in the broad definitions of congregational culture used by others. But the Geertz-inspired instinct to treat virtually all of a congregation's specific events, practices, and activities as parts of a whole—and labeling that

10

whole a congregation's "culture"—offers no criteria for judging which specific events, practices, or activities contribute more to a congregation's culture than which other events, practices, or activities. The informal chatting over coffee after a service, in conversation circles involving only a few people, becomes as significant in assessing a congregation's culture as the hymn singing involving dozens or hundreds. The Habitat for Humanity project sponsored by the ten-person social action committee becomes as significant as the recitation of a prayer by the entire congregation. Seeing all of a congregation's specific activities as aspects of a more or less coherent whole motivates careful observation and rich description of the nooks and crannies of congregational life, but it does not facilitate empirically based judgments about the relative importance of different types of activities for the life of the congregation, nor does it enable rigorous analysis of sources and consequences of variation in the specific activities themselves. Because I am interested in these latter kinds of judgments and analyses, I focus on a central part of congregations' cultural activity rather than on the whole. I examine what kinds of culture congregations *practice* in worship events, not what kinds of culture they *are*.

My emphasis on the centrality of worship in congregational life is not original, but my strategy for analyzing worship is more so. I conceptualize worship services as events that are assembled from a repertoire of specific worship practices. This conceptualization enables me systematically to examine variation in worship practices among congregations as well as sources and consequences of that variation.[7] It leads me to highlight what happens in worship services rather than what is said in worship services. This is not to deny the importance of what is said in worship services, and there are moments, of course, when the distinction between "what happens" and

11

"what is said" dissolves because spoken words ("I baptize you . . ." "I now pronounce you . . .") themselves perform an action. But it also is clear that some of what happens in worship happens through practices which themselves carry meaning beyond whatever meaning is conveyed directly by spoken words. A sixty-minute sermon conveys something different than a ten-minute sermon, whatever the similarities or differences in content. Worship practices such as children's sermons, speaking in tongues, electric guitar music, and communion tell us something important about the worship events in which they occur even if we do not know what was said or sung at these events.

In emphasizing how congregations produce and reproduce religious meanings through the practices that constitute worship services, I am following a movement in the sociology of culture away from the interpretation of subjective meaning and toward the observation and analysis of concrete cultural objects and practices in which meanings are enacted, embodied, and conveyed (Wuthnow 1987, 1994; Ammerman 1997b; Warner 1997); away from investigations aimed at understanding how meanings, objects, collective practices, and individual consciousnesses together constitute holistic cultural forms and toward the study of how repertoires of ideas and practices are strategically deployed in social life (Swidler 2001; Mohr and Duquenne 1997);[8] away from a focus on the symbolic and expressive aspects of cultural objects and practices and toward a focus on the social arrangements by which these objects and practices are produced and institutionalized (Peterson 1994; Wuthnow 1989); away from an emphasis on meaning carried by content and toward an emphasis on meaning carried by form (Berezin 1994; Cerulo 1995).

In Chapter 5, which explores worship events in detail, I show what can be gained by focusing on how those events are constructed from a repertoire of practices. As we will see, the selection of elements from the repertoire is hardly random, and much of Chapter 5 examines the institutional and social sources of structure in that selection. I address questions such as: What is the nature and source of variation in congregational worship practices? How does this variation influence the movement of individuals among religious traditions? How does it influence the ways that denominations position themselves with respect to one another, compete with one another, and thereby shape the American religious ecology? All in all, the discussion illustrates how this approach, in which the central question is how concrete worship events are constructed from a repertoire of available worship elements, opens productive new directions for research and theorizing about the social and cultural ecology of American religion.

Focusing on the specific practices from which worship events are constructed renders the connection between congregations and the arts more visible and more open to empirical investigation. Congregations produce their worship services—indeed, they produce *religion*—partly by deploying artistic elements and activities; individuals can hardly help but participate in the arts when they attend religious services. Moreover, congregations facilitate a good deal of arts activity outside of worship, as when a congregation's space is used for art exhibits or performances, or when a congregation's drama group or choir performs outside worship, or when a congregation organizes groups of members to attend professional performances or exhibits. In Chapter 6 I explore these connections, contributing to a renewed conversation about religion and the arts by addressing questions such as: What is the extent of congregational facilitation of the arts? How does that participation vary across religious traditions?[9]

Religious education is, of course, a major activity for congregations, and I document its importance in Chapter 7. The main agenda in that chapter, however, is to argue that three overlapping aspects of congregational culture—the worship events they produce, the religious knowledge they transmit, and the artistic activity they facilitate—occupy more congregations, engage more people, use more resources, and contribute more significantly to communities than either congregations' social service or political activities. From a perspective internal to congregations, I argue that worship, religious education, and even the arts (largely but not only because of their intimate connection with worship) are their central activities. From a perspective external to congregations, I argue that congregations, because they are sites for so much artistic activity, account for a substantial share of all the live arts occurring in American society, and I argue, more tentatively, that congregations' share of all live artistic activity in American society is larger than their share either of all social service activity or of all political activity in the society. If we ask what congregations do, the answer is that they mainly traffic in ritual, knowledge, and beauty through the cultural activities of worship, education, and the arts; they do not mainly pursue charity or justice through social services or politics. I also conjecture, but not without some basis, that if we look for the secular arena of American social life in which congregations are most a part, we will find it in the arts, not in social services or politics.

In most of this book I treat congregations as coherent and at least somewhat independent organizational units. We can make much progress in this way—indeed, for some purposes we can make progress only in this way—but this approach also has limits. On the one hand, treating congregations as coherent organizational units obscures the fact that they also are aggregations of individuals, and many congregational activities are the activities of a subset, sometimes a very small subset, of these individuals. On the other hand, treating congregations as largely independent organizational units obscures the fact that most congregations are instantiations of larger religious traditions and movements, and much of what they do originates in the extra-congregational institutions associated with those traditions and movements. It would be too strong to say even of congregations in the most centrally controlled denominations that they are merely local franchises charged with implementing models developed at denominational corporate headquarters, but the fact remains that much of what occurs in congregations is more or less strongly shaped by the traditions, institutions, and movements in which they are embedded. In the concluding chapter I explore what might be learned by moving beyond a conception of congregations as coherent and independent units of analysis in order to appreciate more fully the ways in which congregations are shaped by the people in them, by the institutions that surround them, and by the movements that wash over them.

❧ 2 ❧

Members, Money, and Leaders

Congregations are ubiquitous in American social life, but this does not guarantee that their basic features and characteristics are well known. This chapter lays the groundwork for the analyses and arguments to follow by providing an overview of American congregations at the turn of the twenty-first century. I begin by describing two of the most important dimensions on which congregations vary: size and connections to denominations and religious traditions. These are not the only important dimensions on which congregations vary. Racial and ethnic composition and urban versus rural location come immediately to mind as additional key sources of variation. Still, size and religious tradition influence virtually everything congregations do, from the nature and extent of their social services to the nature of their political and public engagement to the kinds of religious culture they produce and reproduce. Furthermore, clearly communicating certain counterintuitive facts about congregations' size and denominational connections requires sustained attention to these two dimensions of congregational variation. Other sorts of variation among congregations will be discussed where they are relevant throughout the book.

The second part of this overview focuses on three key resources congregations need to survive: members, money, and leaders. Congregations perennially face the challenges of maintaining a membership base, securing adequate revenue, and recruiting talented leaders, but these challenges take different shapes at different historical moments. They change as the nature and supply of these resources change. These are not, of course, the only resources congregations need, and the challenges of obtaining members, money, and leaders are not the only ones congregations face. But these three resources are fundamental to congregations' organizational well-being, and they provide convenient hooks on which to hang a portrait of American congregations at the present moment.

Two Key Dimensions of Congregational Variation

I begin by looking in greater detail at congregational size and religious tradition.

Size

Congregations define "members" differently, making it difficult to examine their size meaningfully in terms of official membership. I prefer to use a less official measure—the number of individuals regularly participating in a congregation's religious life—to examine congregational size. This measure is less implicated than "membership" in congregations' and denominations' bureaucratic ways of counting people, and consequently it provides a measure of size that is more comparable across congregations of various denominations and religious traditions.

By any measure, most congregations are small. Fifty-nine percent of U.S. congregations have fewer than one hundred regular participants, counting both adults and children; 71

percent have fewer than one hundred regularly participating adults. The median congregation has only seventy-five regular participants and only fifty regularly participating adults.[1]

The small size of most congregations represents only half the story, however, since the size distribution of American congregations is very skewed. That is, even though there are relatively few large congregations with many members, sizable budgets, and numerous staff, these large congregations contain most of the people involved in organized religion in the United States. To put it succinctly, although most *congregations* are small, most *people* are associated with large congregations—those with many members, sizable budgets, and numerous staff. The median congregation has only seventy-five regular participants, but the median person is in a congregation with four hundred regular participants.

Table 2.1 provides more complete information about the size distribution of congregations in the United States. The third column tracks the distribution of congregations; the middle column tracks the distribution of people in congregations. The key double-aspect nature of congregations' size distribution can be grasped by imagining that we have lined up all congregations from the smallest to the largest, and we are walking up this line of congregations, beginning with the smallest. When you have walked past half of all congregations, you are facing the median congregation—a congregation with only seventy-five regular participants. But even though you have walked past half of all congregations, you have walked past only 11 percent of all people who regularly attend religious services. If you start walking from the other end of the line, after you have walked past half of *all people* in congregations, you will be facing a congregation with four hundred regular participants, but you will have walked past only 10 percent of all congregations. The largest 10 percent of congregations

Table 2.1 Congregational size distribution

Percentile	People who attend religious services are in congregations of indicated size or smaller at stated percentile of distribution	Congregations of indicated size or smaller at stated percentile of distribution
10	75	20
20	125	30
30	180	40
40	275	55
50	400[a]	75[b]
60	600	100
70	1,000	140
80	1,700	200
90	3,000	350
93	—	450
95	—	550
97	—	800

Note: These size distributions are based on the number of regularly participating individuals, counting both adults and children.

a. This number, the median, means that 50 percent of religious service attenders attend congregations with 400 or fewer regularly participating individuals.

b. This number, the median, means that 50 percent of congregations have 75 or fewer regularly participating individuals.

contain about half of all churchgoers. This illustrates a basic point concerning congregations and size: most congregations are small, but most people are associated with large congregations.[2]

Resource distributions are similarly skewed. The median congregation has an annual budget of only $56,000, but the median person is in a congregation with an annual budget of $250,000. Forty percent of congregations, containing 15 percent of religious service attenders, have no full-time staff; 24 percent, with 7 percent of the people, have no paid staff at all. Only 25 percent of congregations have more than one full-time staff person, but 65 percent of the people are in those congregations.

Similarly with wealth. Although some congregations hold very substantial endowments, the well-endowed congregation is a rarity. The median congregation has about $1,000 in a savings account, and even the median person's congregation has savings of only $20,000. Only 7 percent of congregations have endowments or savings that total twice their annual operating budget; only 13 percent have a one-year cushion. Although this might make congregations slightly more financially secure, on average, than other nonprofit organizations—one analyst (Brody 1997) estimates that only 2 percent of nonprofit organizations have endowments sufficient to cover at least two years of budget—it is clear that the well-endowed religious congregation is atypical. As with people and income, the wealth distribution among congregations is very skewed. Some congregations hold significant wealth, but the vast majority operate on the money they raise each year. This dependence on voluntary giving is, of course, a major aspect of congregations' revenue challenges, as I describe in more detail later on.

Understanding the size distribution of congregations is important because size influences almost everything congregations do, and larger congregations, not surprisingly, are able to do much more in almost every arena than are smaller congregations. This may seem obvious, but, as we will see in Chapter 3, it is a point that has often been missed in public discourse about congregations' social service activities, where the substantial activities of some very large congregations are taken to be typical of congregations as a whole. David Horton Smith (1997) has pointed out that, like the natural universe, the universe of nonprofit organizations contains much "dark matter"—small organizations that are not visible through the usual lenses that focus on the largest organizations. This certainly is true of congregations, and a comprehensive understanding of congregations' features, activities, and capacities requires seeing past the largest, most visible congregations to the more typical ones that compose the bulk of American congregations. Some congregations, typically large ones, are extensively engaged in social service work, but these are rare, and it is a mistake to represent their inclinations and organizational capacities as typical. One result of this mistake is to imagine that a large reservoir of as yet untapped congregational resources could be directed toward human service activities. No such reservoir exists, and imagining that it does leads both to a distorted view of congregations and to misguided public policy initiatives. In Chapter 3 I return to this subject in detail. For now I note only that clearly understanding key features of how people are distributed into large and small congregations is of more than academic interest.

Denomination and Religious Tradition

Another major source of variation among congregations is their affiliation (or lack thereof) with denominations and religious traditions. Organizationally, individuals do not, in general, directly become members of denominations. They belong to congregations, most of which are in turn attached to umbrella religious organizations: denominations.[3] The character of these attachments varies substantially. In some denominations, congregations are wholly independent local organizations, owning their own property, fully in charge of decisions about hiring clergy and other staff, and in no way subject to the authority of a denomination's regional or national bodies. In other denominations, congregational property is legally owned by a unit of the denomination, clergy are assigned to congregations by denominational officials, and congregational policies and practices are subject to denominational oversight. Many varieties and mixed forms exist between these two extremes.

Congregations are embedded in more than their denominations, and it is helpful to distinguish two overlapping but distinct ways in which congregations might connect with larger religious worlds: formal affiliation with an organized denomination versus embodiment of a recognizable religious tradition. I will use *denomination* to mean the concrete national religious organizations to which congregations may have formal ties, and *religious tradition* to refer to the larger traditions with which congregations may be associated, with or without formal ties to a denomination. These two aspects of a congregation's embeddedness often overlap. A congregation formally part of the Presbyterian Church (USA)—an organized denomination—will also partake of Presbyterian religious tradition. A congregation formally part of the African Methodist Episcopal Church—another organized denomination—will carry Methodist religious tradition. And so on.

Distinguishing denomination from religious tradition is important, however, because some congregations embody a recognizable religious tradition even though they are not formally connected to any specific denomination. Many Baptist congregations, for example, are independent, eschewing formal affiliation with specific Baptist groups such as the Southern or National Baptist Conventions. For some analytical purposes we may want to highlight the nondenominational aspect of these congregations; for other purposes we may want to highlight their Baptist religious tradition. Several religious traditions, moreover, are represented in the United States by more than one formal denomination. The Evangelical Lutheran Church in America (ELCA), for example, is a distinct denomination from the Lutheran Church–Missouri Synod, though both are Lutheran in religious tradition. For some purposes we may want to distinguish ELCA from Missouri Synod congregations; for other purposes it may be sufficient to know that both are Lutheran. This situation is not unique to Lutherans. There are at least thirty-one Pentecostal denominations in the United States, twenty-one Baptist denominations, fourteen Methodist bodies, and nine Presbyterian bodies. Even smaller religious traditions sometimes generate multiple denominations: there are, for example, twelve Mennonite and six Quaker denominations in this country (Lindner 2001:162–164).

Table 2.2 gives the distribution of American congregations' denominational affiliations. Table 2.3 aggregates some of these denominations into families, and includes in these families congregations within the same religious tradition but with no formal ties to any specific denomination. Baptist congregations, for example, that are not part of any particular Baptist denomination or convention appear in the third line of Table 2.2—included with other congregations that have no denominational affiliation—but they are included in the Baptist line of Table 2.3. Each table shows this distribution from two perspectives. The first numerical column in each table gives the percentages *of people* in congregations associated with particular denominations and religious traditions. The second column gives the percentages of *congregations* associated with each denomination or religious tradition, without respect to how many people are in those congregations. These two percentages are most different for Roman Catholics. On the one hand, nearly 29 percent of religious service attenders in the United States attend Catholic congregations; on the other hand, only 6 percent of U.S. congregations are Catholic. The difference between these two numbers reflects the fact that Catholic congregations are much larger, on average, than non-Catholic congregations.[4]

Another fact from Table 2.2 is worth emphasizing: 18 per-

Table 2.2 Denominational distribution of U.S. congregations

Denominational affiliation	Percent of attenders in congregations with listed affiliation	Percent of congregations with listed affiliation
Roman Catholic	28.6	6.2
Southern Baptist Convention	11.2	16.9
None	9.7	17.9
United Methodist Church	9.2	12.0
Evangelical Lutheran Church in America	4.4	3.1
Other Baptist denominations	3.1	4.8
Three Black Baptist conventions	3.0	2.8
Presbyterian Church (USA)	3.0	2.3
Episcopal Church	2.5	3.2
United Church of Christ	2.0	1.9
Other Pentecostal denominations	1.9	2.3
Lutheran Church–Missouri Synod	1.9	1.5
Jewish	1.6	1.0
Non-Christian and non-Jewish	1.6	2.6
Assemblies of God	1.5	1.9
Other or unknown Lutheran denominations	1.3	0.9
Jehovah's Witnesses	1.1	1.6
Church of God (various denominations)	1.0	1.3
American Baptist Churches	0.9	0.9
Church/Churches of Christ	0.9	1.4
Church of the Nazarene	0.8	1.3
Three Black Methodist denominations	0.7	1.1
Latter-day Saints	0.7	1.0
Eastern Orthodox denominations	0.7	0.5
Disciples of Christ	0.7	0.5
Unitarian Universalist Association	0.5	0.9
Church of God in Christ	0.5	1.4
Church of the Brethren	0.5	0.8
Evangelical Church	0.5	0.3
Seventh-day Adventist	0.5	0.7

Table 2.2 *(continued)*

Denominational affiliation	Percent of attenders in congregations with listed affiliation	Percent of congregations with listed affiliation
Two Mennonite denominations	0.3	0.4
Reformed Church in America	0.3	0.4
Christian and Missionary Alliance	0.3	0.8
Other Methodist denominations	0.3	0.5
Other Presbyterian denominations	0.3	0.4
Other Christian denominations[a]	2.0	2.5

Notes: These distributions represent congregations with formal ties to a denomination. Except for the final "Other Christian" category, they are listed from the most to least numerous categories in the NCS sample. These percentages are based on the 1,236 congregations in the NCS data set.

Percentages in column 2 use data weighted to take account of duplicate congregational nominations.

Percentages in column 3 use data weighted inversely proportional to congregational size to take account of the probability-proportional-to-size feature of the NCS sample. See Appendix A for details about weights.

a. Includes congregations affiliated with denominations but not elsewhere classified in this table. No denomination in this residual category contains more than three congregations in the NCS sample.

cent of congregations, containing 10 percent of those who attend religious services, are formally affiliated with *no* denomination. If the unaffiliated congregations were all in one denomination, they would constitute the third-largest U.S. denomination in number of participants—behind the Roman Catholic Church and the Southern Baptist Convention—and the largest in number of congregations. Although most congregations are attached to denominations, a noticeable minority of American congregations are not formally affiliated with any denomination. We do not have national data with which to assess whether the number of independent congregations is in-

Table 2.3 Religious tradition distribution of U.S. congregations

Religious tradition	Percent of attenders in congregations within listed tradition	Percent of congregations within listed tradition
Roman Catholic	29	6
Baptist	21	30
Methodist	11	16
Lutheran	8	6
Presbyterian/Reformed	7	7
Pentecostal	6	10
Episcopal	3	3
Adventist	2	2
Jewish	2	1
Non-Christian and non-Jewish	2	3
Church/Churches of Christ	1	2
Mennonite/Brethren	1	1
Mormon	1	1
No identifiable tradition	1	2
Christian, not elsewhere classified	7	9

creasing or decreasing, but research in one New England city found that more recently established congregations were much more likely to be nondenominational than those established longer ago (Hall 1999:233). As we will see in later chapters, there are other important differences between newer and older congregations, including their worship styles and the extent to which they engage communities outside the congregation.

Scholars debate the extent to which denominational and religious tradition differences among Protestant congregations remain sociologically significant in American society. Those who see a declining significance of denominations tend to highlight the extent to which individuals move among various

Protestant denominations over the course of a lifetime, increasing religious intermarriage rates, and other ways in which denominational boundaries appear permeable (see, for example, Wuthnow 1988:chap. 7). Others, sometimes examining a wider range of denominations, emphasize continuing differences in the social composition of denominations, with some being much more urban than others, some having many more college-educated members than others, and so on (see, for example, Roof and McKinney 1987).

Whatever the nature of differences among specific denominations and traditions, virtually all observers agree that the division between theologically moderate or liberal religion, on the one hand, and theologically conservative or evangelical religion, on the other hand, crosscuts denominations and religious families and structures congregational life and activities in important ways. Although the "liberal" and "conservative" labels are somewhat tired, they nevertheless point to a long-standing divide within American religion (Ahlstrom 1972; Hutchison 1976; Marty 1991). Whether labeled premillennialist versus postmillennialist, fundamentalist versus modernist, or conservative versus liberal, American religion has long been characterized by a difference between, on the one hand, religion that places spiritual value on reformist engagement with state and society and, on the other hand, religion in which the primary spiritual goal is salvation for individuals through religious and moral discipline. This division is not limited to Protestantism nor to American religion; indeed, every major religious family in every part of the world has both modernist and traditionalist manifestations. In this book, as in American society, however, the distinction is most empirically important for distinguishing among white Protestants. The "liberal" Protestant denominations are the inheritors of a religious tradition, perhaps reaching its peak in the Social

27

Gospel movement at the beginning of the twentieth century, that encouraged wide-ranging institutional engagement between religious organizations and the world. What we now call "conservative" Protestant denominations are the inheritors of a religious tradition that discouraged such institutional engagement in favor of evangelism and an emphasis on individual morality rather than social reform or social service. Using congregations' denominational and religious family affiliations to categorize them into broadly liberal or broadly conservative religious traditions, we find that 56 percent of American congregations (containing 38 percent of those who regularly attend religious services) affiliate with predominantly white, conservative, and evangelical Protestant religious traditions. Approximately one quarter of both congregations and regular attenders affiliate with moderate to liberal Protestant religious traditions.[5]

The liberal-conservative divide is not completely reducible either to sets of denominations or to particular religious families. As mentioned earlier, this distinction is relevant beyond white Protestantism, and even within white Protestantism it crosscuts denominations and religious families. Indeed, the social salience of this distinction within denominations and religious families led Robert Wuthnow (1988) to argue influentially that this liberal-conservative line, cutting across denominations, has replaced denominations and religious families as the most sociologically significant religious boundary within American society. Construed in terms of congregations' self-identification, without regard to denominational affiliation, 59 percent of congregations (containing 53 percent of the regular attenders) are theologically "more on the conservative side," 11 percent (containing 10 percent of the people) are "more on the liberal side," and 29 percent (containing 38 percent of the people) say they are "right in the middle." Only a small minority of American congregations think of themselves as theologically "liberal."

As we will see in later chapters, this basic distinction between two major religious traditions—whether construed as a distinction between two sets of Protestant denominations or as a theological self-understanding that crosscuts denominations and traditions—corresponds to strong differences in several areas of congregational practice and activity, not least the concrete ways in which they connect with the world around them. Later chapters document this in detail. For now, let it suffice to note that this basic distinction continues to structure American religion in important ways.

Three Resources Needed by American Congregations

Size and denomination or religious tradition influence virtually everything about congregations, and it is tempting to let the substantial variation among congregations on these and other dimensions overwhelm any attempt to summarize the state of American congregations. I resist that temptation, however, in favor of presenting an overview of American congregations organized around three resources virtually all congregations need in order to survive: members, money, and leaders.

Members

Religious congregations are voluntary membership organizations, and their fortunes are very directly affected by demographic changes that influence participation in voluntary associations, broadly construed. Although the prevalence of conventional religious belief remains very high in the United States—more than 90 percent of Americans believe in some sort of higher power, more than 60 percent have no doubts about God's existence, almost 80 percent believe in miracles, 70 percent believe in heaven, and almost 60 percent believe in hell (Gallup and Lindsay 1999) stable high levels of religious belief do not guarantee stable trends in participation.

Some researchers have argued that religious participation has increased over the long haul of American history (Finke and Stark 1992). This claim is based on increasing rates of church *membership*. In 1789 only 10 percent of Americans belonged to churches, a figure increasing to 22 percent in 1890 and reaching 50 to 60 percent in the 1950s. Today, about two thirds of Americans say they are members of a church or synagogue. These rising membership numbers, however, are potentially misleading about underlying religious participation because congregations have become much less exclusive clubs than they were at earlier points in our history. Today, fewer people attend religious services than claim formal membership in religious congregations, but that situation was reversed earlier in our history. Thus, a historic increase in formal church membership may not be a valid indicator of a historic increase in religious participation. The changing meaning of and standards for official church (and synagogue) membership make it difficult to know what long-term trends in membership imply about trends in religious participation, and the historical record is too spotty to say anything definitive about long-term trends in participation. Still, one prominent historian of American religion who has reviewed the available historical evidence has argued that "participation [as opposed to formal membership] in [U.S.] congregations has probably remained relatively constant" since the seventeenth century (Holifield 1994:24).

Rising *membership* rates notwithstanding, self-reported *attendance* has appeared remarkably stable for as long as we have survey research on this topic. The Protestant rate has hovered around 40 percent since the 1940s. Although self-reported church attendance among Catholics declined markedly during the 1960s and 1970s—from about 70 percent reportedly attending weekly to about 50 percent—the Catholic numbers too have been stable for about twenty-five years (Greeley 1989). These remarkably stable survey numbers are the basis for the standard view that church attendance in the United States has been essentially constant, at least throughout the last third of the twentieth century.

Several studies, however, have shaken the view that religious service attendance in the United States has been stable in recent decades. Indeed, as mentioned in Chapter 1, research strongly suggests that participation in organized religious activity probably has declined since the 1960s. One study, drawing on time-use diaries completed by individuals, found that weekly religious service attendance declined continuously from approximately 40 percent in 1965 to approximately 25 percent in 1994 (Presser and Stinson 1998). Another study (Hofferth and Sandberg 2001) found a similar decline—from 37 percent in 1981 to 26 percent in 1997—in church attendance reported in children's time-use diaries.

Additional evidence of decline comes from Robert Putnam's monumental book (Putnam 2000) on civic engagement in the United States. Putnam combines survey data from five different sources and finds the same decline in religious participation evident in the time-use diaries. This is important in itself. But perhaps even more compelling, because of the context it provides, are his findings about a whole range of civic and voluntary association activities that are close cousins to religious participation. Virtually every indicator of civic engagement currently available shows decline in the last third of the twentieth century. A partial list of indicators that follow this pattern includes voting, attending a political meeting, attending any public meeting, serving as an officer or committee member in any local club or organization, participating in a local meeting of any national organization, attending a club meeting, joining a union, participating in a picnic, playing sports, and working on a community project.

The details vary for specific items, but the consistency across many different indicators drawn from many different sources is impressive. For item after item, trend line after trend line, the decline starts sometime in the last third of the twentieth century and continues into the present. This casts new light on the religious participation trend. Religious participation is a special case of something more general: civic engagement. Decline in religious participation, it seems, is but one part of a broader decline—one that began sometime in the last third of the twentieth century—affecting a range of civic and voluntary associations that are close cousins to religious congregations. The decline in virtually all sorts of civic engagement since the 1960s, together with the direct evidence for decline in some of the best data on religious participation itself, strongly suggest that religious participation in the United States has indeed decreased in recent decades. In this context, it would be a great surprise if religious participation, alone among all sorts of civic engagement, has failed to decline. Those wishing to maintain that religious participation has been stable over the last three or four decades must explain how it could be that religious trends are so different from trends affecting virtually every other type of voluntary association.

Evidence also converges on an important demographic aspect of this trend: recent generations attend religious services at lower rates than did previous generations when they were the same age. Putnam finds this pattern across a strikingly wide range of activities, including church attendance. Declining participation in all sorts of voluntary associations, including religious ones, is occurring not so much because individual people have become less involved over the last three or four decades. Rather, more recently born cohorts engage in less of this activity than older cohorts, and those born earlier are inexorably leaving the scene, being replaced by less civically engaged recent generations. Even if not a single individual changes his or her behavior over time, it is still possible for widespread social change to occur via generational turnover, and this seems to be largely what is happening with civic engagement in general, and with religious participation in particular.[6]

There is, of course, variation in these patterns across religious groups, perhaps the most important of which is between evangelical and liberal Protestants. It is well known that evangelical or conservative Protestant denominations have grown in recent decades while mainline and more liberal denominations have declined. While the percentage of American Protestants claiming mainline affiliation decreased from 57 percent in the early 1970s to 47 percent in the late 1990s, conservative Protestant denominations grew from 43 percent of all Protestants to 53 percent in the same period. This shift is often attributed to people fleeing liberal denominations for the supposedly warmer confines of evangelical churches, but recent research shows that perhaps as much as 80 percent of this shift is produced by differential fertility rather than by religious switching. In every birth cohort for which we have the relevant data, women affiliated with conservative Protestant denominations have more children than women affiliated with moderate and liberal Protestant denominations (Hout et al. 2001).

Nor is it the case that televised religion is successfully competing for members of traditional congregations. Research from the 1980s, at the height of televangelism's popularity, showed that, except for some elderly and infirm people who would not be able to attend conventional churches anyway, religious television was watched disproportionately by people who were regular churchgoers (Bruce 1990:chaps. 5 and 6). Religious television does not, in general, compete with congregations; watching it is better understood as a kind of leisure activity that supplements, rather than substitutes for, congregation-based religious practice.

Religious switching is relevant to the different fortunes of evangelical and liberal Protestants, but not in the way many people think. The most important trend in religious switching is that conservative denominations are losing fewer people to moderate and liberal denominations than in previous decades, perhaps because upward social mobility no longer prompts switching from being, say, Baptist, to being Presbyterian or Episcopalian. Evangelical denominations and congregations have, with their people, become firmly middle class, even affluent. Conservative denominations are also losing fewer people to secularity.

In sum, conservative Protestant denominations have indeed been doing better than moderate and liberal denominations in recent decades, but *not* because many people have switched from one to the other. The main dynamic is demographic, and there also is evidence that evangelicals are slowly losing their demographic edge. Evangelical birthrates, though higher than liberal birthrates, are declining, as is the fertility gap. Moreover, the rate at which evangelicals lose people to secularity and to religions other than Protestantism, though still lower than for moderate and liberal Protestants, is increasing.[7]

Variations within American religion are interesting and important, but the key point for this overview is that the growth of evangelical denominations—with their higher levels of religious participation—is not sufficient to offset liberal losses and thereby change the general picture I have painted. This picture is one in which fewer people engage weekly in religious activity, but without believing less in the supernatural, and

34

without becoming less concerned about spirituality. Interestingly, this pattern characterizes many countries around the world. Although the United States has more participation in organized religion than most other advanced industrial societies, and although advanced industrial societies vary quite widely in their aggregate levels of religious participation and religious belief, many of these countries have experienced the same basic trends in recent decades: down on religious participation, stable on religious belief, and up on thinking about the meaning and purpose of life (Inglehart and Baker 2000).

Although generational differences in religious participation suggest that many congregations will, in general, see smaller pools of active members in coming years, another demographic trend will push in the opposite direction. Religious participation increases with age, and so the projected aging of the American population over the coming decades is good news for congregations. Whether the bump in overall participation produced by an aging population will offset the downward pressure exerted by the inexorable replacement of older people by their less civically engaged children and grandchildren remains to be seen.

Increased immigration is another demographic development affecting the membership base of congregations. Recent immigrants may not be present in the majority of congregations, but they are shaping a visible minority of congregations. The National Congregations Study found that 14 percent of congregations—containing 24 percent of religious service attenders—had a worship service at which Spanish was spoken. Twelve percent—containing 21 percent of churchgoers—had a service within the past year in which a language other than English, Spanish, Hebrew, or Latin was spoken. The growing Hispanic population in the United States is especially consequential for Catholic churches: one third of Catholic congregations reported having a worship service within the past year in which Spanish was spoken.

The current immigration wave is different from the early-twentieth-century wave in that recent newcomers are more likely to be from Latin America and Asia, but there is continuity in that religion remains an important vehicle for both preserving ethnic identity and facilitating assimilation (Yang and Ebaugh 2001). Recent immigration also is responsible for increasing numbers of non-Judeo-Christians in the United States. There probably are twice as many Muslims, Buddhists, and Hindus in the United States today as there were in the 1970s. The percentage remains tiny—these three groups combined still make up less than 2 percent of the U.S. population (Sherkat 1999; Smith 2001)—but their numbers are growing, and it is safe to say that religious diversity will continue to pose both opportunities and challenges for American congregations.

Money

The vast majority of congregational income comes from individual donations. Three quarters of congregations receive at least 90 percent of their income from individual donations, and about 80 percent of all the money going to religious congregations comes from individual donations.

Because religious congregations depend almost entirely on donations from individuals, declining participation ought to produce declining revenue. But this does not seem to be happening. Although there is a long-term decline in the percentage of their income that Americans give to congregations, per capita religious giving among those individuals attached to congregations has increased in recent decades, outpacing inflation and producing an overall *increase* in the total amount of income received by congregations. An analysis of overall giving in twenty-nine denominations found that total giving, adjusted for inflation, increased 63 percent between 1968 and 1998.[8] Evangelical giving is higher than liberal giving, but the trend is the same across the board. Those who remain in congregations are as generous as ever, perhaps more so, producing overall increases in the total number of dollars received by American congregations.

At the same time, congregations have been using more and more of their income to maintain their local operations. An analysis of spending in twenty-nine denominations found that the percentage of congregations' income spent on maintaining the local operation rose from 79 percent in 1968 to 84 percent in 1998.[9] In-depth studies of several denominations find a similar, or more dramatic, shift toward spending on congregations' internal operations.[10] In part this trend probably is produced by increased clergy salaries. The median annual salary, in constant 1999 dollars, for full-time clergy with graduate degrees rose from $25,000 in 1976 to $40,000 in 1999 (McMillan and Price 2003).[11] It also seems likely that increases in other expenses, such as health insurance and energy, have led congregations to spend more to maintain their basic operations. All in all, it seems that people remaining in congregations are giving more mainly in order to meet internal budgetary needs.

If increased giving to congregations is mainly a response to the increased cost of items necessary for organizational survival, then such increased giving should not be interpreted as an easing of financial pressure on American congregations. As mentioned previously, the median congregation has only about $1,000 in a savings account, and only 13 percent have as much as a one-year cushion of monetary savings. Moreover, the most common issues around which congregations seek help from their denominations or any other outside consultants are financial ones. Forty-four percent of all religious service attenders are in congregations that sought outside consulting on financial matters in 1998. Of those congregations seeking outside consulting of any sort, one fifth sought advice about financial matters. Many congregations feel financially pressured, notwithstanding the aggregate increase in overall contributions.

Financial pressure is not new for American congregations. It is, rather, perennial, and it would be difficult to find a moment in American religious history when there was no hand-wringing about the financial health of many congregations. Although there certainly is variation over time in the size of congregations' income streams—the 1930s, perhaps not surprisingly, was a particularly difficult decade for congregations[12]—the fact of financial pressure for many congregations seems to change less than the typical strategies for relieving that pressure. Pew rents, dues systems, sales of goods, investment income—not to mention, in an earlier day, public support through taxation—all, in greater or lesser degree, have been part of congregations' funding streams.

Today, perhaps the most important kind of secondary income source for many congregations, after individual donations, is the sale or rent of property or space in their buildings. Although only a minority of congregations—23 percent, comprising 38 percent of religious service attenders—received 1998 income from the sale or rent of buildings or property, this is substantially more than the number receiving income from their denominations (12 percent), from foundations (4 percent), or from government (3 percent). Also, congregations that received such income received it in amounts that are not trivial for small organizations. Thirty percent of congregations with 1998 income from the sale or rent of buildings or property received at least $5,000 from this source, 20 percent received at least $10,000, and 10 percent received at least

$25,000. Thirty percent of congregations receiving sale or rental income received at least 5 percent of their annual income from this source, and 15 percent received at least 10 percent of their annual income from this source.

It is difficult to know whether income from the sale or rent of property has become increasingly important for congregations over time. It seems safe to say, however, that although income from this source remains small for the majority of congregations, for a notable minority it seems to be an important way to make ends meet. More generally, we might expect congregations to respond to financial pressures exerted by demographic changes by seeking to reduce their dependence on individual donations. Increased sales of congregations' auxiliary properties or buildings, and increased renting of congregations' building space, seems likely. Congregations with property in desirable locations might, with this strategy, be able to sustain themselves for many years even in the face of dramatically dwindling membership. The desirability of this sort of trajectory is, of course, another matter.

Leaders

Attracting quality leadership is another perennial challenge for congregations. Some evidence points to a long-term and continuing decline in the average talent of individuals choosing clerical careers. Smaller proportions of Phi Beta Kappans and Rhodes scholars become clergy now than in previous decades, and the number of individuals taking Graduate Record Examinations who say they are headed to seminary declined 20 percent between 1981 and 1987. Moreover, the average verbal and analytical GRE scores of prospective seminary students declined during the 1980s, a decade in which average scores increased for all test takers. Prospective seminary students score significantly lower than the national average on the quantitative and analytical sections of the GRE, though only male prospective Master of Divinity students score lower than the national average on the verbal section of the test.[13]

Of course, these indicators of academic skill do not exhaust the meaning of "quality leadership." Finding relevant measures of talent and excellence is especially difficult for clergy, however, because congregations and denominations differ qualitatively in the kinds of training, skills, and personal characteristics they consider desirable for their clergy, with some valuing religious zeal in clergy more highly than their level of formal education. It certainly is true that many gifted individuals continue to enter the priesthood, ministry, and rabbinate. Still, it is noteworthy that several indicators of one kind of talent, partial and imperfect as they are, point in the same direction.

Not incidentally, the gender differences in GRE scores among prospective seminary students are substantial, with females consistently outperforming males, a fact that perhaps is a basis for optimism, at least for religious groups whose clergy is increasingly female. American congregations have been predominantly female for centuries, and they still are today. In the median congregation, 60 percent of the regular attenders are women. In some denominations recent cohorts of seminarians are 50 percent female, although only 10 percent of American congregations are led by women.

The challenge of attracting quality leadership is not equally shared by all denominations. As with participation, there are major differences across religious traditions. Jewish congregations—which pay their clergy better, on average, than Christian congregations—appear to be least affected by this challenge.[14] The Roman Catholic Church, by contrast, appears most affected, but it is worth noting that Protestant congregations are in fact more likely than Catholic congregations to be without either clergy or full-time staff. Seven percent of Protestant congregations (accounting for 5 percent of Protestants) are without a clergyperson or religious leader, compared with 1 percent of Catholic congregations (accounting for 2 percent of Catholics). Thirty-nine percent of Protestant congregations (with 18 percent of Protestants) have no full-time staff, compared with 33 percent of Catholic congregations (with 7 percent of Catholics).

Leaderless Protestant congregations are concentrated among Baptists, Pentecostals, and congregations with no denominational affiliation, but congregations within other major Protestant denominations are, in general, as likely as Catholic congregations to have neither clergy nor paid staff. Perhaps Protestant denominations, despite on-the-ground similarity with Catholics in proportions of leaderless congregations, do not understand themselves as experiencing a clergy shortage because, in most denominations, the total number of clergy continues to exceed the total number of congregations. At the same time, however, many clergy do not work in congregations. The United Methodist Church, for example, reported 35,609 congregations in 1999 and 43,872 total clergy, but only 24,998 clergy were serving in congregations (Lindner 2001). The same pattern is evident in many other Protestant denominations. The situation is one in which, although there are sufficient qualified clergy to meet the labor needs of congregations, there are substantial numbers of congregations unable to attract those clergy—mainly, it is safe to say, because they are unable to provide adequate compensation or because they are located in places where many clergy do not wish to live.

Numerical similarities notwithstanding, however, clergy shortages of equal magnitude create more significant organizational and theological problems for Catholics than for Protestants, since one can be a fully practicing Protestant without a minister but one cannot be a fully practicing Catholic without a priest available to perform the sacraments. All things considered, the clergy shortage probably is most severe in the Catholic Church, but it is not unique to the Catholic Church. Declining participation in congregations, along with other social changes influencing the status and authority of clergy, seem to have reduced the attractiveness of spending one's life leading a religious congregation.

The demographic changes I have described suggest that there will be a growing number of congregations too small to be able to employ full-time clergy. This clearly is occurring in at least one major denomination, the Evangelical Lutheran Church in America, which in 1998 had 270 more congregations with fewer than 50 attendees than it had in 1988. Consequently, the number of Lutheran congregations without pastors increased over this period from 10 percent in 1988 to 19 percent in 1998. Of the congregations in this denomination with fewer than 175 members, 38 percent have no pastor (*Ministry Needs and Resources in the Twenty-First Century*, 2000). Part of the problem is a decline in absolute numbers of ordained clergy and new clergy recruits, but that decline is not sufficient to account wholly for the increase in pastorless congregations. It seems likely that this kind of situation—in which the allocation of clergy is as problematic as the overall supply, and perhaps more so—characterizes other denominations as well.

In every religious tradition the challenge of attracting quality leadership is most acute for rural congregations and, whether rural or urban, for the smallest and least well off congregations. Small and rural congregations long have been disadvantaged in the clergy labor market, but this disadvantage is exacerbated, at least for Protestants, and probably also for Jews, by two recent developments.[15] First, the growth of two-

42

career families constrains geographic mobility, making rural congregations less attractive than they might be if one did not have to worry about meaningful employment for a spouse. Second, an increasing proportion of new clergy have entered the ministry in mid-life, as a second career. This enhances labor supply problems for small and rural congregations because such individuals often demand higher salaries and are less geographically mobile than younger people. In the Evangelical Lutheran Church in America, to give just one example, the average age at ordination increased from 29.5 in 1980 to 37.8 in 1998 (*Ministry Needs and Resources in the Twenty-First Century*, 2000).

The main point here is that the challenges of attracting high-quality leadership are unequally distributed among congregations. The congregations hit hardest by demographic changes will be those crossing a threshold below which they can no longer attract the kind of leadership they would like to have. Ecumenical agreements that make it easier for congregations of different denominations to share clergy are, in part, driven by recognition of this problem.

No chapter-length overview of congregations can be comprehensive. As we will see, however, the congregational features examined in this chapter—size, denomination, religious tradition, human and material resources—strongly shape congregational activities. This is nowhere more evident than with congregations' social service activities, the subject of the next chapter.

≫ 3 ≪

Social Services

Congregations' social service activities—how much they do and how they do it—have been of interest to scholars and religious leaders at least since the Social Gospel movement of the early twentieth century.[1] The more recent wave of interest in these activities has been prompted by efforts aimed at expanding religious organizations' participation in publicly funded social service programs, efforts commonly referred to as "faith-based" or "charitable choice" initiatives. These efforts, pushed forward largely by evangelical Protestant lawyers, scholars, activists, and politicians, achieved their most visible success when, in the opening days of his administration, President George W. Bush signed two executive orders, one establishing a White House Office of Faith-Based and Community Initiatives and another establishing Centers for Faith-Based and Community Initiatives in five federal agencies (Bush 2001a, b). Prior to this, the charitable choice movement's most visible achievement was the inclusion of section 104 in the Personal Responsibility and Work Opportunity Reconciliation Act of 1996—the welfare reform bill. The charitable choice language in this legislation required states to include religious organizations as eligible contractees if states contract with nonprofit organizations for social service delivery using funding streams established by this legislation. Similar language has since been included in legislation affecting other federal funding streams.[2]

Perhaps the most significant consequence of these events is the activity they have inspired within state and local governments and also among a wide range of nongovernmental actors, both secular and religious. Many states, for example, now have "faith-based" liaisons, offices, or task forces within their social service bureaucracies charged with increasing religious organizations' involvement in publicly funded social services. These offices provide grant-writing and other sorts of technical assistance to religious organizations seeking public funds, publicize funding opportunities through mailings to religious organizations and meetings of clergy and other religious leaders, advocate the incorporation of charitable choice language into state law, establish "demonstration projects" through which religious organizations receive funds, and so on.[3] All this activity is directed at channeling more public resources to religious social service providers, and there even have been attempts at both the national and state levels to create public funding streams for which only religious organizations are eligible (Workforce Development Branch 2000; Department of Health and Human Services 2001a).

Whatever the eventual fate of this movement, it has renewed attention to long-standing normative and empirical questions concerning church-state relations, the role of religion in our social welfare system, and—most relevant for this book—religious institutions' social service activities. In this chapter I engage these questions by providing a portrait of congregations' social service activity. Several aspects of this portrait contradict assumptions about congregations held by both advocates and critics of the charitable choice movement, and I do not hesitate to call attention to those contradictions when they arise. My primary aim, however, is to describe fundamental and enduring features of congregations' social service activities and thereby provide a portrait whose value is not limited to whatever direct relevance it may have to a contemporary, but likely fleeting, policy debate.

This chapter is organized around six key claims about congregations' social services:

1. Congregations typically engage in social services in only a minor and peripheral way.

2. Congregations' typical involvement in social services involves small groups of volunteers carrying out well-defined tasks on a periodic basis.

3. Congregations, when they do perform social services, mainly help to meet individuals' emergency needs in a way that involves minimal contact between congregation members and the needy. They are not especially holistic—indeed, they are not especially *religious*—in their approach to social services.

4. The rare congregations that engage more intensively in social services do so mainly in collaboration with a wide range of religious organizations, secular nonprofit organizations, and government agencies. It is more accurate to say that congregation-based social services depend on secular social service agencies than to say that they constitute an alternative to those agencies.

5. Congregations were not more intensively involved in social services in the early part of the twentieth century than they are now, nor did their social service activity ever represent an alternative to government-provided services, nor has there been a displacement of religious social services by secular services.

6. Collaborating with government, including receiving public funding, does not appear to dampen congregations' "prophetic voice" by discouraging their political and advocacy activities.

In developing these claims, I refute a number of popularly held assumptions about congregations' social service work.

Intensely Involved in Social Services?

How deeply or intensively are congregations involved in social services? Table 3.1 presents the percentage of congregations participating in or supporting various social service programs. The table also includes the percentage of attenders who attend congregations that participate in or support these programs. Although a majority of congregations report some type of social service activity—57 percent of congregations, comprising 75 percent of attenders, participate in or support some type of social service program—the percentages engaged in any specific kind of program are rather small.[4] Food programs, for instance, are the most common kind of activity, but they involve only 32 percent of congregations and 50 percent of attenders. Food programs are followed in popularity by programs for housing or shelter (18 percent of congregations, 32 percent of attenders) and clothing (11 percent of congregations, 18 percent of attenders). Well behind these are programs in the areas of health, education (excluding religious education), domestic violence, substance abuse, tutoring/mentoring, and work/employment. Fewer than 10 percent of congregations participate in or support programs of this sort.[5]

Table 3.1 disguises a great deal of variation in the intensity with which congregations are involved in social service activity. The 32 percent of congregations supporting or participating in

Table 3.1 Congregations' social service activities

Activity	Participating congregations (%)	Attenders in participating congregations (%)
Any program	57	75
Program type:		
Food	32	50
Housing/shelter	18	32
Programs specifically aimed at children or students	16	26
Clothing	11	18
Homelessness	8	16
Programs specifically aimed at either women or men	8	16
Habitat for Humanity	7	13
Support for the sick	7	13
Education (not including religious education)	6	10
Programs for elderly	6	10
Cash to needy	5	10
Programs for needy, not elsewhere classified	5	8
Health programs	4	10
Domestic violence	4	6
Disaster relief	4	4
International programs	3	8
Household support	3	5
Ethnicity (heritage or antiracism)	2	4
Family support	2	4
Social or political activism	2	4
Prison-related programs	2	4
Clean highways or parks	2	3
Substance abuse	2	3
Community safety	2	2
Recreation	1	3
Tutoring or mentoring	1	3
Community service, not elsewhere classified	1	2
Employment	1	2
Immigration support	1	2
Job training	< 1	1
Quality of contact with needy:		
Long-term and face-to-face	9	17
Short-term and fleeting	35	54

food programs, for example, encompass a wide range of involvement levels, from donating money to a community food bank, to supplying volunteers for a Meals on Wheels project, to organizing a food drive every Thanksgiving, to operating food pantries or soup kitchens. Similar variety is evident among housing programs and programs to serve the homeless. Regarding housing, specific activities range from providing volunteers to do home repair for the needy, to assisting first-time home buyers with congregational funds, to participating in neighborhood redevelopment efforts, to building affordable housing for senior citizens. By far the most common housing-related activity engaged in by congregations is participation in a Habitat for Humanity project: 41 percent of the housing-related activities reported by congregations refer to Habitat projects. Regarding serving the homeless, congregational involvement ranges from donating money to a neighborhood shelter, to providing volunteers who prepare dinner at a shelter on a rotating basis with other congregations, to actually providing shelter for homeless women and children in the congregation's building. Here the most common activity is providing money and/or volunteers to shelters administered by other organizations.

How intensively do congregations engage in these activities? Not very. The median congregation mentions participating in or supporting only one social service program. Even if we limit attention to congregations that mention at least one program, the median number of programs mentioned is only two. The median attender is in a congregation that participates in or supports two programs. Of course, the total number of programs reported by congregations is not the only possible measure of the intensity with which a congregation engages in social services, since a congregation might engage in only one program but may do so intensively. Other indicators make clear, however, that the vast majority of congregations are involved in social services only in a peripheral way. Only 6 percent of congregations, for example, have a staff person devoting at least 25 percent of his or her time to social service projects. Focusing on the subset of congregations reporting some degree of social service involvement, we find that only 12 percent have a staff person devoting that much time to social service projects. The median dollar amount spent on social services by these more active congregations is approximately $1,200, or less than 3 percent of an average congregation's total budget.[6]

Time-use studies of clergy find that they spend very few hours on community activities of any sort,[7] and even volunteer involvement in social services is small-scale for most congregations, with the median active congregation involving only ten volunteers in these efforts. In 80 percent of the congregations engaged in these activities, thirty or fewer volunteers were mobilized for social service work in the past year. As with money and staff time, the vast majority of congregations devote very small percentages of their volunteer energies to social service activities.

The peripheral nature of social services for most congregations also is clear from the case study literature. Very typical is the Church of God congregation that responded to increased economic need in the community by "establishing a Social Needs Committee and restocking the Helping Hands Cupboard more often than usual" (Ammerman 1997a:130) or the Baptist church which "created a local missions budget of 2 percent of all contributions available for those in need" and used that money mainly to give small cash grants to individuals in times of need (Flynt 1994:147). Omar McRoberts (2003:124) found that only two of the twenty-nine churches located in Boston's high-poverty Four Corners area "housed programs that specifically addressed the neighborhood's social and economic needs." Lowell Livezey summarized results from case studies of seventy-five Chicago congregations, reporting: "Most of the congregations principally serve their own members, with service to the wider community and advocacy for public causes relegated to small committees and discretionary portions of annual budgets . . . . [P]rograms of social service and social action account for but a fraction of the religious contribution to the quality of urban life" (Livezey 2000a:20).

In emphasizing the slight social service involvement of the vast majority of congregations, I do not mean to trivialize congregations' contributions in the human service arena. Two points of context should be borne in mind. First, it is clear that, however small the percentage, some congregations are deeply engaged in social services, and even if only one half of 1 percent of the more than 300,000 congregations in the United States are so engaged, that still represents at least 1,500 congregations.[8] A very small percentage of actively involved congregations still adds up to a substantial amount of activity. Second, properly assessing congregations' social service contributions requires comparing their level of effort to the level of effort observed in other organizations, especially other membership organizations whose main purpose, as for congregations, is something other than charity or social service. In what other organizational population do the majority of units engage in social services, however peripherally? What other organizations whose primary purpose is something other than charity devote, on average, more than 2 percent of their income to charity?[9] In what other organizational population do as many as 32 percent of the units organize food donations, 12 percent distribute clothing, 8 percent engage in some sort of service to the homeless, or 6 percent have staff devoting a quarter of their time to social service activities? From this comparative perspective, congregations emerge as more committed to social services than other organizations whose main purpose is neither charity nor social service. Somewhat ironically, recognizing that social service provision is not central to congregational life enhances our appreciation of the small amounts of social services that they do.

The congregation actively delivering social services is a rarity, but it is one worth understanding more deeply. One obvious question is, Which types of congregations do more social services? Four patterns are particularly important.[10] First, congregations with more resources do more social services. Controlling for other things, we find that larger congregations and congregations with larger budgets do more social services. Congregations with one thousand regular participants, for example, report participating in or supporting two more social service programs than the median congregation of seventy-five people. The direction of this relationship is not surprising, but its magnitude—the extent to which social service activity is concentrated among the largest congregations—should be emphasized. Looking at the money spent on social services, for example, we find that the largest 1 percent of congregations spend one fifth of all the money congregations spend on social services; the largest 10 percent spend more than half.[11]

Second, the social class of both the neighborhood and the congregation influence social service activity, but in a counterintuitive fashion. Congregations in poor neighborhoods perform more social services than congregations in non-poor neighborhoods, but congregations with many low-income members do no more social services than congregations with few low-income members. Congregations with more college-educated members perform more social services. Interestingly, however, controlling for other variables, we find that congregations with particularly high income constituents do *fewer* social services. If we take these results together, it appears that the most active congregations are those that are located in poor neighborhoods but whose members are more middle than lower class. The downtown congregation filled with people who commute there from middle-class suburbs is a familiar feature of American cities. Although the social distance between such congregations and their immediate neighbors may be substantial, these congregations in fact provide more social services than the churches in the same neighborhoods that are peopled by those who live in those neighborhoods. It seems that the human and material resources provided by a middle-class constituency trump social embeddedness when it comes to the extent to which congregations provide social services.[12]

Third, religious tradition matters. Moderate and liberal Protestant congregations, as well as Catholic and Jewish congregations, perform more social services than conservative Protestant congregations. Without regard to denominational affiliation, self-described theologically liberal congregations also perform more social services than self-described conservative congregations. Whatever their denominational affiliations, congregations in denominations that are described by their leaders as theologically liberal report participating in or supporting two more social service programs on average than congregations that are described as theologically conservative. This might not sound like a substantial difference, but consider this comparison: the difference in social service involvement between self-described liberal and self-described conservative congregations is about the same as the difference between a seventy-five person congregation and a thousand-person congregation. This pattern is consistent with previous research on both congregations and individuals, showing that theologically liberal individuals and congregations are, in a variety of ways, more connected to their surrounding communities than are individuals and congregations associated with more evangelical or conservative traditions (Wuthnow 1999; Ammerman 2002; Beyerlein and Hipp 2003). It is a theme that will recur throughout this book.

Fourth, there is no generic race difference. Predominantly African American congregations do not, on average, perform more social services than predominantly white congregations. African American congregations are, however, more likely than white congregations to engage in certain important types of activities, such as education, mentoring, substance abuse prevention, and job training or employment assistance programs (Tsitsos 2003).

So far I have argued that the vast majority of congregations engage in social services only marginally. At the same time, some congregations perform more social services than others, and I have identified key correlates of congregational involvement in this sort of activity. Beyond the question of which congregations do *more* social services, we might also ask about the *nature* of congregational social services among the most active congregations. When congregations engage in social services, what does that activity look like? In addition to its intrinsic interest, this question is important because the debate prompted by the charitable choice movement has rested on certain assumptions about the nature of congregation-based social services. In the next three sections I compare these assumptions with empirical reality.

A Vast Reservoir of Volunteers?

American congregations are sometimes conceptualized as a vast reservoir of volunteer labor. There is a sense in which this is true. When congregations do more than donate money or canned goods or old clothes, they are most apt to organize small groups of volunteers to conduct relatively well defined tasks on a periodic basis: fifteen people spending several weekends renovating a house, five people cooking dinner at a homeless shelter one night a week, ten young people spending two summer weeks painting a school in a poor community, and so on. Half of all congregations say that they support social service activities via the provision of volunteers. Of congregations engaged in social service activity, 90 percent report supporting at least one activity in the form of volunteer labor from the congregation. In this light, it probably is not an accident that the highest levels of congregational involvement occur in arenas—such as food and housing—that also have organizations (such as homeless shelters and Habitat for Humanity) able to take advantage of congregations' capacity to mobilize relatively small numbers of volunteers to carry out well-defined, bounded tasks. Programs or projects able to adapt to this model are likely to be more successful at drawing congregations into their efforts than programs or projects in which this model is not appropriate.

Although providing volunteers is a common kind of congregational involvement in social services, the total number of volunteers provided by the typical congregation is small: ten individuals in the average active congregation. Observations emphasizing how few individuals are involved are typical in the case study literature: "Few church members volunteer at the soup kitchen, but they take pride in it" (Laudarji and Livezey 2000:95). "A core of two dozen or so members [out of about one hundred regular attenders] is active in various church affairs . . . A similarly small number are involved in the one outreach ministry in which the church has been engaged in recent years. On one Wednesday each month, members provide a meal for the residents of Cascade House, a shelter for homeless women and children" (Ammerman 1997a:153). "While Holman is a remarkably active church, it accomplishes its ministries through the efforts of only a handful of its members" (Ammerman 1997a:144).

In one congregation the small Peace and Justice Committee sponsors many activities. Members of this committee "recognize that not everyone in the parish shares their concerns, but they are anxious to get as many people as possible involved" (Ammerman 1997a:173). In another congregation, "several attempts to begin a peace and justice group in the parish have fizzled . . . The St. Vincent de Paul Society [which manages a thrift store] and the new pro-life group are the two points where St. Lawrence members attempt to reach out to problems and issues beyond their experience. Both are relatively small groups" (Ammerman 1997a:296–297). In a United Methodist Congregation that supports a women's shelter, inner-city ministries, and a home for the elderly with donations and volunteers, "only a small portion of the church's twenty-four hundred members are more than nominally involved" (Ammerman 1997a:254).

Margaret Harris, summarizing the situation in four congregations she studied in England, noted that congregational welfare projects' "continuity may be dependent on the enthusiasm and personal circumstances of just one or two committed people" (Harris 1998:193). Lawrence Mamiya (1994:241) studied a very active African Methodist Episcopal Church and commented, "It is very rare for an entire congregation to become involved in social ministry, beyond contributing funds or attending meetings. Most of the daily work of congregational social ministries is carried out by a few members who are highly motivated and display individual initiative."

Even large-scale congregational programs do not necessarily imply a large volunteer base, and, interestingly, congregational programs that indeed use many volunteers do not necessarily draw those volunteers from the sponsoring congregation. Large-scale programs often are run by professional staff whose salaries are paid by grants and contracts from non-congregational sources, including government. David Roozen and his colleagues (1984:151), for example, described the situation in an "activist" congregation they studied: "Although the membership approves of the social action ministry, the staff appears to do most of the work. Laypeople sit on the outreach board and endorse plans; several also serve as volunteers in various programs . . . But it is the dynamic, hard-driving staff that is most often out front . . . [T]he situation is of concern to many members, in part because 'it makes the programs dependent on such a small group.'"

Matthew Price studied several very active Chicago congregations. One offered a large tutoring program that received 75 percent of its funding from foundations, 20 percent from government, and only 5 percent from individual contributions. It used more than three hundred volunteers, only four or five of whom were members of the sponsoring church. The social distance between the program and the sponsoring congregation was dramatized "when a representative of [the program] came to the church to talk on Ministry Sunday [and] it became obvious that she had no idea [that the church] and the program she worked for had ever been connected" (Price 2000:68). Price concludes that social services at this and other congregations are best understood as a product of the "professionalization of urban ministry, with the full-time staff assuming the major responsibilities" (Price 2000:68).

There are, of course, congregations in which more than a handful of individuals are involved in social service activities, but such congregations are the exception, not the rule. The image of a congregation united behind a social service project and devoting its collective energies to it is misleading if it is taken as the typical situation. On the contrary, most congregation-based social services, especially programs that are more demanding, are driven by paid staff and small cadres of volunteers. This pattern is so pervasive that we might wonder if it is appropriate to speak of "congregation-based" social services when such activity typically involves only a few people in the congregation.

A Holistic Approach?

Some have claimed that religious organizations specialize in, or are particularly well suited for, a certain kind of social service activity: holistic service delivery that focuses on personal transformation and provides long-term, lasting solutions to poor people's problems. This assumption is evident in the ur-text of "compassionate conservatism" (Olasky 1992), and it is invoked repeatedly by advocates for expanding the role of religious organizations in our social welfare system. The idea is that there is a distinctively religious approach to social services, one that—even when there is no explicit religious content involved—is relational, morally compelling, and personable; provides love, guidance, and friendship; and helps people transform their lives.[13] This laudable approach to social services is assumed to come more naturally to religious organizations than to government agencies or (in some accounts) to secular social service providers, not least because religiously based services are thought to be more likely to integrate needy people into communities of faith, which are best able to deal holistically with individuals' material, emotional, and spiritual needs. These claims are made about religiously based social services in general, not just about congregations. It is, however, appropriate to ask whether congregations manifest a distinctively holistic or transformational approach to social service delivery. If such an approach has an elective affinity with religion, it ought to be visible in the activities undertaken by the organizations—that is, congregations—where religion is most central, and where the connection between the social services and a concrete community of faith is most direct.

Look again at Table 3.1. I noted earlier that congregations participate in or support some types of programs more than others, but now I want to emphasize a pattern in this variable participation: congregations are much more likely to engage in activities that address the immediate, short-term needs of recipients for food, clothing, and shelter than in programs requiring more sustained and personal involvement to meet longer-term needs, such as programs in the areas of health, education (excluding religious education), domestic violence, substance abuse, tutoring or mentoring, and work or employ-ment.

There are, of course, more or less holistic or personalistic ways to engage in the same activity. Congregations might feed homeless people, for example, by moving them quickly through a cafeteria-style serving line and making sure they leave promptly upon finishing their meal, or they might feed homeless people in ways that foster more interaction between the homeless people and the volunteers, perhaps by having dif-ferent serving stations for each food item, or by having volun-teers eat at tables with the clients (Sager et al. 2001). Table 3.1 also shows the results from a preliminary effort to measure these stylistic differences directly rather than infer them sim-ply from an activity's purpose.[14] The picture is the same. Pro-grams that appear to involve only short-term or fleeting kinds of contact with the needy are far more common among con-gregations than programs that involve more intensive or long-term, face-to-face interaction. Only 9 percent of congregations (comprising 17 percent of attenders) are involved in the more personal kinds of programs. By contrast, fully 35 percent of congregations (including over 54 percent of attenders) participate in or support the more fleeting kinds of activities.

Not incidentally, although congregational surveys vary regarding the overall frequency with which congregations perform social services, all such surveys agree on three points: (1) the majority, perhaps the vast majority, of congregations engage in something that might be called "social services," however sporadic or limited; (2) only a tiny percentage perform social services in an intensive way that takes up significant amounts of their resources; and (3) congregations are far more likely to support emergency services focused on immediate needs for food, clothing, and shelter than to support services requiring more sustained interaction with poor people and focused on long-term problems and needs.[15]

Case studies of congregations that are more actively involved in social services sharpen the picture that emerges from survey results. This body of research shows that even when congregations are more actively involved in social services, that activity rarely brings the needy into the life of the congregation. The more typical situation is one in which the people served by a congregation's human needs programs remain at quite a social distance from the congregation's members. If the holistic and personalistic character of congregation-based social services is meant to emerge from the integration of the needy into a faith community, it is important to recognize how rarely this happens.[16]

Isaac Laudarji and Lowell Livezey (2000) studied twelve churches within walking distance of Henry Horner Homes, a public housing complex in Chicago. Only one "claimed participation of Henry Horner residents as members or regular attenders, although several spoke of ministries to them, including evangelization and social services." Similarly, residents of Henry Horner "mentioned only [the one church] as a church they attended [although the others] were known for their soup kitchens, food pantries, and free clothing" (p. 91). This pattern cut across racial and denominational lines. "Children in the neighborhood partake of the summer afternoon lunches provided through the [African Methodist Episcopal] church but seldom join in the Sunday school or other church activities oriented to member families" (p. 94). At a Roman Catholic church the "school, soup kitchen, and women's shelter provide major resources for the residents of Henry Horner and for the homeless who survive on the streets [yet] the social ministries are offered with minimal contact between the recipients and the members and staff of the church" (p. 95). A Baptist church provides a feeding program, a clothing closet, and a tutoring program, but "the volunteer service providers do not seem to have continuing social contact with the recipients, and the recipients do not participate in the worshiping community" (p. 96). These churches clearly help relieve the day-to-day deprivations of the poor, but they also "find it very difficult to include the socially isolated poor as participants as well as recipients" (p. 91).[17]

This same pattern occurs again and again in the case study literature. In one Roman Catholic church which runs a school that is 30 percent nonwhite and has five hundred volunteers involved in its outreach programs (many of whom are not actually members of the parish), "nonwhite parents are not visible in the congregation [and] [d]espite the extensive volunteering in the poor areas of the city, it is hard to spot anyone [at services] without a middle-class appearance" (Wedam 2000:228). Observers of a Congregational church deeply involved in social services found that "the congregation had not created any stable identity as a community *church*." Rather, "instead of being a *part* of the community in which they existed, they had almost become a detached service agency" (Stout and Brekus

1994:88). Nancy Ammerman describes a predominantly African American United Methodist church whose members "actually find their immediate neighbors rather mysterious . . . [T]hey did not know much about who was now in the neighborhood . . . they were pretty sure that their neighbors were different from themselves and had different needs, [and] they were not quite sure what those needs might be" (Ammerman 1997a:142). At a Presbyterian church on Chicago's "Gold Coast" that is very intensely involved in social services, "few families or individuals from Cabrini-Green [the nearby low-income housing complex] cross the social boundaries between the Gold Coast and Cabrini-Green except during tutoring." This congregation's outreach "is designed to help others, not to integrate them into the community . . . [It is] an ideal form of the lay liberal ethos that gives individuals the opportunity to help others without making the contact too intimate" (Wellman 1999:172–173).[18]

Even congregation-based social service activity that begins with self-conscious and well-intentioned strategies aimed at creating more personal contact between clients served by programs and congregations does not often sustain that approach. Sometimes this is because the effort is superficial, as in the Disciples of Christ congregation in which "members recently decided to put an information table in a place where people coming for [the welfare program that rents space from the congregation] could learn about the church" (Ammerman 1997a:112). At other times, however, less superficial efforts also fail. A new associate pastor in a Baptist congregation, for example, "put together a lively Wednesday evening program for children and youth that began to draw as many as a hundred participants, many of them otherwise unchurched and many of them African American children from the neighborhood." But this event disrupted a "midweek fellowship dinner traditionally enjoyed by one hundred or so longtime members [who] were unwilling to put up with the disruption." The associate pastor left, and "Wednesday night returned to normal" (Ammerman 1997a:119–120).

Mississippi's "Faith and Families" program, designed to connect needy families with mentors in religious congregations, proved ineffective and by 2003 was no longer in operation (Bartkowski and Regis 2003). And an in-depth case study of a congregation's mentoring effort in Wisconsin found that people in the congregation experienced great difficulty connecting with and knowing how to help the poor people in the program. This congregation gave up on its mentoring efforts after only seven months, and the larger program of which they were a part, which involved several congregations, folded after three years (Lichterman 2004). It seems that even when congregations set out to provide more holistic care, those efforts often flounder on the rocky shore of social boundaries and complex realities.[19]

As rare as holistic or transformational approaches to social services are in congregations, perhaps they are even more rare among secular voluntary associations engaged in social service work. Systematic comparisons between congregation-based social services and social services provided by other sorts of organizations are needed to judge whether or not a 10 percent likelihood of long-term or face-to-face programs still might represent an elective affinity, however weak, between an organization's religious base and this sort of social service work. Although I do not have the evidence that would be necessary to make such comparisons, studies of social services in religious organizations other than congregations suggest that these comparisons would not change the basic picture. Stephen Monsma and Carolyn Mounts, for example, surveyed welfare-to-work service providers in four cities. In addition to the standard job-oriented services, such as GED (General Educational Development) test preparation, vocational training, and job placement services, for each provider they measured the extent to which they also attempted to influence "the behavior, attitudes, and values of welfare recipients" through activities focused on "work preparedness, life skills, and mentoring." The key result in the current context is that the religious organizations did no more of this activity than the secular nonprofit, government, or even for-profit providers. This null result holds even when religion-based programs that integrate explicitly religious elements into their programming are isolated. At least among providers of welfare-to-work services, there is no evidence that religious organizations are more likely to do things "holistically" (Monsma and Mounts 2001).[20]

Returning to congregations, one might be tempted to argue that a distinctively holistic style of social services is not generically religious but is rather particular to conservative or evangelical religious traditions. Perhaps the greater emphasis in these traditions on saving lost souls might encourage more personalistic styles of interacting with the needy. In this event such an approach would occur more often in conservative or evangelical congregations than in others. But this is not the case. The evangelistic urge, when it is channeled through social services, is shaped and limited by the same social boundaries that shape and limit congregation-based social services for which the evangelical urge is more distant. One evangelical congregation that fed homeless people, for example, was self-consciously engaged in this activity primarily to save souls, but, in practice, the volunteers directed their most personal and intensive conversionist efforts—engaging in long conversations, extending invitations to other events—toward other middle-class volunteers, not toward the homeless individuals, at whom they mainly preached (Sager et al. 2001).

Table 3.2 compares the social services offered by conservative or evangelical Protestant congregations with the services offered by other congregations. The results are unambiguous: There is, in fact, *no* specific type of social service activity, including the more intensive types, that conservative congregations are more likely than other congregations to perform.[21] On the contrary, conservative congregations do fewer of almost all types of social services. I called attention to this pattern earlier. Here let me emphasize that the lower levels of social service involvement by conservative and evangelical congregations includes those activities which appear to be more holistic or personalistic.

So, as we have seen in this section and the previous one, there is indeed a common style by which congregations involve themselves in social services, but it is not the style envisioned by those who characterize religiously based social services as a holistic alternative to secular social services. Congregation-based social service involvement is more typically composed of small groups of volunteers who are enlisted to carry out well-defined periodic tasks, usually focused on a very specific need. They do not, in general, require more than fleeting personal contact with needy people, entail a particularly holistic approach to individuals' crosscutting needs, or aim at character transformation. Congregational social services are much more commonly characterized by attention to short-term emergency needs, especially for food, clothing, and shelter. These programs do not, in general, bring the poor into community with the people of the serving congregation. If congregations' social services are imagined to be more effective than secular social services because they are more holistic, neither quantitative nor qualitative evidence supports that idea.[22]

There is a larger lesson here. Congregations are embedded in society. Among other things, this means that their activities, however well intentioned, are shaped and constrained by the

Table 3.2 Conservative/evangelical versus other congregations' social service activities

Activity	Conservative/ evangelical congregations (%)	Other congregations (%)
Any program	50	74
Program type:		
Food*	27	46
Housing/shelter*	15	28
Programs specifically aimed at children or students*	13	23
Clothing*	9	14
Homelessness*	7	13
Programs specifically aimed at either women or men*	6	14
Habitat for Humanity*	6	12
Support for the sick*	4	15
Education (not including religious education)*	4	13
Programs for elderly*	5	11
Cash to needy	5	4
Programs for needy, not elsewhere classified	5	7
Health programs	4	5
Domestic violence*	2	11
Disaster relief	3	7
International programs	2	5
Household support	3	2
Ethnicity (heritage or antiracism)*	2	4
Family support	2	3
Social or political activism*	1	4
Prison-related programs	2	3
Clean highways or parks*	1	3
Substance abuse	2	2
Community safety	1	2
Recreation	1	2
Tutoring or mentoring*	1	3
Community service, not elsewhere classified*	< 1	2
Employment	1	1

Table 3.2 (continued)

Activity	Conservative/ evangelical congregations (%)	Other congregations (%)
Immigration support	< 1	1
Job training	< 1	1
Quality of contact with needy:		
Long-term and face-to-face*	7	17
Short-term and fleeting*	30	50

* Difference between conservative/evangelical and other congregations is statistically significant at $p \leq .05$.

same social inequalities that shape and constrain other organizations' activities, and their operations are governed by the same pressures toward social homophily that operate in the rest of society. To put it bluntly, there is little reason to expect congregations to be better than other voluntary membership associations at forging genuine and lasting connections among people across social and cultural boundaries or at developing social services that achieve or are based on such connections. From this perspective, it ought not surprise us to learn that congregations' social services do not, in general, take a distinctively holistic or transformational form. One would expect otherwise only if there were reason to believe that religious organizations transcend the social constraints operating elsewhere in society.

An Alternative to Secular Social Services?

Religiously based social services often are portrayed as a valuable alternative to government or secular social services. They might constitute an alternative if religiously based services existed in an organizational world that is separate from the world of government and secular social services, or they might constitute an alternative if religious organizations that keep their distance from government and secular social service providers were better able to approach social services in a distinctive way, which in this context usually means a more holistic and personal way. In this section I show that collaboration with secular and government organizations—not separation from them—is the norm for congregation-based social services, and that such collaboration does not further reduce the (already low) likelihood that a congregation approaches social services in a more holistic manner. Given these realities, it is difficult to credit the notion that congregations, or religious organizations in general, might offer a genuine alternative to the social service system already in place.

Table 3.3 shows that congregational social service activity is mainly done in collaboration with other organizations.[23] Eighty-four percent of congregations that perform social services have at least one collaborator on at least one program. Seventy-two percent of all programs are carried out in collaboration with others. Although other congregations are the single most common type of collaborator, congregations that engage in social services are as likely to collaborate with some sort of secular organization (57 percent of congregations, 38 percent of programs) as with some sort of religious organization (55 percent of congregations, 40 percent of programs). Although only 3 percent of congregations currently receive government financial support for their social service activity, about a fifth of those with programs collaborate in some fashion with a government agency. Clearly, when congregations engage in social services, they mainly do so in collaboration with others, including secular and government agencies.[24]

Congregations are not equally likely to collaborate. Large, mainline Protestant, theologically liberal congregations with

Table 3.3 Patterns of collaboration in the provision of social services

Type of collaborator	% of congregations with service programs collaborating with:	% of programs administered in collaboration with:
Any collaborator	84	72
Any secular collaborator	57	38
Governmental agency	20	7
Nongovernmental secular collaborator	49	31
Any religious collaborator	55	40
Other congregation(s)	41	25
Noncongregational religious collaborator	27	17

more college graduates are significantly more likely than others to collaborate on social services. Here is yet another manifestation of the same religious variation in civic engagement we have seen before. In addition to being less likely to perform social services, when conservative and evangelical congregations do engage in this work, they also are less likely to collaborate with others. There thus appear to be enduring differences in levels and types of civic engagement among religious traditions.

Interestingly, although there are no race differences in the likelihood of collaborating in general, predominantly African American congregations are significantly more likely than white congregations to collaborate with *secular* organizations on social services, perhaps because, as I noted earlier, African American congregations are more likely to have the types of programs—mentoring, substance abuse prevention, job training, or employment assistance programs—that would involve congregations with secular collaborators.

The great extent to which congregations collaborate in social service work also is evident in qualitative investigations of congregations' social service work. Consider, for example, programs that feed the hungry. The soup kitchen is one of the most common forms of congregational involvement in social services, and, on the surface, it appears to be the quintessential case of a social service provided largely by religious organizations operating on their own, supported only by their own material and volunteer resources. But this surface appearance is misleading. A study of congregation-based feeding programs in Tucson, for example, revealed that virtually all of these programs used food that came from the local food bank, a secular nonprofit organization, and virtually all relied on grants from the city to pay someone to cook the food and someone else to deliver it to the congregations each evening, where volunteers then distributed it to hungry people (Sager et al. 2001). The congregations are an important part of this system—they provide volunteers to serve the food and space in which people can eat it—but they would not be able to do this work absent a three-way collaboration among the congregations, a secular nonprofit organization, and the city.

This situation is typical. Nancy Ammerman describes a Seventh-day Adventist congregation that runs a food pantry. The pantry is staffed by church volunteers, but it also "receives money from the Federal Emergency Management Agency and contributions from a food bank" (Ammerman 1997a:102). Robert Wuthnow studied twenty nonprofit organizations and sixty congregations in Pennsylvania and found many examples of church-based activity, including food banks, that depended on collaborations with secular nonprofits and government. He reported that "none of the [congregation-based soup kitchens or food distribution programs] would be possible without Second Harvest," a large secular food bank which itself is tied to the state's food distribution program (Wuthnow 2000:28).

Congregation-based feeding programs, far from existing on their own and relying solely on congregational resources, are in fact dependent on a complex mix of collaborations. Although such programs may exist physically in congregations, the apparently simple act of ladling a cup of soup into a homeless person's bowl in a church basement typically depends on a web of secular, religious, and government agencies, a mix of volunteers and paid staff, and a blend of public and private money.

Collaboration is the norm for all kinds of congregation-based social services, not just food programs. Furthermore, although collaboration with secular organizations and government, including financial collaboration, is present at every level of congregational social service involvement, it is particularly evident among the most active congregations. Church-based child care programs, for example, often work closely with secular agencies to coordinate services in various ways (Wuthnow 2000). One congregation with $30,000 to spend did so in "close cooperation with the town's Social Service Department, . . . with the department doing initial screening of needs and making recommendations for grants" (Roozen et al 1984:111). Another congregation ran a tutorial program with "grants from the state and from foundations, corporations, banks, and utility companies," not to mention a Head Start program and a summer youth program, both run with federal funds (Roozen et al. 1984:170). Yet another congregation "rarely undertakes a project alone . . . Their partners include the regional ecumenical association, the housing coalition, Christian Outreach Appeal (a local provider of services to people in need), and various AIDS organizations, with funding from local businesses, civic groups, even federal and state sources" (Ammerman 1997a:178–179). In another, "much of the legwork for the feeding and youth programs comes from

Boston College (BC) volunteers, while the mayor's office and local merchants supply funding and food, respectively, for other programs" (Ammerman 1997a:203). A very active Roman Catholic church in San Francisco "became home to several federally sponsored programs [as well as] War on Poverty programs and programs sponsored by the Economic Opportunity Council." The congregation's school "received funds for field trips, books, reading assistance, and bilingual education." Head Start as well as two other federal programs were housed in the congregation's building (Burns 1994:427).

Another typical pattern is for several congregations to support a coalition which in turn provides social services in collaboration with other organizations and government agencies. Examining congregation-based social services in Hartford in the 1980s, David Roozen and his colleagues observed that much of this activity occurred through a coalition of ten churches which ran "three different meals programs; classes for senior citizens seven days a week; tutoring, recreation, and summer job programs for youth; a drop-in center for street people; two overnight shelters; an adult job training program; and a recently begun counseling-referral program." This organization had a budget of close to $600,000, "much of that from federal grants" (Roozen et al. 1984:156).[25] Another observer calls Chicago's Northwest Community Organizations (NCO) "the most significant community group of the [1960s and 1970s]. Significant here is that the NCO "included twenty-two Roman Catholic churches, fifteen Protestant churches, schools, settlement houses, local business leaders, and fifteen civic organizations" (Shaw 1994:384). Substantial social service and community work usually requires collaboration across these boundaries.

This pattern of close collaboration between congregations and secular, including government, agencies also is evident outside the United States. In England, Margaret Harris described a congregation that was able to shift from providing homeless people "a roof for a night or two" to refurbishing houses, making it possible to "put people into flats for longer periods" as a result of a grant from a local government authority. She also observed congregational social service activities that, by their very nature, depend on collaborations with other, mainly secular organizations: a monthly drop-in session in order "to refer people to other places where they could get the information they needed"; a choir concert to raise money which was given to charity; and involvement in "coordinated local welfare efforts" with several organizations (Harris 1995:57–59).

Collaboration with other organizations, including secular organizations and government agencies, is the norm when congregations provide social services. The quantity and depth of these collaborations indicate that congregation-based social services often are integrated into community social welfare systems. They are, in other words, part of the larger system, not an alternative to that larger system.

There is, however, another sense in which congregation-based social services might provide a genuine alternative to secular options. Even if most congregations collaborate with secular and government agencies when they do this work, religiously based social services might still offer a valuable alternative if the congregations that refrain from collaborating retain a distinctive style or approach in this work. It is important to ask, then, whether collaborations with secular or government agencies alter the character of congregations' social services in ways that make them less distinctive in their approach.

As noted earlier, a holistic or personalistic approach often is attributed to religious social services. Those who believe that religiously based social services are distinctively holistic—and

73

therefore constitute an important alternative to social services delivered by nonreligious, especially government, agencies—also tend to worry that this alternative approach is potentially undermined by collaboration with such agencies. We are cautioned in this regard that "religious nonprofits that contract with the state may, as a result, shift their purpose from the transformation of lives to the mere delivery of services," or that the "drawbacks of state funding go deeper than the loss to welfare recipients of the benefits of a spiritual ministry," or that charitable choice "is an innovative public policy measure intended to ensure that when churches and religious nonprofits cooperate with government, they will remain alternatives to it" (Sherman 1995:58, 60; Carlson-Thies 1999:31).

This sort of claim sometimes is offered by critics of the charitable choice movement, who use it to warn religious organizations against partnering with government (as in Treadwell 2000). It also is sometimes offered by charitable choice advocates, who use it to support the notion that religious organizations partnering with government should be able to do so under more lax monitoring and accountability regulations that will protect their distinctively holistic approach from government meddling. Either way, instances of this claim emphasize the threat to religiously based social services posed by partnering with government agencies.

Although claims of this sort usually emphasize the possible consequences of *government* collaborations, the underlying logic implies that collaborations with secular nonprofits also risk undermining religious organizations' distinctive approach to social services. If there is a distinctive approach to social services taken by religious organizations, that approach will not be shared by secular nonprofit collaborators any more than it will be shared by government collaborators. Moreover, many, perhaps most, of the secular nonprofits with which congregations may collaborate are themselves funded by government and may transmit the government virus (and its characteristic symptoms of bureaucracy, impersonality, and unresponsiveness) to their religious collaborators, especially if those collaborations involve formal contracts or subcontracts. The basic idea behind this line of thinking is that collaborations with secular organizations—government or nonprofit—will, if firewalls are not present, place religious social services at risk of losing or diluting their holistic emphasis.

I argued earlier that holistic and more intensive kinds of social services are very rare among congregations. But that approach is not completely absent, and if it is in fact more common among congregations that refrain from partnering with secular or government agencies when doing this work, that would support the notion that congregation-based social services might constitute an alternative to services delivered under other auspices. It is worth examining, then, whether congregational social service activity looks systematically different in relevant ways when secular, especially government, collaborators are involved. Is there evidence that a holistic approach to social service is undermined by collaboration with nonreligious, especially government, agencies?

Table 3.4 examines this question by cross-tabulating the types of organizations with which congregations collaborate with the nature of the social service programs in which the congregations participate. The table looks at this relationship from the perspective of each program associated with a congregation. That is, for each program we can ask: With whom does the congregation collaborate on that program? And does that program take a more holistic approach, one involving longer-term, face-to-face interaction with needy people? Table 3.4 cross-tabulates the answers to those two questions. The upper section of the table examines whether programs with

Table 3.4 Type of collaborator by type of social service program

Type of collaborator	Percent of programs that are long-term and face-to-face
Secular	9.8
Nonsecular	6.8
	chi-square = 9.99, p = .002
Government	8.9
Nongovernment	7.9
	chi-square = .37, p = .54

Note: This analysis is based on the 3,728 social service programs reported by congregations. Programs with no collaborators are included in the "nonsecular" and "nongovernment" categories.

any type of secular collaborator are more likely to be holistic than programs without secular collaborators. The lower section compares programs with and without government collaborators.

The results are clear. Programs involving secular collaborators are slightly, but significantly, *more* likely (9.8 percent versus 6.8 percent) to involve personal or longer-term relationships with the needy than programs involving nonsecular collaborators, or no collaborators. Programs involving government collaborators are no less likely to be more personal and long-term.[26] This analysis is limited, especially because the categorizing of programs as holistic or not is based on very brief descriptions of those programs. Still, these results clearly do not support the notion that collaborations with secular or government agencies *discourage* holistic social services. The differences are either null or in the opposite direction from that implied by that assertion. Thus, there is no evidence here that collaborating with secular organizations in general, or with government agencies in particular, makes congregations less likely to engage in the more personalistic social service activities that some think are more likely to occur within a religious sphere that guards its autonomy. Indeed, such collaborations may even encourage the more holistic types of activities some claim to be the distinctive province of religious organizations.

There are, of course, other dimensions of congregations' social services that might be altered by collaborations with secular and government agencies even if those collaborations do not make a holistic approach less likely. The presence of explicitly religious content in social service programming is perhaps the most obvious that comes to mind. It is worth noting, however, that many, perhaps most, religiously based and even congregation-based social services do not include explicitly religious content (Farnsley 2001; Monsma 1996; Monsma and Mounts 2001; Smith and Sosin 2001). Like the assumption that religiously based social services are particularly holistic, the assumption that religiously based social services are particularly *religious* also is questionable. ← really ?

Still, it seems likely that collaborations with secular nonprofits and, especially, government could be consequential for congregations and other religious organizations in ways that do not directly involve the nature of their social services. Collaborations with government, for example, particularly those involving funding, might prompt structural changes within religious organizations, as they do within secular nonprofit organizations (Grønbjerg 1993; Smith and Lipsky 1993). The evidence presented here suggests that discouraging crosscutting, holistic, and personal approaches to social services is not among the consequences of collaborating with secular and government agencies, but I do not mean to imply that such collaborations are without *any* potential consequences for congregations.

The key conclusion here is that congregation-based social services are not, in general, isolated from larger community

human welfare systems; on the contrary, they are deeply embedded within a larger arena of nonprofit organizations and
government agencies. Moreover, this embeddedness, when it
occurs, does not appear to discourage a more holistic approach
to social services. Congregation-based social services do not
present us with a meaningful alternative to the services already
provided by our community welfare systems. Congregations
often are an important component of those systems, but they
do not, in general, stand apart from them. On the contrary, it
is more accurate to say that, far from providing an alternative to the social services offered by secular and government
agencies, congregations' social service activity, especially activity that goes beyond meeting short-term emergency needs,
often *depends* on collaborations with secular and government
agencies.[27]

More Involved in the Past Than Now?

At present, most congregations engage only minimally in social services, and typically the few that do engage more deeply
rely heavily on paid staff, involve relatively few congregational
volunteers, and conduct their efforts in collaboration—including financial collaboration—with secular and government
agencies. Perhaps, however, congregations were more centrally
involved in social services at some point in the past, in which
case our current situation is the consequence of a secularization process by which a growing government has wrested
social services away from religious organizations, replacing
personalistic, religiously based community services with bureaucratic, government-provided services. Expanding religiously
based social services, including those provided by congregations, would in this case be to return to the institutional arrangements of an earlier, more communitarian time.

The historical reality, however, is that at no time in the twentieth century were more than a tiny minority of congregations deeply involved in social services. H. Paul Douglass and his colleagues surveyed congregations in the 1920s. Even though their nonscientific sample overrepresented large urban congregations—the ones most likely to do social services—similarities to the contemporary picture are striking. Fewer than 10 percent of the urban congregations in their sample provided the more serious social services of the day: dispensaries or clinics, day nurseries, English classes, health classes, visiting nurses, or employment offices (Douglass and Brunner 1935:140). They categorized only a very small percentage of the churches in their sample as "socially adapted," the label they use for congregations that "definitely undertake to become agencies of social ministry to especially handicapped populations" (p. 143):

[Such churches] with all-around social programs ministering to health, education, recreation, cultural and material necessities of their dependent populations are estimated as constituting not more than 4 percent of the urban total, while the more narrowly specialized enterprises of the Christian center type, carrying on with fragmentary rather than all-around welfare programs, may reach as high as 13 percent. Only about one church out of one hundred will be found operating a dispensary or clinic, and only three or four out of one hundred engaging in any other form of health ministry. (p. 190)[28]

Studies of specific cities in the 1920s and 1930s paint the same picture. A 1926 survey of congregations in Springfield, Massachusetts, found that churches "were giving only about $150 worth of direct aid annually on the average." A Chicago survey "at the peak of the depression demand in 1933 also showed an average of $150 per church in cash for direct relief, with an estimated value of second-hand clothing, etc., raising the estimate to $200 per church. The resulting total is infinitesimal within the total community expenditures for direct relief" (Douglass and Brunner 1935:190).[29] Moreover, clergy in the 1920s apparently spent as little of their time on community activities as today's clergy: "According to an extensive collection of work records, the average minister actually gives very little time to extra-parochial service of any sort. While a few gifted and influential ministers are much in evidence in these fields, they stand in striking contrast with the average" (Douglass and Brunner 1935:189).

In the 1920s as today, there was a substantial amount of religiously based social service delivery, but again as today, this mainly occurred via freestanding organizations dedicated to social services, not via congregations. In the words of Douglass and his colleague Edmund Brunner: "When social-welfare ministries, especially in their more technical forms, are contemplated, it is almost sure that they will be carried on through orphanages, hospitals, old people's homes and special chaplaincies and not through local churches. As activities of the church at large, such things are relatively frequent, as activities of the single parish, decidedly infrequent" (p. 141). In sum, in the 1920s, "the direct material aid and relief rendered by the average church is not impressive" (p. 189). Rather, "the more specialized forms of welfare work are very infrequent in local Protestant churches and are generally carried out through specialized agencies" (p. 190).

Like many of today's observers, Douglass was particularly interested in how that small minority of "socially adapted" congregations did their work, partly because he recognized that "the novelty of the programs of socially adapted churches, rather than their number, has given the type so large a place in the imagination" (Douglass 1926:243). Again the similarities to the current situation are striking. There was, for example, no evidence that services provided by congregations—or, more generally, religion-based social services—were more effective or efficient than services delivered through other organizations. On the contrary, the quality of services provided by religious organizations was often found wanting, and "many an agency has to cry for protection from the dabbling religious volunteer" (Douglass and Brunner 1935:196).

Also as today, congregations' social service activities did not involve large numbers of congregation members even in the most active churches. Douglass and Brunner observed that "many activities listed as the church's activities are actually, in large measure, merely the activities of semi-independent constituencies" and "participation [in these activities] is much more limited than the scope of the opportunities provided" (Douglass and Brunner 1935:155–156). Social separation between the congregations' members and the people they served also was common, as it is today. Douglass noted that "frequently socially adapted churches had two constituencies, only one of which was peculiar or in need of specialized ministries," and "the social separation of the two constituencies is sometimes painfully extreme and complete" (Douglass 1926:171, 189). Social service–delivering congregations in the 1920s apparently were no better at integrating the needy into their communities of faith than they are today.

As today, the most active congregations of the 1920s did not constitute an alternative social service system but worked collaboratively with government and other community agencies. Three of the four congregations profiled in Douglass's chapter on "socially adapted" churches received significant financial support from Community Chest and other public funding sources (Douglass 1926:chap. 9), and "the majority of city churches report somewhat systematic relationships with community social agencies" (Douglass and Brunner 1935:189).[30]

An early 1930s survey of 609 urban black churches shows that African American congregations were no more deeply involved in social services in the first third of the twentieth century than either their descendants today or their white contemporaries. This unscientific survey, like Douglass's, clearly oversampled large and more active congregations, but still, although virtually all reported some sort of "poor relief," very few reported more specific kinds of serious services: only 3 percent fed the unemployed, and 1 percent or fewer sponsored day nurseries, employment agencies, visiting nurses, health classes, or homes for girls, old people, or orphans (Mays and Nicholson 1933:122–123).

When African American churches were more deeply involved in social services, collaboration was the norm, as it was for other congregations then and is now. One case study of an African Methodist Episcopal congregation found that, in 1930, it "let the social welfare department of the city of Baltimore use its half-acre church basement for feeding and sheltering unemployed and poor people, as well as for providing industrial, educational, and social programs for them" (Mamiya 1994:254). Benjamin Mays and Joseph Nicholson summarized their survey results by highlighting how active congregations "cooperated with other churches, or with community institutions and agencies, through ministerial alliances and associations; in religious educational activities; in cooperative humanitarian movements; in social welfare, poor relief, and the like; and in obtaining preventative and corrective legislation and administration in civic affairs" (Mays and Nicholson 1933:157).

Informed observers did not consider substantial congregational involvement in social services to be a realistic possibility even in the 1930s. As Mays and Nicholson put it: "The Negro Church today is often challenged to do things that need to be done in the community . . . In reality, however, the church is so limited by lack of funds, equipment and personnel that it could not adequately assume all of the responsibilities the public might place upon it" (1935:164–165). They go on to note how an interested congregation might be expected to act in this arena: "There are two methods, among others, which the church may use to meet the challenge of its community. First, it may cooperate with existing agencies . . . Secondly, it may serve its community by its contribution to the conduct and ideals of its members" (1935:165). To Mays and Nicholson, collaborating with existing agencies and focusing on the moral character of its own members seemed the realistic options for a congregation in 1935. The possibility of congregations providing social services on their own apparently did not seem likely enough to warrant explicit mention. As with white churches, black churches in the pre–New Deal decades of the twentieth century were not, in general, any more deeply involved in their community's social service systems than they are today.

Robert and Helen Lynd's study of Muncie, Indiana, provides more support for the claim that congregations were no more involved in social services in the early twentieth century than they are now. More important, their description of how social services changed in Muncie between the 1890s and the 1930s clarifies the nature of social services' secularization. Social services did indeed secularize in Muncie, but not because religious organizations did less or because government took over functions and services previously filled by religious organizations. Let me explain.

Congregations were not very involved in local social services when the Lynds visited Muncie in 1924, or when Robert Lynd returned in 1935. In 1924 their detailed examination of three large church budgets found that, on average, only 5.6 percent of the "benevolence" budgets stayed local; the vast majority went to denominational offices (Lynd and Lynd 1929:463). Nor did congregational activities or contributions constitute a significant part of the town's social service work. Less than 3 percent of the Social Service Bureau's budget—raised at this time through community donations—came from churches, and the head of the Social Service Bureau reported that "the only time [the churches] take an interest in our work is at Thanksgiving and Christmas, when some of them send to us for names of needy families" (pp. 462–463). After the 1935 visit they wrote that "individual church members are strong supporters of these [social service] agencies, but the churches as organizations accept the role of spiritual agents rather than leaders of group care for the needy" (Lynd and Lynd 1937:306). Interestingly, they noted that the "two exceptions to this position among Middletown's religious groups are the Salvation Army and the Middletown Mission" (p. 306). Both of these organizations were supported by the Community Fund. As we have seen in other times and places, the rare congregations that are more deeply involved in social services often depend on collaborations, including financial ones, with secular and public agencies.

Although congregations constituted only a tiny percentage of Muncie's social service sector in the 1920s, they had constituted a much larger share of it in the 1890s. The precursor to the Social Service Bureau was "Associated Church Charities," formed during the depression of 1893. It dropped "Church" from its name in 1900 and became the Community Fund in 1925. In 1890 "all [charity] cases in any way affiliated with a church were turned over directly to the church," and "one's church contribution covered much local charity" (Lynd and

Lynd 1929:462, 466). By 1924, however, "Middletown families support local charity through one big subscription made once a year as a civic duty often under considerable social pressure" (pp. 462, 466). In addition to the centralization of social service funding in the quasi-public, secular Community Fund, there also was increased involvement of the city government, which established a city-run orphans' home and oversaw the "recent transfer of kindergartens from private charity to the public schools" (p. 468). The Lynds summarize these developments by noting that Middletown's churches "are less conspicuous in local charity today . . . [T]he trend toward secularization is an outstanding characteristic of Middletown's charity in the last thirty-five years" (p. 462).

This is secularization, but it is secularization of a particular sort. Social service activity expanded after the 1890s in response to increased need. The churches' share of social services was indeed lower in the 1920s than in the 1890s, but not because secular and governmental agencies took over what previously were church-based activities. Rather, by the 1920s there was more money for social services generated through centralized giving, and consequently there were more social services delivered by others. In 1925 the Community Fund used citywide voluntary giving to support nine social welfare agencies, including the Salvation Army. This compared to "the struggling church mission sewing school and the charity kindergarten supported by 'penny collections' and similar devices which constituted the local organized charity of 1890" (p. 465). Church-based social services indeed constituted a smaller percentage of Muncie's human service arena in the 1920s than in the 1890s, but that was because there was much more social service activity occurring by the 1920s, not because congregations were doing less than they had done in the 1890s.

This dual development—a decline in the relative role of

religious and other private charity organizations along with growth in the total amount of social service activity—accelerated with the New Deal. Robert Lynd documented this acceleration when he revisited Muncie in 1935. Whereas 46 percent of direct relief spending in Muncie had been through the Community Fund in 1928, that figure had declined to 15 percent by 1935. The significant point here, however, is that the relative decline in the role of religious and other private charity occurred because so much more was being done by government. The total amount spent on antipoverty work in Muncie increased from $39,086 in 1928 to $173,372 in 1935, with new government spending accounting for the vast majority of that increase. Government spending on social services in Muncie increased 600 percent in this period, from $21,214 to $148,186, compared with only a 41 percent increase in Community Fund spending, from $17,872 to $25,186. This increased spending represented real increases in social services delivered. In 1928, only 613 families required relief; by 1933, 3,506 were being helped. The Social Service Bureau handled 2,000 appeals in 1928; in 1933 it handled 91,585 (Lynd and Lynd 1937:541, 126, 133).

Thus, the Lynds conclude, the "slow transformation of sporadic private 'Christian charity' over the past generation into an increasingly secularized, institutionalized service" (Lynd and Lynd 1937:102) occurred because the small-scale efforts of religious and private charity could not meet the expanding need for social services. The result was secularization of charity and social service work in the sense that, at the end of the day, a smaller percentage of this work was being done by congregations and other religious organizations. But this percentage did not become smaller because the work previously done by religious organizations was taken over by government. It became smaller because government and government-funded organizations began new activities, with the result that much more antipoverty work was accomplished. The secularization of social services was driven by the emergence of new secular and government-funded efforts, not by the displacement of existing religious efforts by secular agencies and government. Post–New Deal congregations still performed the small-scale and minor services they had always provided, but over time, much more came to be done through other means, first through secular, centralized fund-raising efforts and then through government. When evoking a past in which charity and social services were mainly religious, we should not overlook the fact that much less charity and fewer social services were thereby available to the needy. Congregations did not retreat from social services over time; government and secular organizations started doing more. That is an important nuance.[31]

Secularization aside, the historical record shows that the vast majority of congregations, like the vast majority today, did very little social service in the 1920s and 1930s. Moreover, the exceptional congregations that engaged more deeply in social services did so in ways strikingly similar to contemporary patterns: this activity was largely staff driven, it was carried out largely in collaboration with secular and government agencies, and it often depended on public funding.[32] At least from the 1890s to the present, the history of congregational involvement in social services is characterized more by continuity than by change.

Government Funding Dampens Prophetic Voice?

Those on the political right tend to worry that collaborations with government, especially financial collaborations, will dampen religious organizations' holistic approach to social services. Those on the political left also worry about the consequences for congregations of financial partnerships with government, but they tend to focus on a different potential consequence: the loss of congregations' "prophetic voice."[33] Although the concern expressed here uses the theological language of "prophetic voice," and although this is a concern that has been heightened for religious organizations by the charitable choice movement, this is a special case of a more general concern with the consequences of government funding for nonprofit organizations' political activity.[34]

As with nonprofit organizations in general, there are good reasons to expect that receiving government funding might decrease congregations' political activity. The most obvious mechanism is resource dependence: congregations dependent on government funds for part of their operations might refrain from political activity or advocacy that could be perceived as critical of that source. There clearly are instances in which government funding has had this consequence. Fredrick Harris, for example, traces the relative passivity of some of Chicago's major African American churches during the civil rights movement to their financial dependence on Mayor Richard Daley's patronage. One minister who, with the mayor's help, received city and federal funding to build low-income housing was criticized for failing to protest police brutality, even though he was on the city's civilian police board and was also president of the local NAACP chapter (Harris 2001:152). More generally, Harris notes that the mayor "used the largess of federal monies designated for [President] Johnson's War on Poverty and the city's department of Human Services to undermine clergy dissent." One result of this patronage was that "Martin Luther King Jr. failed to recruit influential ministers in Chicago for his campaign against open housing in 1966." A contemporary put it this way: "You don't eat at the mayor's table and fight the mayor. Quite naturally had they allowed Dr. King in their pulpit they were not an ally to the mayor" (Harris 2001:153).

At the same time, however, there are plausible mechanisms by which government funding might *encourage* congregations' political activity. Government agencies might be dependent on congregational providers of necessary services, thereby creating an incentive for a congregation to exploit its power through attempts to exert political pressure. Religious leaders whose organizations receive government funding also are likely to be more knowledgeable about the political arena and about community needs, and so more able to effectively direct political effort. Congregations receiving government funding also might have increased motivation to participate in the political process in order to protect their own funding streams. This last mechanism is the flip side of the patronage relationships I have described. That is, involvement in patronage networks might discourage political activity critical of the patron at the same time that it encourages political activity—voter registration drives, candidate rallies, and so on—in support of the patron's political machine.

The point here is that congregations that collaborate with government are likely to face *conflicting* incentives regarding whether or not to involve themselves in political activities. The key question, then, is this: Overall, do the complex cross-pressures that come with government funding lead, in the aggregate, to more political activity by congregations or less?

In the next chapter I examine congregations' political activities in detail. Here, however, two observations are key. First, as with social services, most congregations do not engage in political activity to a great extent. Even the most common types of activity—informing people at worship services about opportunities for political action and distributing voter guides—are engaged in by only 26 percent and 17 percent of congregations, respectively. Fewer than 10 percent of congregations have organized or participated in a demonstration or march, registered people to vote, lobbied elected officials, or had candidates as visiting speakers. It is not clear, in other words, that there is in fact much "prophetic voice" expressed by congregations that might be at risk of suppression by government funding.

A notable minority of congregations do engage in political activities, however, and so a second observation is relevant: When congregations that do collaborate with government are compared on various types of political activity with those that do not, either there is no difference between the two groups in the likelihood of engaging in these activities or, when there is a difference, congregations receiving public funds in support of their social service work are *more* likely to engage in political activities than those that do not have such collaborations. Although government funds might discourage political activity for some specific congregations, in the aggregate congregations receiving government funds are not less politically active than congregations without such funds. They may even be more active.[35]

There are ambiguities here. Perhaps government spending suppresses political activities other than those measured in the NCS. Or perhaps government funding reduces the intensity with which congregations engage in political activity without reducing the likelihood that they do it at all. This is something that would not be picked up here since, unlike for social services, the NCS measures only whether or not congregations engage in each political activity, not the intensity with which they engage in them. Or perhaps there is a threshold effect such that government funding suppresses congregational political activity only if a congregation receives a very substantial portion of its income from government. In the NCS sample no congregation received more than 30 percent of its income from government, and the median congregation that received any public funds received only 5 percent of its funds from that source. Perhaps a suppressing effect on political activity would be present at higher levels of dependence on government funds. I also do not know the content of any of the political activity reported by congregations, and so I am not able to assess the extent to which congregational political activity was narrowly self-interested versus broadly public-spirited. Perhaps government support increases the former but decreases the latter, a subtlety I am not able to address with the data at hand.

These qualifications notwithstanding, the available evidence suggests that government financial support does not suppress congregations' political activity. It may even enhance it. Although government funding of congregations' social service activities sets in motion some forces that discourage political activity, it also sets in motion other forces that encourage that activity. It appears that the latter forces, on balance, are stronger than the former.

In this chapter I have examined congregations' social service activities and challenged several key assumptions behind recent debates concerning "faith-based" social services. Some congregations certainly play an important role in communities' social service systems, but the intensively involved congregation is the exception, not the rule. Congregations do have a distinctive approach to social services, but their typical approach is not the one commonly highlighted. When they do more than donate money or collect canned goods at Thanksgiving, congregations typically provide small numbers of volunteers to carry out well-defined tasks on a periodic basis. Contrary to the claim that religiously based social services are distinctive in their holistic or personal approach, congregations are most likely to engage in social services requiring only fleeting contact, if any at all, with needy people, and they are most likely to participate in or support programs aimed at meeting short-term emergency needs, especially the need for food, clothing, and shelter.

When congregations provide social services in a more intensive way, that work is typically driven by staff rather than by volunteers, and it is done in collaboration with other organizations, including secular and government agencies. Congregation-based social services do not occur in isolation from larger community welfare systems. And these collaborations (even when they involve funding) discourage neither a holistic or transformational approach (as some on the political right fear) nor congregations' political activism (as some on the political left fear). Indeed, some evidence points to the possibility that collaborations with government and with secular organizations might actually encourage both political engagement and a deeper involvement with more holistic and transformational kinds of social services.

I have emphasized the point that, far from offering an alternative to the social services provided by secular and government agencies, congregations' social service activity, especially activity that goes beyond meeting short-term emergency needs, often *depends* on collaborations with secular and government agencies. In this light, the relationship between religiously based social services and a larger, secular and governmental social services arena seems akin, both empirically and conceptually, to the relationship between the nonprofit sector and government. Lester Salamon (1995a) has shown that, empirically, the American nonprofit sector, far from being an alternative to government, flourishes because of the funds government makes available to nonprofit organizations. Conceptually, he has shown how the common rhetoric portraying the voluntary sector as a substitute for, or even in conflict with, the state—as a sector operating most prominently and effectively where the state is absent—obfuscates the empirical reality of cooperation and mutual dependence between government and nonprofits.

Similarly, it seems that the congregational social service arena, far from offering an alternative to secular nonprofit activity, in fact is deeply embedded within and even dependent on the world of secular social services and government. Perhaps ironically, congregations seem to be most tightly connected to that world precisely when they are doing the social service work some consider most distinctively religious. Religiously based social services are not, in general, an alternative to secular or government-supported social service delivery. They are, rather, part of that world, likely to rise and fall with it rather than in counterpoint to it. Like the rhetoric portraying nonprofits in general as an alternative to government, the rhetoric portraying religious organizations as bearers of a social service alternative obfuscates the empirical reality.

Overstating the extent of congregations' social service work and mischaracterizing its nature misleads about the intersection between religion and social services, but it also misleads about the nature of congregations. For the vast majority of congregations, social services constitute a minor and peripheral aspect of their organizational activities, taking up only small amounts of their resources and involving only small numbers of people. We fundamentally misunderstand congregations if we imagine that this sort of activity is now, was ever, or will ever be central to their activities. The Social Gospel image of congregations deeply engaged in serving the needy of their communities has been for many a compelling normative vision for more than a century, but we should not let notions of what congregations *ought* to look like influence our assessment of what they *do* look like.

❦ 4 ❦

Civic Engagement and Politics

Congregations engage their communities in ways that go beyond providing social services to the needy. Indeed, social service activity is just one of many avenues—and, as we saw in the previous chapter, it is mainly a minor one—by which congregations might contribute to civil society, build social capital, or simply have a public presence in their communities. Many observers now see religion and religious organizations as springs of voluntarism, community resources, and civic skills that can be deployed in a wide variety of secular arenas. In this chapter I examine congregational participation in a broad range of civic activities, focusing especially on political activities and attending particularly to differences among religious traditions in their rates of participation in civic and political activities. Three patterns emerge. First, congregations embedded in theologically moderate and liberal religious traditions participate more than other congregations in virtually all kinds of civic activity. In the previous chapter we saw this pattern with regard to social services; here we will see that it emerges in other arenas as well—with one exception.

The exception—and this is the second pattern I highlight in

this chapter—is politics. Unlike in other arenas, moderate and liberal congregations do not, in general, engage more in political activities than congregations in other traditions. When it comes to political involvement, Catholic and predominantly African American congregations outpace both liberal and conservative white Protestants. These differences, however, seem more a matter of variations across traditions in the typical *styles* by which their congregations engage in politics than a matter of variation in the *extent* to which they engage in politics. In the political arena, qualitative differences across religious traditions seem more significant than quantitative differences.

Third, as with social services, the overall extent to which congregations engage in politics is rather meager. Just as the charitable choice movement of the 1990s focused attention on congregations' involvement in social services, the rise of the religious right in the 1980s focused attention on congregations' political activities. There are interesting patterns in these political activities, and I describe them in this chapter, but we should not lose sight of a larger point: public attention notwithstanding, politics is not an arena in which most congregations actively participate. Politics remains, for most congregations, a peripheral activity.

Civic Engagement

Discussions of civic participation often note that not all voluntary associations contribute positively to civil society, not all community resources are deployed to advance the public good, and not all voluntarism is outward-looking. In one influential formulation, the political scientist Robert Putnam distinguishes between "bonding" and "bridging" forms of civic participation. "Bonding" participation tends to keep individuals within the groups or associations to which they are primarily attached. "Bridging" participation, by contrast, tends to build connections between groups or associations. In this chapter I focus on religious differences in various kinds of bridging civic activities engaged in by American congregations. Such bridging activity is one important way that religion and religious organizations might be civically engaged.

Religious groups vary in the extent to which they value, pursue, or encourage civic engagement. Previous research suggests that, among Christians in the United States, such variation is systematically tied to long-standing differences among theologically liberal or moderate Protestants, theologically conservative or evangelical Protestants, and Catholics. Moderate and liberal Protestants are more likely than conservative Protestants or Catholics to join nonreligious voluntary associations, work actively in those organizations, and volunteer in support of secular activities and organizations. Historically, moderate and liberal congregations appear to have been much more likely than congregations in other traditions to give rise to secular associations of various sorts. In short, liberal and moderate Protestantism has appeared to encourage more bridging forms of civic engagement than either conservative and evangelical Protestantism or Roman Catholicism.[3] Previous research on religion and a broader civic engagement has mainly examined *individuals'* civic activities. Here, as throughout the book, I focus on *congregations'* activities. Are the same religious patterns we see in individuals' civic activities visible among congregations' collective activities?

The NCS gathered data on a wide range of congregational activities and characteristics that can reasonably be interpreted as indicators of bridging sorts of activities. I have organized several dozen specific items into six arenas of activity: social services, education, religion, arts, community, and politics.

The specific items included in each of these arenas are not all equally apt as indicators of congregations' connectedness to the world around them. Having a school, for example, may or may not indicate a congregation's effort to connect itself or its people to others in the community. A religious school might indicate just the opposite: an attempt keep a congregation's children isolated—or, from the congregation's point of view, protected—from the wider community. Without knowing more about how a congregation's school actually operates, it is difficult to know, from the mere fact of its existence, whether to interpret it as bridge-building or barrier-erecting.

Although this and other interpretive questions can be raised about some of the specific items examined in this chapter, there is value in examining a broad range of activities that bear on the question of congregations' engagement in bridging sorts of civic activity. Although these items were selected without respect to what the data show about religious differences on each of them, we will see that differences among religious traditions are (with the exception of political activities) strikingly consistent across these arenas. This consistency is not a consequence of any selective choice of items.

Table 4.1 gives the percentages of people within four religious traditions who are in congregations participating in the specified activity.[4] This table gives results for five activity arenas; political activities are presented in later tables. It would be tedious to inventory every number and comparison in this table. Instead, let me emphasize a single compelling pattern: moderate and liberal Protestant congregations and Jewish synagogues are most likely to engage in bridging sorts of civic activity, followed by Catholic congregations, followed by conservative and evangelical white Protestant congregations.[5] On some specific activities the key fault line lies between Protes-

Table 4.1 Religious tradition differences in congregations' civic activities

Activity	Percent of congregants attending congregations with specified program/activity				Significance level for diff. bet. moderate/liberal Protestant congreg. and all other congreg., controlling other characteristics
	Moderate and liberal Protestants (n = 336)	Conservative and evangelical Protestants (n = 551)	Roman Catholics (n = 299)	Jews (n = 20)	
Social services					
Total number of social service programs (mean)	3.9	2.2	3.5	3.9	**
Participation in any social service, community development, or neighborhood project	86	68	87	90	**
Had a representative of a social service organization as a visiting speaker	58	24	46	60	**
Group/meeting/class/event to organize or encourage people to do volunteer work	59	45	79	80	ns
Sponsored or participated in any:					
food programs	59	39	59	58	**
housing programs	50	22	33	53	**
clothing programs	19	15	19	16	ns
homelessness programs	20	12	17	26	*
health programs	12	5	14	37	ns

Education					
Has an elementary or high school	5	14	55	25	**
Gives money to any college, university, or seminary	56	45	39	30	**
Had an academic or professor as a visiting speaker	42	33	38	80	ns
Has an education-related group or program (not including religious education)	19	9	19	32	*
Sponsored or participated in mentoring program	6	2	2	5	*
Religion					
Group/meeting/class/event to discuss or learn about another religion	39	26	25	50	**
Had clergy from another congregation as a visiting speaker	72	78	61	75	ns
Participated in joint worship with another congregation	74	66	60	75	**
Participated in joint worship with a congregation of another religious tradition	37	15	49	60	*
Participated in joint worship with a congregation of a different racial or ethnic makeup	31	33	27	40	ns

Table 4.1 (continued)

Activity	Percent of congregants attending congregations with specified program/activity				Significance level for diff. bet. moderate/liberal Protestant congreg. and all other congreg., controlling other characteristics
	Moderate and liberal Protestants (n = 336)	Conservative and evangelical Protestants (n = 551)	Roman Catholics (n = 299)	Jews (n = 20)	
Culture					
Hired singers or other musicians to perform at a worship service	59	42	56	80	**
Visitors sometimes come to view the building's architecture or artwork	62	41	68	80	ns
Group/meeting/class/event to discuss a book other than the Bible	64	33	33	80	**
Group/meeting/class/event to attend a live musical or theatrical performance outside the congregation	61	55	40	70	**
Outside groups have used the building for rehearsals or performances of musical or theatrical works	43	18	33	37	**
Outside groups have used the building for exhibits of paintings, photography, or sculpture	18	6	12	25	**

Community

Any outside groups use or rent space in the building	81	55	73	90	**
Group/meeting/class/event to:					
plan or conduct an assessment of community's needs	51	43	53	45	ns
discuss pollution or other environmental issues	23	6	16	20	**
discuss race relations in our society	31	17	21	45	**
Any special rules or norms regarding what sorts of groups outside the congregation people can join	7	25	23	15	**

Notes: For most of the activities and programs in this table, congregations were asked if they occurred within the past year. Given the small number of synagogues in the NCS sample, percentages in the "Jews" column should be interpreted cautiously. The 95% confidence intervals around percentages in this column range from ±10 percentage points (for percentages near 0 or 100) to ±22 percentage points (for percentages near 50). The 95% confidence interval around percentages in the other columns is never more than ±6 percentage points.

Significance level based on logistic regressions with the following control variables: logged size; logged amount of annual income; theologically conservative, liberal, or right in the middle; percentage of regular participants living in households with annual income under $25,000; percentage of regular participants living in households with annual income higher than $100,000; percentage of regular adult participants having at least a four-year college degree; racial composition; geographical region; rural/nonrural location; located or not in a census tract where more than 30% of the people fall under the official poverty line; percentage of regular adult participants younger than 35; percentage of regular adult participants older than 60; and founding date.

ns: $p \geq .05$;   * $.05 > p \geq .01$;   ** $p < .01$

tants and Catholics, while on other activities Catholics and liberal Protestant congregations appear to be fairly similar when compared to conservative Protestants. Still, the general though not universal pattern is that moderate and liberal Protestant congregations and Jewish synagogues are most likely to expose people to bridging civic activities, other Protestants are least likely, and Catholics fall in between.[6]

In regard to social service activities, for example, moderate and liberal Protestants appear significantly more engaged on six of the nine social service items.[7] On the activities where this overall difference is not present—organizing or encouraging volunteer work and participating in clothing or health-related programs—liberal to moderate congregations are noticeably more likely than conservative Protestants to do these things, but the overall difference is washed out because Catholic congregations are at least as likely as liberal Protestants to engage in them as well. When it comes to organizing or encouraging volunteer work, Catholic congregations are substantially more likely to do this than even moderate and liberal Protestants.

Some of these differences are sizable. Fifty-eight percent of people attending moderate to liberal congregations, for example, are in a congregation that had a representative of a social service organization as a visiting speaker within the previous year, compared to 46 percent of people attending Catholic congregations and only 24 percent of people attending conservative and evangelical Protestant congregations. In general, the differences between liberal and conservative Protestants are larger than the differences between liberal Protestants and Catholics. For some kinds of activities—hearing someone from a social service agency speak, participating in some kind of housing activity (often a Habitat for Humanity project), sponsoring or participating in some kind of health-related program—liberal Protestant congregations are more than twice as likely as conservative Protestant congregations to expose their members to these ventures.

A similar pattern is evident in the education items. Moderate and liberal Protestant congregations are significantly more likely than other congregations to engage in three of the five items: giving money to an institution of higher education, having education-related programs or groups, and sponsoring or participating in youth mentoring programs. Liberal Protestant congregations are significantly more likely than conservative Protestants—but not more likely than Catholic congregations—to have an academic or professor as a visiting speaker.[8]

Given the long history of Catholic schooling in the United States, the priority given to school building by Missouri Synod Lutherans (but not the Evangelical Lutheran Church in America), and the more recent emergence of private schooling among evangelicals and fundamentalists, it is not surprising to see that moderate and liberal congregations are least likely to sponsor elementary or high schools. More than half of all Catholics are in congregations that sponsor schools, compared to 14 percent of conservative Protestants and only 5 percent of moderate and liberal Protestants. From one perspective this could be seen as a dimension of civic engagement on which liberal Protestant congregations fall behind other groups. From another perspective, as mentioned earlier, to the extent that school sponsorship indicates wagon circling rather than bridge building, this result is consistent with the larger pattern in which liberal Protestants are more likely than others to connect their congregations to other parts of the community. Moderate and liberal Protestant congregations are less likely than others to build institutional enclaves for their people.

Contemplating the meaning of religious schools prompts another observation. Institutions or practices that begin as efforts to separate a religious community from the surrounding world may develop into institutions or practices that enhance the connectedness of the religious community to others. The fact that some urban Catholic elementary schools, which began as an effort to shield Catholic children from public schools dominated by Protestants, now educate large numbers of non-Catholic children from the surrounding neighborhoods is, perhaps, a case in point. Religious institutions, it always is worth mentioning, can generate long-term consequences that are unintended and unforeseen by their founders.

The set of items indicating bridging to other religious communities presents a slightly more mixed picture, but one that still is consistent with the developing theme. Although moderate and liberal Protestant congregations are not more likely than others to have clergy from other congregations as visiting speakers, the connections pursued by liberal Protestants are more likely to cross important religious boundaries than are the religious connections pursued by other kinds of congregations. Moderate and liberal Protestant congregations are significantly more likely than other congregations to hold a group or meeting or class to discuss or learn about another religion. They also are more likely than other congregations to expose people to joint worship with another congregation, and they are about twice as likely as conservative Protestant congregations to expose their people to joint worship with a congregation from another religious tradition (meaning a Catholic or non-Christian congregation). Interestingly, liberal Protestant, conservative Protestant, and Catholic congregations are equally likely to sponsor joint worship that crosses ethnic or racial boundaries: approximately 30 percent of the people within each group are in congregations that had such a joint service in the previous year.

The culture and community items tell an unambiguous story. Moderate and liberal Protestant congregations are substantially more likely than other congregations to connect to the secular art world in various ways, from hiring musicians to perform in worship services, to organizing groups to attend live performances, to allowing outside groups to use the congregation's building for rehearsals, performances, or exhibits. They are also more likely—by substantial margins—to permit outside groups to use or rent space in their building, and they are more likely to hold groups, meetings, classes, or events to discuss environmental issues or race relations. On only two of the culture and community items are liberal Protestant congregations statistically indistinguishable from other congregations, and in both cases this is because a sizable intra-Protestant difference is balanced by the fact that on these measures Catholic congregations are very similar to liberal Protestant congregations. Moderate and liberal Protestants are more likely than conservative Protestants to have visitors view their building's architecture or artwork, and they are more likely to have a group or meeting focused on assessing the surrounding community's needs, but in both cases Catholic congregations outpace even liberal Protestants.

Strikingly, only 7 percent of participants in moderate and liberal Protestant congregations are in congregations reporting special rules or norms regarding what sorts of outside groups people can join, compared to 25 percent in conservative and evangelical Protestant congregations and 23 percent in Catholic congregations. On this rather direct measure of whether or not congregations actively discourage other kinds of civic engagement, it is clear that liberal and moderate Protestants are far less likely than others to receive this sort of discouragement from their churches.

All in all, these results support the basic conclusion that moderate and liberal Protestant congregations are substantially more likely than other congregations to create and encourage connections between churches and their surrounding communities. Although the small case base for synagogues leads me to refrain from comparing synagogues on an item-by-item basis, the numbers in Table 4.1 nevertheless suggest a signal that can be discerned through the noise generated by the small subsample: Jewish synagogues' patterns of civic engagement most closely resemble the high levels of engagement observed for moderate and liberal Protestant churches.

Table 4.1 categorizes congregations by their denominational affiliation, but it is important to note that, over and above denominational affiliation, self-described theologically conservative congregations within every denomination also are less likely to engage in bridging sorts of civic activities. Whether conceptualized in terms of denominational traditions or more local congregational cultures, theological liberalism enhances many kinds of civic engagement while theological conservatism suppresses that engagement.

Only in terms of political activities does the picture I have been painting look dramatically different. When it comes to politics, moderate and liberal Protestant congregations are *not*, in general, significantly more active than other congregations.

Political Activities

The emergence and continuing presence of the Christian right in American politics has generated a great deal of social scientific research about the relationship between religion and political activity in the United States.[10] Much of this research has used surveys of individuals to document substantial differences among religious groups in voting likelihood, voting choice, political attitudes, and overall levels of civic skills.[11] The primary conclusion emerging from this literature is that religion-based political differences among individuals are not reducible to other characteristics—race, social class, education, gender, and so on—known to generate political variation.

The vast majority of empirical research on religion and politics, however, examines individuals' political attitudes and activities abstracted from the institutional and organizational contexts in which much religion-based political activity occurs. Occasionally, research based on surveys of individuals provides glimpses into congregations' activities, as when Sidney Verba and his colleagues (1995:373) reported that, over a five-year period, 34 percent of members or regular attenders of congregations were asked by someone in authority in their congregation either to vote or to take some other form of political action, or when Andrew Kohut and colleagues (2000:108) reported that 27 percent of monthly religious service attenders were exposed in their congregations to information on political candidates or parties. More commonly, however, previous research does not permit even indirect answers to two basic questions: To what extent do congregations' engage in political activities? And in what ways do religious traditions structure congregation-based political efforts?[12]

The NCS provides leverage on both of these questions via data on nine types of congregational political activity: (1) whether people at worship services have been told within the past twelve months of opportunities for political activity, including petitioning campaigns, lobbying, or demonstrating; (2) whether voter guides have ever been distributed to people through the congregation; (3) if voter guides have been distributed, whether they were produced by Christian right organizations;[13] whether the congregation had a group, meeting, class, or event, within the past twelve months, to (4) organize or participate in a demonstration or march either in support of or opposition to some public issue or policy, (5) discuss politics, (6) get people registered to vote, or (7) organize or participate in efforts to lobby elected officials of any sort; and whether, within the past twelve months, (8) a candidate for political office or (9) an elected government official was a visiting speaker at the congregation, either at a worship service or at another event.

How Many Congregations Engage in Political Activities?

Table 4.2 shows that religious service attenders are most frequently exposed to three kinds of political activities in congregations: being told at worship services about opportunities for political participation (such as petition campaigns, lobbying, or demonstrating), receiving voter guides, and being mobilized to participate in a demonstration or march in support of or opposition to some public policy. Thirty-seven percent of religious service attenders are in congregations where opportunities for political activity were mentioned at worship services, while roughly a quarter of congregations, taken as units without respect to size, mentioned such opportunities at worship services. Approximately one fourth of religious service attenders are in congregations that distributed voter guides, and one fifth of religious service attenders are in congregations in which a group participated in a demonstration or a march. No more than 13 percent of religious service attenders are in congregations engaging in any of the remaining political activities.

Are these numbers large or small? On the one hand, the level of congregation-based political activity seems low. Fifty-eight percent of congregations, containing 40 percent of religious service attenders, engage in *none* of these political activities. Scholarly and media attention to politically active congregations and congregation-based political mobilizing notwithstanding, the majority of religious congregations do not engage in political participation. Furthermore, only three

Table 4.2 Congregations' political activities

Activity	Percent of attenders in congregations that:	Percent of congregations that:
Told people at worship services about opportunities for political activity (within the past 12 months)	37	26
Have ever distributed voter guides	27	17
Of those distributing voter guides, have distributed Christian right voter guides	39	47
Have ever distributed Christian right voter guides	7	5
Have had a group, meeting, class, or event within the past 12 months to:		
organize or participate in a demonstration or march in support of or opposition to some public issue or policy	21	9
get people registered to vote	12	9
discuss politics	13	7
organize or participate in efforts to lobby elected officials of any sort	12	4
Have had an elected government official as a visiting speaker within the past 12 months	12	6
Have had someone running for office as a visiting speaker within the past 12 months	6	4
Participated in at least one of these political activities	60	42

of these activities are engaged in by more than 20 percent of all congregations, and only four of them are experienced by more than 20 percent of religious service attenders. As we saw with social services, the vast majority of congregations are not engaged in political activity in any extensive way. On the other hand, a majority of religious service attenders (60 percent) are in congregations that engaged in at least one of these political activities, and a sizable minority of congregations (42 percent) report political activity of some sort.

It is instructive to compare congregational involvement in politics with the involvement of other organizations whose primary purpose is *not* political action. No direct comparisons are possible with existing data, but three indirect comparisons are suggestive. A mid-1990s survey of nonprofit organizations in Minneapolis–St. Paul found that approximately one quarter of organizations reported lobbying efforts in the previous two years (Chaves et al. 2004). Only 4 percent of congregations, by contrast, report direct lobbying activity. A 2000 national survey of nonprofits large enough to file a tax return with the Internal Revenue Service ($25,000 in annual income) found that 10 percent "lobby" and 20 percent "advocate with" government officials at least *twice a month* (Berry 2003:190). Only 7 percent of congregations below that income threshold had lobbied within the past year. Ten percent is not significantly more than 7 percent, but note the difference in intensity. It seems unlikely that many of the congregations reporting some lobbying pursued that activity twice a month on an ongoing basis.

Another national survey of nonprofit organizations found that 16 percent spent money on some sort of advocacy activity (Salamon 1995b, cited in Reid 1999:301). As I just noted, 42 percent of congregations reported political activity of some sort in 1998, but most of these activities do not involve spending money, and it seems very likely that the proportion of congregations spending money on advocacy or political activity is much smaller than 16 percent. These comparisons are tentative, but they suggest that congregations engage in less of at least some types of political activity—especially direct lobbying of government officials—than other nonprofit organizations whose primary purpose is something other than poli-

110

tics.[14] At the same time, I should note that the very largest congregations report lobbying at a rate that approaches that of nonprofits in general. Approximately 20 percent of the largest congregations (those with more than four hundred people) reported lobbying in the past year.

Rather than comparing the extent to which congregations enter the political sphere *as congregations* with the extent to which other nonpolitical organizations enter the political sphere *as organizations*, we might instead compare the extent to which congregations and other organizations offer opportunities for political action to individuals. Verba and colleagues (1995:373) asked a sample of individuals whether they were asked to be politically active by someone in their congregation, by someone at work, or by someone from other nonpolitical organizations to which they belonged or contributed. Thirty-four percent of people affiliated with congregations said they had been asked in religious settings to be politically active,[15] compared with 19 percent of workers who were asked in the workplace and 9 percent of those associated with other nonpolitical organizations who were asked to be politically active by someone in such an organization. From the perspective of offering opportunities to individuals rather than acting as organizations in the political sphere, congregations seem to be *more* politically active than nonreligious organizations whose primary purpose is something other than politics.

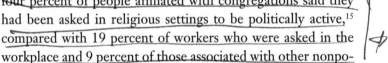

Adding this comparison to the mix suggests a provocative, if tentative, conclusion. On the one hand, congregations' level of political involvement is, in absolute terms, rather low, and congregations *qua congregations* are less likely to engage in certain kinds of political activity than nonprofit organizations whose primary purpose is not politics. On the other hand, however, even at their relatively low levels of activity, congregations still might be providing more opportunities for *individual* political action than other organizations whose primary purpose is non-political. Despite the thorny normative and legal issues associated with congregation-based political action in the United States, congregations engage in a fair amount of such activity. Whether we consider the level of that activity to be substantial or minimal depends somewhat on whether we focus on congregations as unified organizations or as sites at which opportunities for political action are offered to individuals. Overall, it is difficult to reach a stronger conclusion about the magnitude of congregations' political activity than the one reached by Verba and colleagues (1995:146, 373): such activity is "neither the norm nor exceptional" in congregational settings; it is "not frequent, but neither is it rare."

Religious and Race Differences in Political Activities

Table 4.3 continues this chapter's exploration of religious differences in congregations' civic activities. Unlike with other kinds of civic activities, race differences cut across denomination-based political differences in systematic and important ways, so Table 4.3 presents rates of congregational participation across five religious traditions: Roman Catholic, black Protestant, white moderate and liberal Protestant, white conservative and evangelical Protestant, and Jewish. Here, unlike in Table 4.1, Protestant congregations whose regular participants are at least 80 percent African American are included in the black Protestant category whatever their denominational affiliation.

The main message in this table is that religious traditions line up differently on political activity than they do on other kinds of civic engagement. Looking at the bottom line of Table 4.3, we find that approximately 70 percent of both Catholics and black Protestants are in congregations that have engaged

112

in at least one of these political activities compared with approximately 55 percent of white Protestants. And even with the small number of synagogues in this sample, we still may conclude with a great deal of confidence that at least 70 percent of synagogues have engaged in at least one of these types of political activity. With other types of civic activities, Jews lined up on the high end with liberal Protestants; on political activities, Jews still line up on the high end, but now with Catholics and black Protestants.

Beyond this quantitative difference, however, there are qualitative differences among these groups in the nature of their political activity.[16] Although Jewish synagogues seem to be on the high end of participation for each of these activities, Christian churches seem to specialize in particular modes of political participation, and this specialization is strongly structured by race and religious tradition. As before it would be tedious to narrate all the numbers in this table. Instead, I will describe the distinctive patterns of political activity evident within the four Christian traditions represented in Table 4.3.[17]

White Conservative and Evangelical Protestants. White conservative Protestant congregations may, overall, be less likely than Catholic or black Protestant congregations to engage in any political activity, but at the same time they specialize in distributing voter guides, especially voter guides produced by Christian right organizations. Indeed, this is the only political activity in which white conservative Protestant congregations are significantly more likely than others to engage. Thirty-two percent of conservative Protestant religious service attenders are exposed to voter guides in their congregations. Nearly that many Catholic and black Protestant attenders are exposed to voter guides, but the white conservative distinctiveness is especially evident when we consider the source of the voter guides: 70 percent of conservative Protestants in congregations dis-

Table 4.3 Religious tradition differences in congregations' political activities

Activity	Percent of attenders within each tradition who attend congregations with specified political activities				
	Moderate and liberal white Protestants (n = 305)	Conservative and evangelical white Protestants (n = 439)	Black Protestants (n = 143)	Roman Catholics (n = 299)	Jews (n = 20)
Told people at worship services about opportunities for political activity (within the past 12 months)	34	28	47	45	60
Have ever distributed voter guides	20	32	28	26	25
Of those distributing voter guides, percent distributing Christian right voter guides	33	70	8	14	17
Have had a group to organize a demonstration or march	11	14	15	42	10
Have had a group to discuss politics	18	5	17	13	45
Have had a group to get people registered to vote	5	7	35	16	20
Have had a group to lobby elected officials	9	5	10	23	20

Have had an elected government official as a visiting speaker	14	9	25	8	37
Have had someone running for office as a visiting speaker	5	2	27	3	35
Participated in at least one of these political activities	57	52	71	68	90

Notes: Chi-squares associated with each row of this table are significant at least at the .01 level. Given the small number of synagogues in the NCS sample, percentages in the "Jews" column should be interpreted cautiously. The 95% confidence intervals around percentages in this column range from ±10 percentage points (for percentages near 0 or 100) to ±22 percentage points (for percentages near 50). The 95% confidence interval around percentages in the "Black Protestant" column is never more than ±8 percentage points; in the other columns it is never more than ±6 points.

tributing some sort of voter guide are in congregations that distributed voter guides produced by Christian right organizations, compared to only 33 percent of moderate and liberal white Protestants, 14 percent of Roman Catholics, and 8 percent of black Protestants.

The fact that conservative Protestant congregations distribute voter guides but do not engage much in other forms of congregational political activity is not surprising when viewed in light of the political strategies pursued by national Christian right political organizations. Many observers have pointed out that, at least since the late 1980s, conservative Protestant political organizations have embraced electoral politics, even to the point of recruiting candidates and providing campaign support for them (see, for example, Green et al. 2000; Wilcox 1996). Distributing voter guides within religious congregations is an important part of this strategy, one that these results show to have been at least somewhat successful, if (as we saw in Table 4.2) reaching more than 5 percent of church attenders in the country can be considered success. At the same time, despite overt appeals on behalf of many Christian right leaders in recent years to broaden support for their political organizations among Catholics and African Americans, black Protestant and Roman Catholic congregations remain very substantially less likely than conservative Protestant congregations to distribute voter guides produced by Christian right political organizations.

The conservative Protestant use of voter guides has, of course, received substantial attention from both scholars and journalists. This attention notwithstanding, conservative Protestants do not have a monopoly on congregation-based political activity in the United States. On the contrary, as noted earlier, Catholic and predominantly African American congregations are significantly more likely than white conservative (and liberal) Protestants to engage in some form of political activity. Extensive scholarly and media attention to the religious right obscures this fact and hides the important differences in political style typical of congregations in different religious traditions. Congregations within other major religious traditions are not less political than conservative Protestant congregations. Rather, they engage in politics in different ways.

Black Protestants. Reflecting the enduring political activism of black Protestantism at least since the civil rights era, black Protestant congregations are particularly likely to have voter registration drives and to invite political candidates and elected officials to congregations to give speeches. Thirty-five percent of those who attend African American churches are in congregations with voter registration efforts, 27 percent are in congregations that had a political candidate as a visiting speaker, and 25 percent are in congregations that had an elected official as a visiting speaker. All three of these numbers are substantially and significantly higher than the comparable percentages for congregations within other religious traditions. Overall, these results comport well with recent research finding that black Protestant congregations routinely hear speeches from political candidates, organize voter mobilization drives, and expose congregants to various political messages and solicitations (Harris 1999:chap. 6; Patillo-McCoy 1998:778–881; Verba et al. 1995:383–384). African American congregations have embraced electoral politics more than white congregations, and even explicitly partisan involvement in elections seems more common and more accepted among African American churches than among white churches.

Roman Catholics. In recent years Roman Catholics have not been prominent in research on religion and politics in the United States. Table 4.3 shows, however, that Roman Catholic congregations are behind only Jewish synagogues and black

Protestant congregations in the likelihood of engaging in some form of politics, and they also have a distinctive way of engaging in politics. Perhaps the most surprising result in this table is that Roman Catholic congregations are substantially more likely than other congregations to attempt overtly to influence public life by lobbying elected officials and by organizing groups to demonstrate or march for or against some public issue or policy. Forty-two percent of Catholics are in congregations that have participated in a demonstration or march in the past year, three times the rate within any other tradition. Twenty-three percent have lobbied an elected official, more than twice the rate within any other Christian group. Catholics also are substantially more likely than white Protestants, though not more likely than black Protestants, to hear about opportunities for political involvement at worship services.

NCS data do not contain information about the purposes for which congregations are demonstrating or lobbying. Other research, however, suggests that much of this Catholic organizing may be related to abortion (Jaffe et al. 1981:chap. 6; McCarthy 1987; Byrnes 1991:chap. 9; Byrnes and Segers 1992). Catholic churches also may be more open than other congregations to mobilizing efforts by community organizers in the Saul Alinsky tradition (Warren 2001; Wood 2002). Whatever the purpose of this activity, the important point here is that Catholics are *more* likely than white Protestants to be in politically active congregations, and, like congregations in other traditions, they engage in politics in distinctive ways. Specifically, Catholic congregations are more likely than others to engage in the direct action and pressure group politics of demonstrating, marching, and lobbying.

White Liberal and Moderate Protestants. Unlike for other sorts of civic activity, liberal and moderate white Protestant congregations do not stand out from others on *any* form of political

118

involvement, but the overall pattern of results still suggests a distinctively "mainline" way of engaging in politics. These congregations are significantly more likely than white conservative Protestant congregations, but not more likely than blacks or Catholics, to have a group that discusses politics and to have someone running for office visit their congregations to give a talk. Although the high level of clerical activism that some claim characterized liberal Protestantism in the 1960s and early 1970s is not evident here,[18] there is a sense in which these results indicate a certain political continuity in the liberal Protestant religious tradition. Robert Wuthnow and John Evans (2002) have argued that mainline Protestants do not, in general, favor their religious institutions and leaders taking a more active and visible role in public policy issues and politics. Rather, they prefer to influence public life as individuals by working behind the scenes. Thus, while moderate and liberal white Protestant congregations are relatively active when it comes to organizing political discussion groups or offering their people opportunities for political action, they are not particularly likely, relative to congregations in other traditions, to organize for the purpose of directly influencing political or electoral processes.

As is the case with other kinds of civic activities examined in this chapter, the religious traditions represented in Table 4.3, defined in terms of denominational affiliations and race, do not capture all the religious variation in congregational political activity. In particular, congregations described by informants as theologically conservative are more likely to distribute Christian right voter guides than theologically moderate and liberal congregations, whatever their race or religious denomination. This is not surprising, since many attenders in these congregations would have ideological commitments similar to those of the conservative Christian political organizations producing these guides, but it is worth noting yet again that, as Wuthnow (1988) reminded us forcefully, there is a liberal-conservative divide in American religion that crosscuts denominations.

Taken as a whole, Table 4.3 shows that congregations tend to specialize in particular forms of political action, specialization that is structured by race and religious tradition. Conservative white Protestants tend to engage in politics by distributing voter guides, especially Christian right voter guides. Black Protestants tend to register voters and open their doors to candidates and elected officials. Catholics tend to lobby elected officials and organize demonstrations and marches. Mainline Protestants tend to organize discussion groups.[19] Although none of these political activities are completely monopolized by a single religious tradition, clear modalities are present. I do not know whether the source of these affinities between religious tradition and political style lies in the nature of the issues of primary concern to different religious groups, in organizational differences among religious groups, in the preferred political strategies pursued by national leaders within different traditions, in long-term religious differences of political style and strategic repertoire, in variations across religious traditions in clergy-lay relations, in differences among religious groups in proximity to political establishments, or somewhere else. Whatever the source of these differences, it seems clear that race and religious tradition channel congregations' political activity into distinctive and recognizable paths.

This examination of congregations' civic and political activities points to a simple but important fact about American religion: moderate and liberal Protestants—and, indeed, more liberal congregations within every denomination and religious tradition—engage in more civic activity of all sorts *except political activity.* They are more likely to engage in and encourage activities that build connections between congregations and the world around them through delivering social services, sponsoring educational programs (except their own elementary or high schools), interacting with other congregations across traditional religious boundaries, connecting or exposing their people to the arts, and opening their buildings to community groups. Jewish synagogues tend to be similarly highly engaged with the world around them.

Liberal Protestant congregations are not, however, more likely to engage in politics. Political activity is likely to represent taking sides in a partisan conflict, even when, as with encouraging voter registration or distributing voter guides, the activity is ostensibly educational and nonpartisan. From this perspective, we might reach a conclusion stronger than the straightforward observation that liberal congregations are in many ways the most civically engaged of all congregations. It seems that they tend also to encourage bridging and nonpartisan connections with other segments of the community while at the same time avoiding explicitly partisan activities more than congregations in some other traditions. More expansively, we might say that theologically moderate and liberal congregations appear more likely than others to act as stewards of civil society rather than as one competing component of civil society.

The basic contours of religious variation in civic engagement described here are, as I have indicated in previous chapters, consistent with a long-standing divide within American culture between religion that is essentially open to the world around it and religion that is more withdrawn from that world, or at least more skeptical of engaging with it. Interpreters of American religion have offered a variety of explanations for this difference. Robert Wuthnow (1999) has suggested that one source of the difference, at least among Protestants, is that denominations with European roots as territorial churches re-created in America their systems of associations and federations, thereby reproducing their deep involvement in civic affairs. The historian Peter Dobkin Hall (1998) attributes the difference in part to regional differences in institutional culture and to a broader contrast between pro- and anti-institution-building ideologies within different religious traditions. The sociologists John Wilson and Thomas Janoski (1995) have hypothesized that higher levels of otherworldly religious beliefs among conservative and evangelical Protestants might be responsible for lower levels of concern with, and participation in, the community outside the congregation. Generally lower levels of civic activity in Catholic congregations, compared to mainline Protestant congregations, might be an institutional residue of historic attempts to build an encompassing set of Catholic institutions and associations whose purpose was to maintain enclaves rather than build bridges to other communities.

A somewhat less sanguine explanation for high levels of bridging civic activity among liberal Protestants might emphasize the fact that, for much of American history, white Protestant "mainline" congregations were more or less coterminous with a civil society that quite effectively excluded others from full participatory citizenship. If "your" people control public schools, there is no reason to use your congregations to build schools. If the surrounding civil society is mainly composed of associations, federations, and organizations that "your" people lead, there is no reason to discourage congregants from participating in them. The higher levels of civic activity among moderate and liberal Protestants may thus be in part a by-product of mainline Protestant domination of civil society, in which case lower levels of civic activity by other congregations emerge as a long-term consequence of social exclusion from the Protestant establishment. Perhaps congregations become vehicles for bridging civic activity for groups already wholly embedded by other means in the secular institutions of civil society, while they become enclaves and vehicles for achieving social closure for groups that do not have such easy access to the opportunities for action offered by secular civil society. From this perspective, civic engagement is less a product of any internal features of moderate and liberal Protestantism and more a product of the position traditionally held by these congregations within communities' civic hierarchies. Perhaps preferring individual to collective involvement in politics is a luxury more easily available to congregations with historically close ties to the political establishment.

I am not able to assess fully the validity of any of these explanations, but none of them seems adequate by itself. It seems unlikely that there is a strong correlation among denominations between civic participation and historical roots as a state or territorial church. Neither Methodists nor American Baptists nor Jews have these roots, for example, yet their congregations are among the most civically engaged. Nor do regional or theological differences, when assessed in multivariate analyses, fully explain the different patterns of civic activity observed across religious traditions. Catholics' efforts to build enclaves may explain earlier Catholic versus Protestant differences in civic activity, but why would Catholic levels of such activity remain lower than liberal Protestant levels some three or four decades after full Catholic assimilation into middle-class America? As for the Protestant establishment thesis, it works better, prima facie, for some kinds of activities than for others. It is plausible that "establishment" congregations would be less likely to build schools and more likely to do other things, such as letting outside groups use the building, having representatives of community groups as visiting speakers, and support-ing educational programs. But why would links to a broader civic establishment make a congregation more likely to partici-pate in or sponsor social service programs, build or rehabilitate housing for poor people, sponsor soup kitchens, hold meetings about race relations or the environment, or hold joint worship services that cross major religious boundaries? Why would ex-clusion from a civic establishment make a congregation less likely to do these things? And how does the "Protestant estab-lishment" thesis account for the fact that Jewish synagogues—hardly part of any Protestant establishment—are among the most civically active congregations in virtually every arena?

Results from more complex analyses are relevant here. If the religious tradition differences evident in Table 4.1 disap-peared or became much smaller when relevant variables are controlled, this would suggest that the historic and long-noted differences between religious traditions in civic participation might be attenuating as the Protestant establishment erodes and as congregations in all religious traditions face similar pressures arising from suburbanization, high divorce rates, in-creased numbers of families where the adults work two and three jobs, and so on.

The fascinating reality, however, is that the basic patterns of religious variation evident in Table 4.1 are *not* much explained by other congregational characteristics. The right-hand col-umn in that table shows that the differences between, on the one hand, moderate and liberal Protestant congregations and, on the other hand, all other congregations largely remain sta-tistically significant even after controlling for a congregation's size, annual income, theological leanings, social class composi-tion, racial composition, age composition, geographical re-gion, rural versus nonrural location, location in a poor neigh-borhood, and founding date.[20] Thus, the verdict reached from inspecting the simple percentages in Table 4.1 is sustained by more sophisticated analysis: moderate and liberal Protestant congregations are more likely than other congregations to have a public presence encompassing activities that create or maintain connections between churches and communities. The propensity to encourage these kinds of public activities is not reducible to differences in any congregational or community characteristic I am able to examine.

Among the variables examined in these more complex analyses is a congregation's self-described theological bent: whether informants described their congregation's theology as more on the conservative side, more on the liberal side, or right in the middle. I mentioned earlier in this chapter that, above and beyond connection to one or another denomination, a local culture of theological liberalism or conservatism is associated with congregations' civic bridge-building activities. Within each denomination and religious tradition, theologically liberal congregations are more likely to build these bridges than theologically middle-of-the-road congregations, and middle-of-the-road congregations are more likely to build these bridges than conservative congregations. Here I would add that, although a congregation's local theological culture often has its own independent correlation with civic participation, theological variations among congregations do not account for the religious tradition differences in public presence. Those differences remain substantial even when self-described theology is held constant.

These results—the joint presence, in the face of controls, of both denominational and theological effects on a wide range of civic activities—suggest that religious differences in civic engagement are not reducible to any single feature of demography, organization, ideology, or historical background. I am not sure how, ultimately, to account for these differences, but they appear to be deep and stable.

These analyses also provocatively suggest a possible trend

in congregations' level of civic engagement. More recently founded congregations are *less* likely to engage in many of the bridging civic activities examined here, whatever their religious tradition.[21] It is impossible to know whether this implies a trend toward less civic engagement in American congregations, or whether it means only that newer congregations, at any point in time, are less publicly engaged than older congregations. Perhaps a congregation's early years require more inward than outward focus as people work to create a stable organization, and perhaps today's newer congregations will become more publicly engaged as they become more established in their communities. If this is what is happening, we need not worry that in the future America's congregations will, as a whole, be less engaged in civic bridge building than are today's congregations. If, however, the other interpretation is the correct one—if more recently founded congregations are less civically engaged at their core and will remain so even as they age and become more established—then we will see a future in which congregations collectively engage in and encourage less civic activity than currently is the case.

In this chapter and the previous one I developed a dual theme regarding congregations' involvement in social services and politics. On the one hand, congregational involvement in social service delivery and political activism is rather meager; these are peripheral activities for the majority of congregations. On the other hand, relative to other organizations whose primary purpose is neither social service delivery nor politics, congregations engage in a fair amount of at least some types of this activity—enough to warrant exploring its nature and varieties. In the next chapter we turn our attention away from that which is peripheral to most congregations and toward that which is central to virtually all congregations: worship.

5

Worship

Congregations' central purpose is of course the expression and transmission of religious meaning, and corporate worship is the primary way in which that purpose is pursued. In Chapter 7 I document quantitatively the centrality of worship to congregational life, but let me illustrate the point here with a qualitative observation. The regular worship services produced by congregations are tied to the calendar and therefore occur regularly and predictably: every Sunday at 11 A.M., every Friday at 5 P.M., every Saturday at 10 A.M. The anthropologist Roy Rappaport (1999:90) notes that the occurrence of such calendrical rituals does not tell us much about the social group or organization producing them. The *non*occurrence of such a ritual, by contrast, is of great significance:

> The parishioners of the local Methodist church are, after all, not told much by the occurrence of a service at their church at 10:00 AM on Sunday. At best the occurrence of a calendrical ritual is a "match signal" indicating that the system of which the ritual is a part continues to function.

The *failure* of a calendrical ritual to occur, on the other hand, indicates that something extraordinary, probably bad, has happened.

There is a sense in which congregations are organizations whose primary output is the regular worship event. If that event fails to occur, the congregation is in much deeper trouble than if its social service project fails or if voter guides are left undistributed in the narthex. A congregation that stopped producing regular worship services would no longer be a congregation even if it remained an organization that was active, even religiously active, in other ways. Producing collective religious events frequently and at regular intervals is part of what we mean by congregational religion.

Engaging in some manner of collective worship may be nearly universal for congregations, but these events vary tremendously in form and content. Consider these two partial descriptions of worship services, the first occurring in a Roman Catholic church, the second in an Assemblies of God congregation:

> Most congregants genuflect before entering a pew and kneel in prayer before sitting down to wait for the Mass to begin . . . The music is often slow, and congregational participation is sparse. The choir and organ often compete with the coughing, whispering, and fidgeting of the congregation. Although singing is often lackluster, many congregants recite the Apostles' Creed with energy and enthusiasm. And the eucharistic prayer is the one time during the Mass when all parishioners are equally focused . . . Virtually the entire congregation on any given Sunday will receive the Host; the wine is never offered to parishioners here. Most receive the Host in their hands, return

to their seats, and kneel in prayer until communion is over. (Ammerman 1997a:67)

The pastoral staff and greeters hand programs to worshippers as they enter . . . Instead of pews, there are cushioned chairs that can be rearranged for different occasions . . . Singing draws [people's] attention to the front, and congregants stand, often raising one arm heavenward as they join in opening the service. Some songs are favorites, and many attending do not refer to the printed refrains. The tempo is at first upbeat, and everyone claps in time . . . The last songs, which create a peaceful, worshipful mood, are interspersed with times of prayer. Most of the worshippers join in, praying softly but audibly in their seats. A few pray quietly in tongues . . . The offertory prayer and collection follow, while music plays . . . When Pastor Tommy announces that it is time for children sixth grade and under to attend Sunday school, they are escorted out of the sanctuary by their parents . . . The service resumes with some additional singing and Pastor Tommy's sermon . . . When the pastor reads from his Bible, members of the congregation follow along in theirs. (Ammerman 1997a:299)

These two worship events, different as they are, provide only a glimpse of the rich variation in collective religious practice within American congregations. My agenda in this chapter is to investigate systematically the nature and sources of this variation.

I use the notion of "repertoire" to help guide this inquiry. The repertoire concept has been used fruitfully in both the sociology of culture (Swidler 1986, 2001) and the sociology of social movements (Tilly 1978, 1993; Tarrow 1994). In the sociology of culture, culture itself has been conceptualized as a "'tool kit' of symbols, stories, rituals, and world-views, which people may use in varying configurations to solve different kinds of problems" (Swidler 1986:273). In the sociology of social movements, analysts have identified a repertoire of contentious collective action that has, at various times and places, included grain seizures, disruption of ceremonies, petitions, formal meetings, street demonstrations, strikes, public marches, and so on. Repertoires of ideas and actions do not stay constant over time; new elements become legitimated and thereby enter the repertoire, old elements become irrelevant and thereby drop out of the repertoire. Whatever the repertoire of ideas or actions available at a given time and place, neither individuals nor groups draw randomly or in a wholly voluntary fashion from the available repertoire as they construct strategies of action. Social and institutional contexts structure the manner in which elements are selected from the repertoire. Scholars in the sociology of culture and the sociology of social movements have studied how repertoires change and how social contexts influence the selection of elements from a repertoire for deployment in particular times and places.[1]

This chapter focuses on how worship events are constructed out of the repertoire of available worship elements, not on change over time in the repertoire itself. The animating idea is that worship services like the two just described are constructed from a repertoire of "worship elements"—specific practices such as organ music, choir singing, communion, reciting creeds, kneeling, sermons, Bible reading, speaking in tongues, and so on—that are available for deployment in worship services. My analytical strategy is to specify a repertoire of worship elements and then analyze how those elements cluster in systematic ways in actual worship services. This approach is fruitful in at least three ways. It enables me to show that the tremendous variation in congregational worship is shaped simultaneously from "below," by the social characteristics of participants, and from "above," by the denominations and religious traditions in which congregations and their participants are embedded. It leads to a fascinating puzzle about the nature of change in collective religious practice. And it begins to develop a sociology of religious organizations that is at once cultural and ecological, opening new and productive lines of investigation.

The Repertoire of Worship Elements

The National Congregations Study collected data on worship services by asking informants whether or not their congregation's most recent main worship service contained any of twenty-nine different worship elements. For some elements informants were asked whether or not any service within the past year included that practice. Consequently, embedded in this nationally representative sample of congregations is a nationally representative sample of worship events, with information about which of twenty-nine different worship elements was included in each of these services.[2]

Table 5.1 lists the twenty-nine worship elements on which the NCS gathered data, the percentage of congregations having services containing each element, and the percentage of attenders in congregations where services have each element. This is not an exhaustive inventory of worship elements, but it is a fair approximation of the repertoire of worship practices out of which worship services are constructed.

Two of these elements—singing by the congregation and a sermon or speech—are essentially universal in American collective religious events. No other element (except using a musical instrument of any sort, something closely associated with

Table 5.1 Repertoire of worship elements

Element	Percent of attenders at worship services with element	Percent of congregations whose services have element
Singing by congregation	98	96
Sermon/speech	97	95
Musical instrument of any sort	91	84
People greet one another	84	79
Written program	84	71
Silent prayer/meditation	81	74
Laughter	75	74
People speak/read/recite together	75	63
Singing by choir	72	52
People testify/speak about religious experience[a]	72	78
Organ	70	53
Skit or play performed by teens or adults[a]	70	62
Piano	68	69
Applause	59	55
People call out "amen"	53	63
Singing by soloist	50	41
Performance by paid singers or other performers[a]	51	35
People other than leader raise hands in praise	48	45
Communion	48	29
Something specifically directed at children	48	47
Teens speak/read/perform	46	40
People told of opportunities for political activity[a]	37	26
Electric guitar	30	22
Dance performance by teens or adults[a]	29	17
Drums	25	20
People speak in tongues[a]	19	24
Visual projection equipment	15	12
Adults jump/shout/dance spontaneously	13	19
Incense	7	4

a. Percentage of congregations having a service with that feature at any time within the past year. (For other elements, the percentage indicates the percent of congregations whose most recent main service included that element.)

congregational singing) occurs in more than 80 percent of services, but virtually all services include both a speech and collective singing. Moreover, more than half (approximately 60 percent) of all the *time* spent in these events is taken up either with sermonizing or with music of some sort. The worship service experienced by the average attender lasts seventy minutes, and it contains a twenty-minute sermon and twenty minutes of music, so the average worship service is approximately one third listening to the leader talk, approximately one third listening to or making music, and approximately one third other kinds of activities, such as keeping silent, listening to someone read a text, or reciting together.

Whatever else happens at collective religious events in congregations, worship in the United States mainly involves people getting together to sing and listen to somebody talk.[3] Indeed, this combination almost completely distinguishes worship events from other sorts of collective events in American society. Few secular collective events—with the exception, perhaps, of some birthday parties and some political rallies—routinely contain both singing and speech making. And only a few religious services lack one or the other of these elements. Muslim worship, for example, is less likely to involve singing and Buddhist worship is less likely to incorporate a speech. These exceptions notwithstanding, worship services occupy a distinctive niche in American cultural life, a niche that goes beyond their explicitly religious aspects. To put it bluntly, there are few places one can go, other than to a religious congregation's worship service, to sing and hear a speech.[4]

Actual worship events are not random subsets of these elements. Some elements are more likely than others to occur together. It is logically possible, for example, to have a worship event that includes silent prayer, communion, and an overhead projector, but such a combination is far less common (occurring in only 2 percent of worship services) than a service with a sermon, organ music, and singing by a choir (a combination occurring in 33 percent of services), or one in which participants call out "amen," raise their hands in praise, and offer personal testimony (a combination occurring in 35 percent of services). This nonrandom clumping of elements indicates structure in the process by which subsets of these elements are assembled to construct worship events.[5] Some of these elements are more tightly linked in practice than others, and we would like to know how those links are forged. As Paul DiMaggio (1985:557) once put it, "The most substantively important variations in cultural systems have to do with the manner in which elements are assembled, not with their frequency." Interesting as the frequencies in Table 5.1 might be, I want to move beyond them to ask how subsets of these elements come to be assembled into worship events.

Socio-Demographic Sources of Religious Practice

I begin with a well-established finding from the sociology of culture: people with different social class positions have different cultural tastes and engage in different cultural practices.[6] We should expect that worship events, as a form of cultural expression and consumption, are similarly shaped by the social class of individuals participating in them, and indeed, social class often has been considered *the* most fundamental source of religious variation and the engine driving an endlessly repeating process of religious change and renewal.[7] Table 5.2 shows that social class does indeed shape worship. This table gives, for each worship element, the mean percent of adults with incomes under $25,000 and the mean percent with bachelor's degrees in all congregations using a particular element in their collective worship. The elements are listed from those, at the

Table 5.2 Education and income in congregations using specific worship elements

Element	Mean % of people with B.A. degrees	Mean % of people in poor households (< $25,000)
Adults jump/shout/dance spontaneously	15	47
People speak in tongues	16	46
People other than leader raise hands in praise	18	42
Drums	18	43
People call out "amen"	19	42
Piano	22	38
Singing by soloist	23	38
Electric guitar	23	39
Applause	23	38
Visual projection equipment	23	37
People testify/speak about religious experience	24	37
Skit or play performed by teens or adults	24	36
People greet one another	24	36
Teens speak/read/perform	25	32
Sermon/speech	25	37
Singing by congregation	25	37
Singing by choir	26	31
Something specifically directed at children	26	35
Laughter	27	34
Silent prayer/meditation	27	36
People told of opportunities for political activity	27	34
Organ	27	29
People speak/read/recite together	28	36
Written program	28	33
Communion	30	34
Performance by paid singers or other performers	31	33
Dance performed by teens or adults	31	31
Incense	42	29

top, most common among the less educated and less affluent, to those, at the bottom, most common among the more educated and affluent.

A clear pattern emerges from reading down this list. More spontaneous, informal, demonstrative worship occurs in congregations with higher percentages of poor and less educated people. Speaking in tongues, spontaneous jumping and shouting, playing drums, and raising hands in praise, for example, all occur near the top of the list. The less poor and more educated a congregation is, the more formal is its worship, containing elements such as written programs, reading together, organ music, or silent prayer, all of which occur nearer the bottom of the list. Spontaneous jumping, shouting, or dancing, for example, occurs in congregations where only 15 percent of people, on average, are college graduates and where almost half the people had household incomes below $25,000 in 1998. Worship in which there is dance *performance*, by contrast, occurs in congregations where about one third of the people, on average, are college graduates and where only one third are in households with incomes below $25,000. Table 5.2 makes clear that worship elements of different sorts, like other forms of cultural expression, systematically appear in different social class contexts.

Social class is not the only factor around which social and organizational life is organized. Especially when forming voluntary associations, individuals tend to sort themselves into relatively homogeneous groups, and social class is only one dimension, albeit an important one, on which this sorting occurs (McPherson and Smith-Lovin 1987). Age, race, and, in some contexts, gender are other dimensions which, together with social class, create a socio-demographic space; different combinations of social characteristics represent different regions within that space. If voluntary associations of different sorts

136

reside within different regions of social space, so do different cultural forms (McPherson 1983b; McPherson and Ranger-Moore 1991; Mark 1998). This shift from one-dimensional social class to multidimensional socio-demographic space helps to move the sociological analysis of religious expression beyond church-sect theory's nearly exclusive emphasis on social class as the main social source of variation in religious expression.[8]

Figure 5.1, for example, places each worship element in a two-dimensional socio-demographic space defined by the percent of adults in a congregation with B.A. degrees and the percent under thirty-five years old.[9] I locate elements in this space by calculating the mean "percent college educated" and the mean "percent young" for congregations having each element in their worship, and then plotting these means in Figure 5.1. We already saw in Table 5.2 that social class, here operationalized as level of education, shapes worship events. Figure 5.1 shows that social class is not the only socio-demographic source of structure in these events. Congregations with more young adults in them have less formal worship. Reading together, written programs, organs, and choirs, among other elements, all are situated in congregations with older constituents. Speaking in tongues, playing drums and electric guitars, and raising hands, among other practices, all appear among congregations with more young people in them.

Figure 5.1 also suggests that worship elements closer together in socio-demographic space are more likely to be linked *in practice*—that is, they are more likely to occur together in actual worship services. Speaking in tongues, playing drums, and raising hands in praise, for example, are located near one another in the socio-demographic space defined by age and education. These are elements that appear together fairly commonly in Pentecostal worship services, and they co-occur

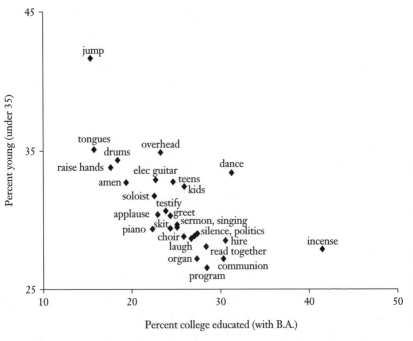

Figure 5.1 Worship elements and congregations' social composition

much more commonly than some of the elements—spontaneous jumping and burning incense, for example—that are more
distant from one another in this social space.

Additional analysis shows that, in general, worship practices
closer together in social space are indeed more likely to co-occur in worship services.[10] This connection emerges because
congregations, like all voluntary associations, tend toward social homogeneity. Since congregations tend toward social homogeneity, individual worship practices attractive to people in
a particular region of socio-demographic space will tend to co-
occur in the same worship services. Since the better educated,
for example, tend to congregate together, if reading together
and using written programs each bears an affinity with the

better educated, these two practices will tend to co-occur in worship services. From the other direction, if individual worship practices tend to occur in the same worship services because a denominational worship tradition places them together, those same elements cannot help but be close together in social space, since congregations and denominations themselves reside in particular regions of socio-demographic space. If Pentecostal worship, for example, by tradition includes both speaking in tongues and raised hands, those two worship elements also will tend to be practiced by those who are socially similar to one another, since Pentecostalism, like all traditions, resides in a particular region of social space.

The key point here is that *congregations' social homogeneity forges links between worship elements.* Speaking in tongues and raised hands are fairly tightly linked in American religious worship because they reside in similar regions of socio-demographic space, congregations tend toward social homogeneity, and so congregations employing one practice also will tend to employ the other practice. The same is true of using written programs and reading together, though this latter pair of practices resides in a very different region of social space than the former pair.[11]

The combination of congregations' tendency toward social homogeneity and the tendency of worship elements to occur more commonly in some rather than other social contexts explains why there is variation of *some* sort in religious expression across social contexts, but it does not explain why that variation has the specific content observed in Table 5.2 and Figure 5.1. Why, for example, do speaking in tongues and raised hands show up more among the less well educated while moments of silence and greetings show up more among the better educated? Why not the other way around? Why is there *this* sort of religious variation across social contexts?

One kind of answer to these questions might focus on the

process by which religious meanings become institutionalized as one rather than another sort of practice. If ideas and expectations about God vary across social contexts, and if these ideas and expectations themselves influence worship practices, then specific practices will reside in particular social locations. If, for example, belief in an active and powerful supernatural is more common among the less educated, worship designed to display and invoke that supernatural—such as speaking in tongues or spontaneous jumping—also will be more common there.

Lynn Smith-Lovin and William Douglass (1992) have documented one kind of link between religious ideas and ritual practice. They accurately predict the ritual content of worship in two congregations solely from information about how congregants view themselves and God. In a congregation in which individuals consider God to be more supremely good, active, and powerful, worship was predicted to be informal and personal, with congregants "applauding" and "amusing" God while God attempts to "satisfy" congregants. In a congregation of individuals who view God in a less active and powerful way, congregants are predicted to "speak to" and "admire" God rather than "applaud" or "amuse" the deity, and the deity is expected to "counsel" and "reassure" rather than "satisfy" or "like" the congregants. The remarkable thing about these predictions is that *they are made by a computer algorithm* solely on the basis of a social-psychological theory holding that individuals' ideas about themselves and others shape interpersonal interactions because people act to keep those ideas intact. The computer algorithm takes numerical measures of how good, powerful, and active individuals consider themselves and God to be, and it finds behaviors that are known to be associated with those combinations of expectations about self and other. The success of this algorithm at identifying aspects of worship in these two congregations—the first associated with the Metropolitan Community Church, the second with the Unitarian

Universalist Association—indicates one process by which religious ideas might shape collective religious practice.

A process that emphasizes only the links between particular religious ideas and particular worship practices, however, cannot by itself account for the observation that class-based variations in religious practice bear striking similarities to class-based variations in other sorts of cultural expression. Pierre Bourdieu's (1984:487–488) characterization of a key dimension of variation between "popular" and "bourgeois" entertainment styles, for example, seems also to describe the class-based variation in religious expression evident in Table 5.2:

> The most radical difference between popular entertainments—from Punch and Judy shows, wrestling or circuses, or even the old neighborhood cinema, to soccer matches—and bourgeois entertainments is found in audience participation. In one case it is constant, manifest (boos, whistles), sometimes direct (pitch or playing-field invasions); in the other it is intermittent, distant, highly ritualized, with obligatory applause, and even shouts of enthusiasm, at the end, or even perfectly silent (concerts in churches).

In several cultural arenas—not just in religion—there appears to be more spontaneity and demonstrative participation among lower classes, more formality and audience-like behavior among middle and upper classes.

Bourdieu's (1984:197–198) description of class differences in eating styles suggests another kind of resemblance between class differences in religious styles and class differences in other sorts of cultural practice:

> In one case, food is claimed as a material reality, a nourishing substance which sustains the body and gives

strength (hence the emphasis on heavy, fatty, strong foods, of which the paradigm is pork—fatty and salty—the antithesis of fish—light, lean, and bland); in the other, the priority given to form (the shape of the body, for example) and social form, formality, puts the pursuit of strength and substance in the background and identifies true freedom with the elective asceticism of a self-imposed rule.

Whether the cultural object is food or religion, as we move up the social class ladder the manner of engaging with that object seems to shift from more emphasis on substance and materiality to more emphasis on form and discipline. If Bourdieu is correct, moving up the social class ladder produces not simply variation in cultural expression but a particular type of variation discernible within multiple arenas, including religion.

If class-based variations in collective religious practice are similar in style to class-based variations in other sorts of collective practice, these variations must be produced by a process that is not specific to religion. Bourdieu (1984:128–129) connects this variation to the relative amounts of economic and cultural capital individuals possess. People will be attracted to cultural practices and styles that make best use of the particular kind of capital they possess. Individuals with relatively high levels of cultural capital but relatively low levels of economic capital (schoolteachers, for example) will display a common sort of style whether the arena of action is religion, sports, theater, or dinner. Among other things, individuals with this particular combination of economic and cultural capital are likely to practice literacy in various arenas, and so it should not be surprising that worship elements connected to literacy, such as using written programs or reading together, would appear in more highly educated regions of social space.

An observation offered by Mary Douglas (1999:239), again

concerning food, suggests a variation on this theme. Douglas points out that household meals are constructed partly by "reaching out to the meal structure of [a family's] cultural environment." People who commonly eat at steak houses will construct different household meals than people who commonly eat at French restaurants, and not just because individuals' restaurant choices and home-cooked meals both reflect underlying tastes. Cultural elements learned, encountered, or practiced in one context can be imported to another context. Many of the practices deployed in worship services, such as electric guitar playing or reading, also have nonreligious manifestations that vary systematically across social space, and those practices are likely to find religious expression in the same regions of social space in which they find secular expression, simply because individuals carry practices from one domain of action to another. This kind of process also would produce specific cultural content in particular social locations, and that content also would crosscut domains of action.

Whatever the exact mechanisms by which socio-demographic context shapes religious expression or, more generally, cultural expression, it is clear that this context structures the process by which worship events are constructed out of a repertoire of worship elements. It is not, however, the only important source of structure in that process.

Institutional Sources of Religious Practice

Denominations and, more generally, religious traditions provide an institutional source of structure in worship. Denominational influence on worship might take the form of published or officially approved readings, prayers, hymns, and orders of service, or it might take the form of habits and norms carried by clergy who are trained in denominational seminaries. Even when worship services are constructed in whole or in part by individuals other than clergy, such as music directors, liturgists, or worship committees, these people almost always are constrained by a more or less explicit charge to construct events that remain faithful to a particular religious tradition and that meet the expectations of the people who will show up for these events.[12]

In order to examine the extent to which denominations and religious traditions shape worship, I use the repertoire of worship elements to build on the common observation that collective worship events—and religious rituals more generally—occur in two main modes. Many observers of religious variation have noted these two modes, though they go by different names, including Max Weber's ([1920] 1978:chap. 14) charismatic versus routinized religion, Ernst Troeltsch's ([1911] 1981) sectarian versus churchly religion, Ruth Benedict's (1934) Dionysian versus Apollonian modes of religiosity, Ernest Gellner's (1969) C versus P syndromes, Stephen Warner's (1988) nascent versus institutional religious forms, Harvey Whitehouse's (1995) imagistic versus doctrinal modes of religiosity, and Michael Chwe's (2001) common knowledge–generating versus non–common knowledge–generating ceremonies. This same distinction even appears in analyses that are not specifically about religious collective action, as in Charles Tilly's (1998:54–56) discussion of thin versus intense ritual.

The multiple versions of this distinction differ in their details, but this is not the place to catalog those differences.[13] Instead, I want to highlight a commonality. In one way or another, attempts to describe two common modes of religious expression distinguish between, on the one hand, religion that is more intellectual, staid, scripted, and reserved, having little emphasis on face-to-face interaction among participants, and, on the other hand, religion that is more emotional, enthusiastic, informal, and demonstrative, having many moments in which participants mutually focus on one another. The worship elements we have been considering here also cluster in ways that correspond to this distinction. I add to the list of labels for these two modes of religious expression by using a pair of terms—enthusiasm and ceremony—that seem particularly appropriate for describing two dimensions of congregational worship present in these data. It is important to recognize, however, that these represent two quite general dimensions of ritual practice.

I do not treat enthusiastic religion and ceremonial religion as two mutually exclusive boxes into which we might sort denominations, congregations, or even particular worship services. Nor do I treat them as two ends of a single continuum, with worship necessarily becoming more enthusiastic the less ceremonial it is, and vice versa. Rather, I treat these as two *independent* dimensions of collective religious practice, both of which occur, to a greater or lesser extent, in virtually every collective religious event. It is possible, in other words, for a single worship event to have high (or low) levels of both ceremony and enthusiasm. This approach avoids the ultimately fruitless categorization and subcategorization plaguing many efforts to describe and theorize religious variation, and it allows us to examine institutional structuring of worship practices in productive ways. Just as I earlier placed worship elements in a two-dimensional socio-demographic space, here I place religious traditions in a two-dimensional *cultural practice* space defined by the extent to which their worship manifests enthusiasm and ceremony.

As we look down the list of worship elements in Table 5.1, it is not difficult to distinguish elements that contribute more to a worship event's "ceremony" from elements that contribute more to its "enthusiasm." Raising one's hands, jumping or shouting, applauding, calling out "amen," speaking in tongues, and giving lay testimony all would increase what I am calling the enthusiasm evident in worship. These are elements that would encourage participants to focus on other participants rather than on their own individuality, a leader, a script, or a performance. Reading together, singing by a formal choir, using written programs, and engaging in silent prayer all would increase what I am calling the ceremonial aspect of worship. These are more scripted or individualistic or performed kinds of elements that are less likely to lead participants to focus on one another.

When all the worship elements are included in a factor analysis—a statistical technique that uses the pattern of correlations among the elements to identify items that tend to occur together—the two factors that emerge correspond very closely to the enthusiasm and ceremony dimensions one would construct intuitively using these worship elements. The nine elements most strongly associated with one factor, for example, are playing drums, raising hands, jumping or shouting, applauding, using overhead projectors, playing electric guitars, saying "amen," speaking in tongues, and giving lay testimony. This is the enthusiasm dimension of worship events. The eight elements identified most strongly with the other factor are reading together, choir singing, organ music, written programs, silent prayer, skit performances, hired musicians, and dance performances. This is the ceremonial dimension of worship events.[14]

These two worship modes define a two-dimensional cultural practice space in which denominations and religious traditions can be placed by examining the worship practices of their congregations.[15] Figure 5.2 shows where selected denominations and traditions fall in this space.[16] Each box can be understood as the niche occupied by that religious tradition in a cultural ecology defined by these two dimensions of worship practice.[17]

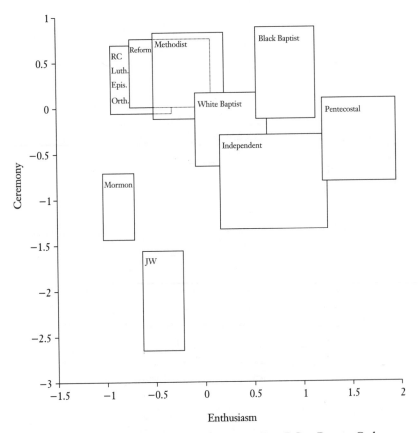

Figure 5.2   Denominatons in worship space. Key: RC = Roman Catholic; Luth. = Lutheran; Epis. = Episcopal; Orth. = Eastern Orthodox; JW = Jehovah's Witnesses

There is much that is fascinating about this figure. Most obviously, it shows that denominations and traditions structure worship. In the upper-left corner of this space are Roman Catholic, Lutheran, Episcopalian, and Eastern Orthodox worship services. Worship in these traditions is on average the most ceremonial and least enthusiastic in the United States. Slightly to the right is the worship of congregations in Reformed traditions (including Presbyterian, Reformed, United Church of Christ, and Unitarian Universalist denominations). Worship in these traditions is just as ceremonial on average as worship in the more high church traditions, but it is slightly more enthusiastic. Methodist worship is another notch more enthusiastic, and so on. These denominational differences in practice are not reducible to other characteristics of their people or congregations.[18] They represent a direct institutional influence on congregations' collective religious practice.

More subtly, the overall pattern of denominational locations in this figure bears a remarkable correspondence to the institutional history of Christianity in the West. The oldest religious traditions reside in the upper-left portion of this cultural space, meaning that their worship tends to be more ceremonial and less enthusiastic. As we move down and to the right across the space—in the direction of more enthusiastic and less ceremonial religion—we come across religious traditions more or less in the historical order in which they entered this cultural field as significant religious movements. The four traditions that are most to the "northwest" in this figure—Catholic, Eastern Orthodox, Episcopal, and Lutheran—are also the oldest of the Christian denominations represented here. Slightly to the "east" are denominations carrying the Reformed tradition, which emerged and consolidated in the sixteenth and seventeenth centuries.

During the eighteenth and nineteenth centuries, the most significant religious movements in the United States were the populist movements of the Methodists and the Baptists, and the uniquely American Mormons. Autonomous African American Methodist and Baptist denominations also were formed. Each of these groups is either less ceremonial, more enthusiastic, or both than the traditions that came before. Methodists moved only slightly further in the enthusiastic direction relative to the Reformed traditions they emerged against, while white Baptist worship practices are noticeably less ceremonial and more enthusiastic than those of any of the groups previously mentioned. Black Baptists, interestingly, are more enthusiastic in their worship than white Baptists, but they also are more ceremonial, while Mormon worship resides in a region of this space occupied by no other group.

Jehovah's Witnesses and Pentecostals arrived on the scene in the late nineteenth and early twentieth centuries. Perhaps because the central regions of the cultural space defined by these two basic dimensions of religious collective practice were by this point fairly densely occupied, each of these movements drew on the repertoire of worship elements in truly novel ways. Pentecostals moved to the extreme on enthusiasm, while Jehovah's Witnesses found a niche that is low on both dimensions.[19]

Some observers consider the growth of independent congregations—free-standing congregations not affiliated with any denomination—to be among the most significant American religious developments in the last decades of the twentieth century. These congregations, on average, are located in a region with noticeably less ceremonial practice and noticeably more enthusiastic practice, but their worship is not, in general, so enthusiastic that it overlaps with Pentecostal practice.

Denominational positioning in this two-dimensional space defined by worship practices more or less tracks the historical development of Christian religious traditions away from the standard set by the Catholic Church in the Middle Ages. It seems that there is a steady, centuries-long movement of Christian worship toward more enthusiastic and less ceremonial practices, with occasional bursts of novelty further away from the main line of cultural development. An early glimpse of this movement can be seen in a 1537 treatise written by the reformer John Calvin ([1537] 1954:53–54) which is worth quoting at length:

> There are the psalms which we desire to be sung in the Church, as we have it exemplified in the ancient Church and in the evidence of Paul himself, who says it is good to sing in the congregation with mouth and heart. We are unable to compute the profit and edification which will arise from this, except after having experimented. Certainly as things are, the prayers of the faithful are so cold, that we ought to be ashamed and dismayed. The psalms can incite us to lift up our hearts to God and move us to an ardour in invoking and exalting with praises the glory of his Name. Moreover it will be thus appreciated of what benefit and consolation the pope and those that belong to him have deprived the Church; for he has reduced the psalms, which ought to be true spiritual songs, to a murmuring among themselves without any understanding.
>
> This manner of proceeding seemed specially good to us, that children, who beforehand have practised some modest church song, sing in a loud distinct voice, the people listening with all attention and following heartily what is sung with the mouth, till all become accustomed to sing communally.

In sixteenth-century Geneva, congregational singing apparently was a great innovation, moving Reformed worship ever so slightly away from Catholic worship in the enthusiastic direction, where it remains to this day. To give another example of this process in action, Grant Wacker's recent history of American Pentecostalism documents how Pentecostals "ratcheted up the intensity even more, endorsing leaping, screaming, and deathlike prostration" (Wacker 2001:99). In addition to its sheer length, early Pentecostal worship was "chaotic and deafening," marked by speaking in tongues, jerking bodies, rapid music, and testifying children. None of these practices, taken as individual elements, was new, but Pentecostalism put them together in new ways. Furthermore, this innovative reshuffling of the repertoire of worship elements into a new package occurred with one eye on the established traditions against which Pentecostals were trying to distinguish themselves. As Wacker (2001:100) puts it, "What distinguished pentecostals . . . was not so much the presence of uninhibited emotion as its centrality," adding, "Any service—indeed any part of any service—that looked like it had been planned seemed a sure sign of nominal Christianity." Although much Pentecostal worship has become, in general, somewhat calmer and regularized over time, Figure 5.2 makes clear that it has remained, on average, much more enthusiastic than the rest of American worship.

What underlying mechanisms of cultural and religious change produce such a striking correspondence between, on the one hand, the extent to which a religious tradition's worship is ceremonial and enthusiastic and, on the other hand, the historical moment of its consolidation as a tradition? Two broad types of answer to this question are possible. The pattern evident in Figure 5.2 could arise if new religious movements always begin with more enthusiastic and less ceremonial worship practices that then become less enthusiastic and more ceremonial over time as the movement becomes more institutionalized. This is the routinization of charisma process first described by Max Weber and elaborated by many others.[20] The pattern in Figure 5.2 also could arise, however, even if religious traditions do *not* move significantly over time in a less enthusiastic and more ceremonial direction. If emergent religions position themselves relative to already existing groups such that their worship is different, but not too different, from prevailing worship practice, and if the worship practices manifest at a movement's origins continue to shape worship in that tradition strongly as time elapses, this sort of process—one resembling an ecological, evolution of species process more than a developmental, routinization of charisma process—also would produce the pattern evident in Figure 5.2. In the first account, variation in religious expression occurs because religious traditions change as they age, and new religions emerge to occupy the cultural niches vacated by the institutionalizing traditions. In the second account, this variation occurs because newcomers adopt somewhat different practices from those already on the scene, and practices adopted at a movement's origins remain more or less constant throughout its history.

These two possibilities are not mutually exclusive. A religious tradition might alter its worship over time in the direction of more ceremony and less enthusiasm *and* its worship might remain strongly similar even centuries later to the worship practiced at its founding. The correct question is not, Which one of these processes is the correct one? The correct question is, What is the relative importance of each of these processes in producing the systematic variation across religious traditions that we see displayed in Figure 5.2?

I cannot definitively answer this question with a single cross-sectional survey like the NCS, but I will develop the ecological side of the answer rather than the routinization side of the answer. I do this for two reasons. First, the routinization process is well known and well established in the sociology of religion. Religious movements that survive beyond their initial flourishing undoubtedly routinize and institutionalize in ways that move their worship in the more ceremonial and less enthusiastic direction. Many examples of this process have been documented by historians and sociologists. At the same time, this process is so well known and so well established that the ecological process has been almost completely overlooked in the literature on religious change, leaving the impression that the routinization of charisma process accounts for 100 percent of the variation in religious expression of the sort evident in Figure 5.2. But the dominance of the routinization model in the sociology of religion is not the result of careful comparison and considered rejection of the ecological model. It is, rather, the result of neglecting to consider ecological processes as potential sources of religious change. I develop an ecological interpretation of Figure 5.2 in part to call attention to a kind of process that has not received adequate attention in analyses of religious change.

A second reason for developing an ecological interpretation is that this strategy allows me to bring insights from larger sociological literatures to bear on the study of religious variation and change. Although the routinization model continues to dominate the sociology of religion, scholars in other areas of sociology have come to recognize ecological processes as important sources of organizational and cultural change. Calling attention to these other literatures may enhance the conceptual, theoretical, and empirical resources available to students of religion.

An ecological interpretation of Figure 5.2 starts with the idea that the creation of new organizations, with new styles, forms, and practices, is a significant source of change in the overall distribution of organizational styles, forms, and practices within a society. We know that organizational change of many sorts occurs in this way,[21] and it seems likely that this applies as well to changing worship practices. From this perspective, new types of worship events emerge when new religious movements or religious entrepreneurs create new congregations with new worship styles, not just via change within congregations associated with already established religious traditions.

Internal change within established traditions certainly occurs, but there also is impressive historical continuity in worship practices within denominations and religious traditions. Catholic worship in the United States, for example, certainly has changed over time. In particular, the significance of momentous changes in Catholic worship brought about by Vatican II should not be understated. At the same time, however, much of today's Catholic worship looks more like Catholic worship of centuries ago than like today's Baptist or Pentecostal worship, neither of which, remarkably, even slightly overlaps Catholic worship in Figure 5.2.[22]

Roman Catholicism is not the only tradition within which worship practices show strong inertia over time. The Directory for Worship used by the Presbyterian Church (USA) and predecessor denominations was changed only eighteen times between 1788 and 2002. There is some indication that the directory's rate of change has increased in recent decades. From 1788 it took 162 years to change the directory nine times, but it took only an additional 52 years to change it another nine times. This increase in the rate of change aside, and acknowledging that change in the official Directory for Worship certainly occurs more slowly than change in on-the-ground worship practices within Presbyterian congregations, eighteen instances of change spread across 214 years bespeaks impressive continuity in American Presbyterian worship practice.[23]

Evident continuity in worship practices within religious traditions suggests that, along with whatever internal change in worship practices occurs within religious traditions, the formation of new congregations and traditions that create and carry new cultural forms also produces a substantial amount of the variation in worship style within American religion. How to worship is a common source of conflict in American congregations.[24] When it comes to assembling a new kind of worship event, it may be easier to start over in a new congregation than fight to change practice in an existing one.

An ecological interpretation of denominational variation in worship practices requires more than organizational inertia. We also need to say why newer traditions situate their worship practice where they do. Figure 5.2 suggests two major types of innovation in worship practice. A striking feature of this figure is that historically more recent religious traditions are situated, in general, in cultural locations that are different—but, with the exception of Mormons, Pentecostals, and Witnesses, not *too* different—from what came before. The progression of worship styles characterizing Catholic to Reformed to Methodist to white Baptist to independent congregations suggests that newer worship tends to overlap considerably—perhaps different by only one or two elements—with what came before. Religious change occurs in part because new religious movements reshuffle available worship elements to situate themselves partially in a cultural practice space that already is occupied and partially in a space that is not yet occupied by established religious organizations of the day. Religious movements and religious entrepreneurs partly innovate, but they also partly seek continuity with major existing traditions in their cultural field. Why?

One answer is that, like new movements and organizations of many sorts, new religious movements must simultaneously be recognizably similar to and recognizably different from existing religions. They must both establish themselves as "real" religion and differentiate themselves from other religious options. Continuity in worship practice declares, "We are religion of a legitimate sort." Innovation declares, "We are religion unlike—and better than—others that you know." This posits an irreducibly cultural engine of religious change, one that, because tomorrow's religious practices are determined in part by today's practices, does not depend only on the fuel of socio-demographic differences among individuals.

This phenomenon—change that occurs through relatively small alterations in existing practice—can be observed in other areas of culture. Stanley Lieberson notes that in the realm of fashion, "new tastes are usually based on existing tastes; what is most appealing is a modest variant on existing tastes." This is true of dress styles, children's names, and even music, where "musical innovations—if they are to succeed—are based largely on an existing set of practices" (Lieberson 2000:93–94). In the realm of social protest, activists "generally innovate at the perimeter of the existing repertoire [of collective action] rather than by breaking entirely with old ways" (Tilly 1993:265–266). In a realm closer to congregational worship practice, Rappaport (1999:32) notes that "rituals composed entirely of new elements are . . . likely to fail to become established . . . 'New' rituals are likely to be largely composed of elements taken from older rituals . . . There is still room for the rearrangement of elements, and even for discarding some elements and introducing others, but invention is limited and the sanction of previous performance is maintained." The dual need for legitimation and differentiation seems likely to be behind many sorts of cultural change.

This legitimation and differentiation mechanism will produce new cultural forms that overlap considerably with current cultural forms, but it will not necessarily produce a series of changes in any particular direction. In addition to the partial overlap among traditions characterizing much of the worship practice variation in American religion, there also appears to be directionality to this variation. It is remarkable that newer

move further in same direction vs. overlap

religious traditions tend to appear further "south" and "east" on Figure 5.2 than older religious traditions. No major religious movement has successfully moved "northwest" in this cultural practice space. What sort of process might produce not just traditions that partially overlap in worship practice with preexisting traditions but also traditions that, one after the other, move further in the same direction on Figure 5.2: less ceremonial and more enthusiastic?

In his analysis of cultural forms, such as skirt lengths and first names, that change relatively quickly and are driven partly by a faddish desire for newness for its own sake, Lieberson (2000:95) identifies a "ratchet" mechanism that moves culture in an identifiable direction rather than in oscillations. Practice moves in an identifiable direction because, "were a new fashion to backtrack . . . then the very newest fashion would be confused with older fashions that had occurred just a few years earlier . . . Fashions that persistently move from the previous fashions in one direction, however, will not be subject to any confusion."

Worship styles do not change as quickly as skirt lengths, and sheer newness, though not irrelevant to the popularity of a worship form, probably is not as salient a feature in the realm of worship as it is in the fashion realms Lieberson has in mind. Still, the basic mechanism—cultural change moving in an identifiable direction rather than randomly so that newer cultural forms are not confused with older forms—can operate even without a fast rate of change or a premium on newness for its own sake. Indeed, in the religious realm, the ratchet might push worship in a particular direction precisely because older worship styles, once established, do not disappear as quickly as last season's dress styles or last year's most popular girls' names. Worship styles endure for centuries, so newcomers have to innovate in a direction that avoids being confused with an entire field of traditions, not just with the most recent entries. Today's independent congregations, for example, have to move further along the main axis of change and develop worship styles more enthusiastic and less ceremonial than those of white Baptists. If they went in the opposite direction, they would risk being confused with Methodists, and this is to be avoided not because Methodists are old-fashioned but because Methodists are still there to be reckoned with. When cultural forms endure, newcomers have little space in which to pursue a legitimation and differentiation strategy except further out on the leading edge of cultural change. The result is change over the long term that moves in an identifiable direction.

We can go one step further. In addition to asking, Why is there change in an identifiable direction? we might also ask, Why is there change in *this* direction? Why is the long-term trend of American worship practice toward decreasing ceremony and increasing enthusiasm? An ecological interpretation suggests that the leading edge of cultural innovation would occur where the resources are richest. In this context, the key resources are individuals who participate in worship practices, and so an ecological explanation of long-term change in the direction of decreasing ceremony and increasing enthusiasm might invoke change over time in individuals' modal cultural tastes. As it happens, there is evidence of a long-term trend toward informality in several cultural domains, including clothing, manners, and naming (Lieberson 2000:77–81). Increasing preferences for informality, in conjunction with worship forms that endure, in conjunction with a legitimation and differentiation process of organizational formation would produce not just new worship styles that partially overlap with previous styles, not just a sequence of overlapping worship styles moving further and further in one direction, but a sequence of overlapping worship styles that move further and further in a particular direction: toward less ceremony and more enthusiasm.

Not all change in worship practice can be characterized in terms of newer groups partially overlapping with older groups. Another type of innovation finds an entirely unexploited region of the relevant worship practice space, as seems to be the case for Pentecostals, Jehovah's Witnesses, and Mormons. It is tempting to relate the positioning of these traditions' cultural practices relative to the "mainstream" of American worship to their origins in deviant and sometimes persecuted religious movements. Perhaps a truly novel combination of worship elements indicates a religious movement intent on establishing a marked distance between itself and the other players in the cultural field.

There is another intriguing possibility, again inspired by Lieberson's analysis of fashion trends. The ratchet tends to push cultural change in a particular direction, but many fashion trends eventually turn around. Skirts can get only so long (or short) before they have to move in the opposite direction. When that turnaround occurs, why is the length just this side of the inflection point not confused with the length just the other side of the inflection point, which in a fashion example like this one occurred only a few years before? Lieberson's answer is that when a trend reversal occurs in one dimension of a style, there are simultaneously "unusually rapid shifts in at least one other fashion attribute [by which] some other feature experienced a rapid change in the direction *away* from its earlier position." By changing, say, a waistline at the same time that skirt lengths are reversing the direction of their movement, today's "dresses are still visibly different from recently popular ones" (Lieberson 2000:97–98).

Perhaps something like this dynamic is behind the positioning of Mormons and Jehovah's Witnesses off the main line of development in American worship practices. If a mid- to late-nineteenth-century religious movement sought collective practice that was less enthusiastic than that of the most enthusiastic groups in the field, it also would have had to innovate in the ceremony dimension in order to differentiate itself from other established groups. Unlike in fashion, the move along two dimensions at once does not emerge from a need to differentiate the new style from the now old-fashioned style of two years ago. In the realm of religion, the simultaneous move along two dimensions emerges from a need to differentiate the new practices from ongoing established traditions. If a group moves "backwards" along one of the dimensions, it has to move simultaneously on another dimension in order to set itself apart from the crowd.

An ecological interpretation of innovation in worship practices does not require intentionally strategic action on the part of religious entrepreneurs. The pattern observed in Figure 5.2 *could* be produced by religious entrepreneurs strategically seeking to locate their innovative movements either near an established, and therefore familiar, tradition or in an entirely unoccupied cultural niche. But these patterns also could be produced by an entirely blind evolutionary process in which religious entrepreneurs, reformers, and charismatic leaders innovate for theological or normative or aesthetic reasons, with no regard whatsoever for strategic concerns. Over time, much as the natural environment favors certain randomly occurring genetic mutations, the religious traditions that survive and thrive will be those that happened to locate in cultural niches that are both relatively unoccupied and also rich with resources in the form of individuals who want to participate in the worship practices offered by the tradition. American religious history probably is filled with groups all over the worship space represented in Figure 5.2, but most of these packages of worship elements do not survive, and only relatively few live long enough and become large enough to appear in data collected in 1998.

As noted earlier, I cannot say how much of the variation in worship practices is explained by the ecological account offered here relative to a more traditional routinization of charisma account (or one of its descendants). I leave that as a puzzle for readers to ponder and future research to solve. But I stand on firm ground when I suggest that Figure 5.2 indicates at least in part an ecological process by which significant innovation in worship practice occurs at a religious movement's beginnings and in relatively unoccupied regions of the worship practice space, regions in which there are individuals to nourish that growth and where the innovations relatively quickly become institutionalized into patterns of worship practice that endure for centuries.[25] This ecological interpretation of Figure 5.2 leads us to view denominations and religious traditions as institutionalized packages of worship elements forever carrying marks of their origins in a particular historical moment of collective religious practice, when they were trying to distinguish themselves, usually not by too much, from the traditions dominating the religious field at that time. They draw on the worship practices (and technologies) available at their time of origin to construct new kinds of collective worship events that, if they find enough people to practice them, retain their basic shape for a very long time. Even recent and sophisticated variants of routinization-of-charisma or sect-to-church theories focus only on change occurring within specific religious traditions. If the ecological story I have developed here is at all plausible, the study of religious change should move beyond a nearly exclusive concern with change *within* religious traditions and assess instead how much of the religious variety we see around us is produced by internal changes and how much is produced by ecological processes of the sort I have described.

Another theme in the foregoing is worth highlighting. In addition to socio-demographic influences on worship practice, there also is an engine of change in religious culture that does not need the fuel of social differences. As with change in some other cultural forms, there seems to be a mechanism of change in worship styles by which a new religious movement, whatever its social origins, develops a package of practices that to some degree is determined by the characteristics of the set of packages against which it is defining itself. In most sociological theories of religious change it is social differences among individuals that drive change, but perhaps there also is an irreducibly cultural engine of religious change, one that is relatively autonomous from social or demographic change, one in which tomorrow's religious practices are determined in part by today's practices, plus or minus a few elements.

Toward a Cultural Ecology of Religious Organizations

Congregations' worship is shaped both by participants' social characteristics and by the denominations and religious traditions in which they are embedded. Neither of these sources of influence is reducible to the other. Denominational differences in worship style remain strong and significant even when I statistically control social and organizational variables, and key social and organizational variables have significant effects on the levels of ceremony and enthusiasm in congregations' worship even when denominational differences are controlled.[26] Congregational worship is simultaneously shaped from above and from below.

Beyond this specific argument, the approach to worship de-

162

veloped in this chapter envisions a sociology of religious organizations that is at once cultural and ecological. The key step in this regard was adapting McPherson's (1983b) strategy for placing voluntary associations in *socio-demographic* space in order to place religious denominations and traditions in a *cultural practice* space. Looking back at Figure 5.2, note that each denomination or tradition can be precisely characterized by (1) where in this worship practice space it is centered, (2) the size of the area it covers, (3) the distance of its center from every other denomination's center, and (4) the extent of its overlap in worship practice space with every other denomination.

Locating religious organizations in this way, and comparing locations with one another, enables investigations that are not otherwise possible. One might use this framework, for example, to investigate whether religious organizations grow in the direction of social or cultural areas containing more people and fewer competing groups (McPherson and Ranger-Moore 1991), whether religious organizations in more densely populated regions of social and cultural space compete more intensely with one another than organizations in less densely populated regions (Baum and Mezias 1992), whether people are more likely to drop or switch their religious participation when they are nearer the edge than the center of their group's social or cultural niche (Popielarz and McPherson 1995), whether religious groups operating in smaller areas respond differently to competition than religious groups operating in larger areas of social or cultural space (Carroll 1985), or whether religious organizations' growth rates depend on how dense or sparse competition is in their region of social or cultural space (Galaskiewicz et al. 1997).

Ecological analysis using only denominations' and congregations' socio-demographic locations might proceed without taking a cultural turn of the sort I took in this chapter. Taking this turn, however, enhances the usefulness of ecological analysis for the study of religious organizations because there is analytical leverage in the fact that a religious tradition's socio-demographic and cultural practice locations are not reducible to each other. It is evident from Figure 5.2, for example, that the Assemblies of God, the largest Pentecostal denomination, is very far in worship practice from the Jehovah's Witnesses even though these two denominations largely overlap in socio-demographic space. This comparison suggests that cultural practices may be a more effective means than social segmentation for religious traditions to differentiate themselves. Indeed, if we compare the overall extent to which a large set of major denominations overlap on dimensions of worship practice (ceremony and enthusiasm) with the extent to which they overlap on socio-demographic dimensions (age, education, and income), they overlap least on the two dimensions of worship practice. Denominations are more dissimilar, more distinctive, in their worship practices than in their demographic composition.

Differences in worship practice, moreover, are salient to individuals. People move back and forth between denominations with similar worship practices more frequently than they move among denominations with dissimilar worship practices, and this pattern holds even after controlling for similarities and dissimilarities in denominations' social composition (Breiger 2002). The point here is that explicitly considering religious organizations' collective worship practices alongside their socio-demographic composition adds something valuable to ecological analysis of interdependencies among these organizations and their people. Attending to worship practices in this way moves us toward a sociology of religion that is simultaneously ecological and cultural.[27]

Using repertoires of worship elements to create cultural

spaces in which congregations, denominations, and religious traditions can be placed is not the only way to conceptualize cultural practices so that they become amenable to productive analysis.[28] Nor does the approach developed here permit every kind of analysis we might like to perform. Among other things, a more fully developed and dynamic framework would enable investigation of how elements enter and exit the repertoire rather than treating the repertoire as static and given, and it would enable investigation of variations in the sequencing of worship elements rather than limiting attention simply to the co-occurrence of elements within events. Whatever the limits of the particular approach to studying worship used in this chapter, it is important to remember that religious traditions, denominations, and congregations are, at one and the same · time, groups of people and collections of practices. We should strive for a sociology capable of apprehending both the social and the cultural aspects of religion, and capable of analyzing their connections without reducing one to the other. This is the route to deeper understanding of the varieties of collective religious expression, its sources, and its consequences.

6

The Arts

No one doubts the historical importance of religion to art. Music, painting, sculpture, and architecture all have been sponsored, produced, and consumed in close connection with religious institutions. Indeed, at some times and places it has been difficult to produce or consume art without simultaneously producing or consuming religion, and the history of art hardly could be written without giving prominent attention to the religious content of artworks, the religious sponsorship of their production, and the religious context of their display or performance (Hauser 1999). As Max Weber put it, "Religion and art are intimately related in the beginning" (Weber 1922 [1991]:242).

Today, by contrast, art and religion are largely institutionally distinct in complex societies, and the sociological study of artistic activity has proceeded without much attention to its connections to religion.[1] To quote Weber again, religion has been "an inexhaustible spring of artistic expressions [but] the more art becomes an autonomous sphere . . . the more art tends to acquire its own set of constitutive values, which are quite different from those obtaining in the religious and ethical domains" (Weber 1922 [1991]:242–243). Sometimes it even seems that religion and art are not just institutionally distinct but even *opposed* to each other, as when public controversies pit artists or art world bureaucrats against religious leaders. This impression of opposition is not completely accurate. The vast majority of artistic displays, exhibits, and performances occur without conflict of any sort, and even when conflict over the arts erupts, religion is a factor in only a minority of cases. Only about one quarter of the public conflicts over the arts in Philadelphia between 1965 and 1997, for example, involved either visible religious participants or explicit religious arguments. At the same time, religious participants in these conflicts were more likely to use attention-getting mass mobilization tactics. Thus, although the overall level of conflict between art worlds and organized religion is low, conflicts involving religion tend to attract more media attention than other conflicts, producing the inaccurate impression that the institutional arenas of art and religion are constantly at odds (DiMaggio et al. 2001).

Even discounting the significance of outright conflict between art worlds and organized religion, however, artistic activity and religious activity now seem to be animated by fundamentally different spirits. Art, after all, strives for innovation, creativity, individual self-expression, and beauty for its own sake, whereas religion mainly preserves tradition, reproduces ritual forms, and values community norms over individual expression. If religious traditions value beauty at all, they tend to value it only insofar as it serves religious goals. In one formulation of the distinction between art and religion, Clifford Geertz (1973:111–112) characterized the "aesthetic perspective" as one which favors "an eager dwelling upon appearances, an engrossment in surfaces, an absorption in things, as we say, 'in themselves.'" The religious perspective "differs from art in that instead of effecting a disengagement from the whole question of factuality, deliberately manufacturing an air of semblance and illusion, it deepens the concern with fact and seeks to create an aura of utter actuality."[2]

Artistic activity and religious activity seem animated by fundamentally different spirits, however, only if we limit "art" to the activity occurring under the auspices of institutions self-consciously devoted to high art. If we expand the concept of art to include popular practices as well as high culture, reserve judgment about artistic quality, and resist the temptation to oppose kitschy popular culture to "real" art, then art and religion seem much less opposed. Stated more positively, if we conceptualize artistic practice broadly as the making or consuming of music, dance, drama, and objects for display, without respect to the venue in which they are practiced or displayed, the skill with which they are executed or constructed, the audience to which they are primarily addressed, the overall quality of the product, or whether these practices are pursued as ends in themselves—art for art's sake—rather than as means to some other end, then connections between the arts and religion, especially religion as it is practiced in congregations, become more clear. Sociologists long have been pointing out that the distinction between high culture and popular culture is difficult to draw by reference to the intrinsic quality or characteristics of objects or activities. This literature criticizes the idea "that only high culture is a culture, and that popular culture is a dangerous mass phenomenon" (Gans 1999:xi). Analogously, for the purposes of this chapter I eschew the notion that only high art counts as "art." Avoiding that narrow view of art—a view that ultimately is more normative than analytical—clears the way for examining the connections between congregations and arts.

From this perspective the secularization of self-conscious art worlds does not negate the fact that substantial amounts of artistic activity—conceptualized broadly—occur in religious congregations. Worship services, most obviously, are constructed in part out of artistic elements such as music, drama, and dance. The case is clearest with music. Large majorities of religious service attenders experience or make music as part of their standard collective religious activity. As we saw in the previous chapter, congregational singing is nearly universal at religious services, and large majorities also experience choir singing (72 percent) and performances on musical instruments (91 percent), which mainly means piano or organ but also might include electric guitar (in 22 percent of services) or drums (in 20 percent of services). In religious services attended by half of all attenders, there is singing by a soloist. Nearly 90 percent of religious service attenders are in congregations with a choir or other musical group that regularly performs. In the average congregation, such groups number eighteen people; the average congregant is in a congregation in which fifty-four people are in such musical groups. The worship service experienced by the average churchgoer in the United States lasts for seventy minutes and includes twenty minutes of music, which means that more than one quarter of congregational worship consists of music.

Although music is by far the most common kind of artistic activity occurring in congregations, it is not the only type of artistic activity to which individuals are exposed in worship. According to the National Congregations Study, almost three quarters (70 percent) of attenders are in congregations in which a skit or play was performed at worship during the past year, and nearly one third (29 percent) are in congregations in which dance was performed at worship within the past year.[3]

Congregational worship and congregational arts activity thus overlap, but not completely. Not everything that happens in worship is usefully conceptualized as art, and not all congregation-based arts activity occurs in worship. Congregations also facilitate a good deal of arts participation outside of worship, as when a congregation's drama group or choir performs outside worship, or when a congregation organizes groups of members to attend professional shows or exhibits. Both through regular collective worship events and through arts activity outside of worship, congregations provide opportunities for individuals to practice and consume art.

Some, but not all, congregation-based arts activities connect congregations with worlds outside themselves. In Chapter 4 I drew on Robert Putnam's distinction between "bonding" and "bridging" forms of civic participation. "Bonding" civic participation tends to keep individuals within the groups or associations to which they are primarily attached. "Bridging" civic participation, by contrast, connects people in one group or association with people in other social locations. Some congregational activities are of the bonding sort; others create bridges to the world outside the congregation. This is as true for congregations' arts and cultural activities as it is for their activities in general. Some congregational arts activities directly connect congregations and their people to secular art worlds; others do not. Having a choir fosters one sort of cultural capital; bringing in professional musicians to sing and perform fosters another sort of cultural capital.

Bridging arts activity can occur either inside or outside of worship. It occurs inside worship, for example, when professional soloists or musicians are hired to perform in worship, something occurring in the congregations attended by approximately half of the churchgoing population. But it also occurs outside worship. More than half of all religious service attenders are in congregations with groups that attend live music or theater performances. Two fifths (42 percent) of people are in congregations with organized groups discussing books other than the Bible, 29 percent are in congregations that provide rehearsal space for unaffiliated performing arts groups, and 11 percent are in congregations that provide space for exhibits of artwork.[4] Fifty-five percent of attenders are in congregations that people sometimes visit to see the congregation's building or to view architecture or artwork. Although this last item does not connect the congregation to secular art worlds, it is an art-based activity through which people within the congregation potentially connect to people outside the congregation.[5]

Congregations and the arts—broadly defined—are clearly entwined. The arts are used to produce religion, and religion provides social and organizational contexts for artistic activity. Congregations expose people to substantial amounts of artistic activity, and they facilitate participation in art worlds beyond the life of the congregation itself. The nature of congregational use and facilitation of arts, however, varies substantially across religious traditions.[6]

Previous research has demonstrated that variation in artistic consumption and participation is strongly shaped by social variables, especially education, but relatively little is known about how religion might influence exposure to and participation in artistic activity.[7] Max Weber observed long ago that, rather than there being a generalized opposition between religion qua religion and art qua art, "particular empirical religions hold basically different attitudes toward art" (1922 [1991]:245). Some types of religion are more hostile toward art than other types of religion: "Sects of ascetic virtuosi [for example] are naturally more hostile to art on principle than are sects of mystical virtuosi." Moreover, there are affinities between particular types of religion and particular types of art: "Orgiastic religion leads most readily to song and music; ritualistic religion inclines toward the pictorial arts; religions enjoining love favor the development of poetry and music."

This last observation cuts to the heart of the matter. Religion that rejects all artistic expression is very rare. More common is religion that selectively rejects certain types of artistic expression while selectively incorporating other types. Weber emphasized religious acceptance or rejection of modes of artistic expression: some religious traditions value pictorial representations, for example, but devalue music; others reverse this valuation. But religions also are selective *within* artistic modalities, rejecting *this type* of music, *this type* of picture, *this type* of literature, *this type* of dance, rather than music, images, literature, or dance in general.[8]

These considerations suggest that when it comes to arts activities wholly internal to congregations, religious variations will appear more as differences of kind than as differences of degree. The types of art employed internally by religious congregations will vary in ways that reflect affinities between certain types of religious expression and certain types of artistic activity, but we should not expect to find large differences across religions in the overall extent to which some sort of art is present in the internal life of the congregation. Religious differences in bridging kinds of arts activities are a different matter.

The upper section of Table 6.1 shows religious differences in arts activities that occur within the confines of the congregation. The lower section shows religious differences in arts activities that, at least potentially, connect people inside a congregation with people outside the congregation.[9] I want to highlight three features of this table. First, most of the within-congregation arts activities occur in worship, and consequently most of the detailed differences among religious traditions' use of art reflect different ritual traditions and styles of worship.

Choirs, for example, are much less common in Jewish worship than in Christian worship, but soloists (in the Jewish context, cantors) are more common in Jewish worship than in Christian worship. Religious differences partly manifest themselves in different artistic practices, and these practices in turn become an important part of a religious tradition's identity, probably a more salient marker to most people than doctrines or creeds. Frank Burch Brown (2000:xiv) offered this observation about art as a marker of identity among Christian groups: "Much of what unites, and much that divides, communities and churches is connected with—though not, of course, reducible to—what various Christians perceive, enjoy, and value aesthetically." Brown was focused on differences among Christians, but the observation that religious identities and traditions are constituted in part by different uses of art surely applies more generally.

A second notable feature of Table 6.1 is that there are much stronger religious differences in facilitating connections to arts activity outside of congregations than in exposing people to art inside congregations. Religious traditions, that is, vary more in bridging than in nonbridging artistic activity. For example, the average percentage point difference between conservative white Protestants and moderate and liberal white Protestants on the seven within-congregation arts items is only 8.7. The average difference between these two groups on the items indicating bridging to secular art worlds is more than twice that: 18.7. When other factors are controlled, religious differences in the total amount of nonbridging arts activity engaged in by congregations almost completely disappear while religious differences in the bridging activities—explored in more detail in Chapter 4—remain strong.[11] Concretely, for example, liberal Protestant congregations are much more likely than conservative Protestant congregations to expose their people to pro-

Table 6.1 Religious tradition differences in congregations' arts activities

Activity	Percent of attenders within each tradition who attend congregations with specified activity				
	Moderate and liberal white Protestants (n = 305)	Conservative and evangelical white Protestants (n = 439)	Black Protestants (n = 143)	Roman Catholics (n = 299)	Jews (n = 20)
Nonbridging arts activities					
Congregational singing at recent worship service	99	99	99	98	90
Choir singing at recent worship service	79	63	87	78	30
Soloist at recent worship service	36	58	52	50	70
Dancing at any worship service within past year	30	23	42	30	20
Skit/play at any worship service within past year	81	75	70	57	50
Some instrument at recent worship service	96	91	91	93	42
Affiliated groups that perform music or theater	59	54	61	51	60

174

Bridging arts activities

Hired singers or other musicians to perform at a worship service	60	45	34	56	80
Visitors sometimes come to view the building's architecture or artwork	65	42	35	68	80
Group/meeting/class/event to discuss a book other than the Bible	67	36	26	33	80
Group/meeting/class/event to attend a live musical or theatrical performance outside the congregation	61	55	57	40	70
Outside groups have used the building for rehearsals or performances of musical or theatrical works	44	19	18	33	37
Outside groups have used the building for exhibits of paintings, photography, or sculpture	17	5	12	12	25

Note: Given the small number of synagogues in the NCS sample, percentages in the "Jews" column should be interpreted cautiously. The 95% confidence intervals around percentages in this column range from ±10 percentage points (for percentages near 0 or 100) to ±22 percentage points (for percentages near 50). The 95% confidence interval around percentages in the "Black Protestant" column is never more than ±8 percentage points; in the other columns it is never more than ±6 points.

fessional singers, books other than the Bible, and outside artists who use the congregation's building for rehearsal, performance, or exhibit.

By contrast, when other factors are controlled, the main religious traditions in the United States do not differ significantly in the extent to which individuals experience art within them—except for Catholics. Catholic congregations are less likely than congregations in any other religious tradition to expose people to artistic activity inside the congregation. This pattern is not evident in Table 6.1 because of the large average size difference between Protestant and Catholic congregations. Catholic congregations, on average, are much larger than Protestant congregations, and larger congregations in every tradition engage in substantially more arts activity than smaller congregations. Hence, size suppresses the underlying Catholic-Protestant difference in arts activity, a difference that becomes visible only when congregational size is controlled.[12]

Exposure to art within Catholic congregations probably is understated in the NCS because there are no measures of visual richness—statues, paintings, sculpted altars, stained glass, and so on—within a congregation's worship space. Still, a similar Protestant-Catholic difference also is evident when we examine the artistic experiences that individuals report having in congregations. When individuals (rather than congregations) are surveyed, Catholics acknowledge significantly fewer within-congregational artistic experiences than Protestants do. More than one third of Jews (35 percent), liberal Protestants (39 percent), black Protestants (39 percent), and conservative Protestants (41 percent) report having experienced the arts at their place of worship. Only 18 percent of Catholics make this same report (Marsden 2001:76). If Catholic churches do offer more visual richness than other congregations, that visual richness does not sufficiently compensate for lower levels of other

176

kinds of artistic practice to produce equivalent rates of subjectively experienced art among attenders. Thus, data about both what congregations do and how individuals experience what they do support the conclusion that the only major religious difference in the quantity of exposure to art inside congregations is that Catholic congregations expose people to less art than do congregations in any other tradition.

A third feature of the results in Table 6.1 is that, with one exception, religious differences in bridging arts activities recapitulate the general pattern we explored in Chapter 4 regarding congregations' bridging activities in multiple arenas. Among major American religious traditions, and even after we take account of the usual social factors known to shape secular arts participation, Jewish and liberal or moderate Protestant congregations provide significantly more opportunities for exposure to professional musicians and outside arts groups than do conservative or evangelical Protestant congregations. The exception again concerns the relative position of Catholic congregations. We saw in Chapter 4 that, in most arenas, Catholic congregations fall between liberal and conservative Protestants in the likelihood of engaging in bridging activities. In the artistic arena, however, conservative Protestant congregations provide significantly more exposure to professional musicians and outside arts groups than do Catholic congregations, which provide fewer such opportunities than any of the other traditions examined here.[13]

These Protestant-Catholic differences in exposure to both bridging and nonbridging arts within congregations do not mean that Catholics participate less in the arts than others do. On the contrary, survey evidence consistently shows that Catholics are at least as likely as Protestants (but less likely than Jews) to engage in arts activities such as visiting an art museum; attending a classical music, dance, or drama performance;

playing a musical instrument; volunteering for the arts; or purchasing art (Greeley 1996:10; Marsden 2001:76; Wuthnow 2003a:138). Catholics apparently participate in the arts as much as Protestants; they just do less of it in their congregations.[14]

Three additional details not evident in Table 6.1 but clear in multivariate analyses are worth mentioning. First, African American congregations, whatever their religious tradition, include more singing and dancing in their worship services than white congregations.[15] At the same time, their arts activities do not connect to worlds outside the congregation any more (or less) than the arts activities of predominantly white congregations. This was also true of the other sorts of bridging activity examined in Chapter 4. African American congregations apparently expose their constituents to more artistic activity than other congregations—a finding consistent with standard observations about the internally rich cultural life of organized black religion in the United States—but African American congregations do not facilitate contact with outside art worlds any more (or less) than white congregations.

Second, as in other arenas, the artistic activity within more recently founded congregations connects less frequently to the world outside the congregation than does the artistic activity within older congregations. We cannot tell from these data if this represents a trend toward declining arts-based engagement between congregations and their communities, but if there is such a trend, it appears to be in the negative direction. Third, I am able to explain 50 percent more variation in congregations' bridging arts activities than in within-congregation arts activity. Variation in congregations' bridging artistic activities apparently is more systematically structured than variation in arts activity occurring within their walls.[16]

Activities that connect people inside a congregation to peo-

178

ple outside the congregation often are assumed to promote positive social consequences, but the religious differences in bridging artistic activities documented here may very well *increase* cultural stratification in American society. Liberal congregations connect their people to secular art worlds, and thereby help to build conventional sorts of secular cultural capital, when they hire musicians and sponsor concerts or exhibits. Conservative congregations resist these connections partly because they wish to replace secular cultural capital—and the criteria for merit and achievement they imply—with explicitly religious cultural capital. From this perspective, the connections between congregations and secular art worlds may reinforce rather than weaken important social and class boundaries, and religious differences in cultural capital formation may exacerbate rather than attenuate cultural inequality.[17]

Whatever their consequences, however, these religious differences in congregation-based artistic activity should not obscure the extent to which congregations in virtually every religious tradition routinely expose people to the arts. I do not mean to imply that all, or even most, of the artistic activity occurring in congregations is subjectively experienced as art by parishioners.[18] Even less do I mean to imply that people in general attend religious services in a self-conscious attempt to experience art. I mean only to say that, whether or not worshipers know it, and whether or not people generally come to congregations and worship services in search of art or beauty, a substantial amount of artistic activity in fact occurs in congregations, and congregations both inside and outside of worship thereby expose large numbers of people to art. If in previous chapters I corrected a tendency to overstate congregations' involvement in social services and politics, in this chapter I correct a tendency to understate their involvement in the arts. In the next chapter I push this agenda further by assessing, on the one hand, the relative importance of worship, religious education, art, social services, and politics to congregations, and, on the other hand, the relative importance of congregations to these arenas of activity.

☙ 7 ❧

Culture in Congregations,
Congregations in Culture

Three overlapping aspects of congregational culture—the worship events they produce, the religious knowledge they transmit, and the artistic activity they facilitate—occupy more congregations, engage more people, and use more resources than either congregations' social service or their political activities. They are the most important means by which congregations involve individuals and connect with the world outside their walls. Looking inside congregations, we see that worship, religious education, and even the arts (mainly but not only through their intimate connection with worship) are their central activities. Looking outward, we find that congregations probably contribute to our society's arts arena more extensively than they contribute to either the social services arena or the political arena. From both of these perspectives, congregations' cultural practices—worship, education, and arts—emerge as their core activities and the most common points of contact between congregations and the world around them.

The Centrality of Worship, Religious Education, and Artistic Activity

It is hardly necessary to document the centrality of worship and religious education to congregational life. The relative importance of arts, social services, and politics to congregations, however, is a more subtle issue. Table 7.1 compares congregations' involvement in worship, religious education, arts, social services, and politics. There is a clear and striking contrast between levels of involvement in the first three types of activities and in the last two types of activities. Whereas approximately 60 percent of congregations participate in some manner of social service activity, and approximately 40 percent engage in some manner of political activity over the course of a year, virtually all congregations engage in worship, religious education, and artistic activity *every week.* With regard to arts, the level of congregational involvement is impressive even if we focus only on activity other than the use of music regularly occurring in worship. More than three quarters of congregations reported having had at least one of the following events or activities in the past year: dance or dramatic performance at worship, a musical or theatrical performance put on by a congregational group other than the regular choir, or attendance at a live performance elsewhere.

Table 7.1 also lists the most common specific activities within each category. The most common kind of social service activity for congregations involves feeding people; 32 percent of congregations reported doing this. The most common kind of political activity is telling people about opportunities for political action (letter writing, lobbying, rallying, voting, and so on); 26 percent of congregations reported doing this. About half of congregations, by contrast, have special classes for prospective or new members and classes focusing on the history and practices of their religious tradition. And virtually all have

Table 7.1 Congregational involvement in worship, religious education, arts, social services, and politics

Activity	Percent of congregations with activity
Worship	
Any worship service in last week	99
More than one worship service in a typical week	72
Religious education	
Any religious education class	90
A class for prospective or new members	56
A class for members about the history/practice of your tradition	45
A class to train new religious education teachers	37
A class to discuss or learn about a religion other than your own	22
Arts	
Any musical activity in last week	96
Any nonmusical arts activity in last year	78
Singing by the congregation last week	96
Musical instrument in worship last week	84
Singing by the choir last week	52
Skit or play at worship in last year	62
Paid singers/performers at worship in last year	35
Group puts on musical/theatrical performance in last year	38
Group attends live performances elsewhere in last year	43
Social service	
Any social service activity in last year	57
Food programs in last year	32
Programs for the homeless in last year	8
Staff person devoting at least quarter-time to social service activities in last year	6
Politics	
Any political activity in last year	42
Mention political opportunities at worship in last year	26
Distribute voter guides ever	17

live music in their worship services every week, with large numbers also reporting other sorts of artistic activity both within and outside of their worship services.

Not only do many more congregations regularly engage in worship, religious education, and the arts than in either social services or politics, but also the former set of activities engage more people than either social service or political activities. In the median congregation with social service programs, only ten individuals are involved as volunteers in those activities. In the median congregation, furthermore, only fifteen people reported participating within the past year in a small group that meets at least monthly *for any purpose* other than worship, religious education, or internal governance or administration.[1] Seventy people, by contrast, attend the main worship service in the median congregation, forty attend a religious education class in a typical week, and, in congregations with choirs, eighteen people participate in those choirs.

These activities also use significantly more staff time. Clergy spend more than fifteen hours per week engaging in or preparing for worship and between five and ten hours per week teaching. By contrast, clergy spend only between one and two hours per week working with community or civic organizations. Other internally focused activities—counseling, pastoral visiting, administration—take up the rest of clergy work time (Carroll and McMillan 2002; Brunette-Hill and Finke 1999).

Worship, religious education, and artistic activity all are prominent in congregations, but the greatest of these is worship. Worship services take up more congregational resources and involve more people than anything else congregations do. Considerations other than numerical ones also point to the centrality of collective worship to congregational life. Worship services are the main point of contact between the congregation and the outside world, and as such they constitute a congregation's most public face, the self-portrait religious congregations offer to the outside world. There also is a sense in which worship events are more truly collective than anything else congregations do. In Chapter 5 I distinguished between enthusiastic and ceremonial aspects of worship, a distinction intended in part to capture the difference between, on the one hand, moments in worship or ritual in which people are aware of one another and directly oriented to the collectivity and, on the other hand, moments in which the gathered are more like an audience. Although worship events generally contain moments of both sorts, and although worship services vary in the relative prominence of ceremony or enthusiasm, worship—however ceremonial or enthusiastic it might be—is likely to be the most enthusiastic moment of a congregation's collective life. However staid the service, it is more collectively effervescent than any other congregational event. However much the service calls for audience-like behavior, the gathered are more congregation than isolated individuals during worship than at any other time, if only because the service almost always contains moments when participants move together—kneeling, bowing, standing, singing, reciting—in coordinated ways.[2]

The intimate connection between collective worship and arts, explored in detail in the previous chapter, makes artistic activity far more prominent in the vast majority of congregations than either social services or politics.[3] There even is evidence that the artistic elements of worship services provide some of the most religiously meaningful moments of those events. Eighty percent of conservative Protestants, 76 percent of liberal Protestants, and 56 percent of Catholics said that they "felt close to God from music during worship," compared with 82 percent, 72 percent, and 62 percent, respectively, who said that they "felt close to God listening to a sermon" (Wuthnow 2003a:141). Artistic activity also is prominent in religious gatherings other than traditional worship services. Thirty percent of people participating in congregation-based small groups, such as Bible studies, prayer fellowships, support groups, and the like, say that their group discusses art or music (Wuthnow 2003a:116).

I do not mean to say that congregations or the people in them intentionally seek to produce or facilitate art in the same way that they intentionally seek to worship meaningfully or educate their people in the ways of the tradition. I mean to say only that artistic activity is a much more common by-product of congregations than either social services or political action.

The Significance of Congregations to Cultural Life

Examining the relative importance of worship, religious education, arts, social services, and politics to congregations is relatively straightforward. Examining the relative importance of congregations to the larger arenas of collective religious expression, education, arts, social services, and politics requires a more indirect approach.

Very little needs to be said about congregations' dominance of collective religious expression in the United States. Weekend worship services remain central religious events for the vast majority of religiously active individuals, and participation in weekend worship events remains by far the most common kind of collective religious activity in American society. When religious service attenders are asked what day they attend, just 2 percent mention a day other than Saturday or Sunday without also mentioning a weekend day. Perhaps more telling, when those who say they did *not* attend religious services in the past week are asked whether they participated in some other type of religious event or meeting, such as a prayer or Bible study group, only 2 percent say yes (although 21 percent of nonattenders say they watched religious television or listened to religious radio).[4] The vast majority of collective religious activity in the United States thus involves attendance at weekend religious services. New forms of religious participation are not taking the place of attendance at weekend worship services. If other sorts of religious activity have increased, that increase is not much at the expense of traditional weekend services.

Congregations' contributions to a wider educational arena also are well known and substantial. Six percent of congregations run schools, the vast majority of them within just two denominations: Roman Catholic and Missouri Synod Lutheran. These schools educate approximately 9 percent of all children, and approximately 80 percent of children who attend private schools. Approximately one fifth of all colleges and universities are religiously affiliated, and these institutions account for about 10 percent of enrollment in higher education (Stewart et al. 2002:109, 125). Congregations are much less directly involved in higher education than in primary and secondary education, although 34 percent of congregations report giving money directly to some college, university, or seminary. That is about the same percentage of congregations involved in feeding the hungry and twice as many as distribute voter guides. All in all, efforts at transmitting religious knowledge to the next generation have led to a significant congregational presence in the larger educational arena, especially manifest, of course, in the Catholic parochial school system.

Congregations' dominance of collective religious life is obvious, and their role in American education is well known, so I will not spend more time on those arenas. I want to concentrate instead on the less obvious and less well known role of congregations in the larger arena of artistic activity. Relevant evidence here is more sparse and indirect than we might like, but I draw on evidence of various sorts to build a circumstantial case that a significant proportion of all in-person artistic activity occurring in American society occurs in congregations, and also, more tentatively, that houses of worship are more significant sites of activity in the larger arena of the arts than in the larger arenas of social services and politics.

We can start by comparing the extent to which people are exposed to arts in worship with the extent of their arts exposure in other contexts. The case is clearest with music. In 1998, two thirds of American adults claimed to have attended a religious service within the past twelve months. More than 95 percent of those attendees participated in a service with singing by the congregation, more than 90 percent heard a musical instrument being played, and more than 70 percent heard singing by a choir. Half of religious service attendees heard a soloist. This means that more than 60 percent of Americans participated in, or at least heard, group singing in a congregation in the past year, 60 percent heard an instrument being played in a congregation, and one third heard a soloist.[5] In that same year, by contrast, 17 percent of American adults claimed to have attended a classical music concert and 39 percent claimed to have attended a pop music concert in the past twelve months. Twenty-five percent saw a musical play, 12 percent saw a jazz performance, and 5 percent saw live opera.[6] If we factor in the frequency with which people attend religious services compared with these other events at which live music is heard, it becomes clear that worship services constitute the vast majority of the live musical events experienced by people in American society. Congregations' worship services, where 60 percent of the population hear live music in a given year, are the single most common type of event at which live music is heard in American society.

The case is strongest with music, but other sorts of art—drama, dance, painting, sculpture—also are experienced in

188

worship services. A substantial proportion, though probably not a majority, of all in-person exposure even to these art forms occurs through religious worship services. Twenty percent of individuals reported attending a dance performance in 1998; 16 percent reported attending a nonmusical play. Seventy percent of religious service attenders, by contrast, are in a congregation that included a skit or a play in worship in the previous year and 29 percent are in a congregation that included dance in worship during the previous year. Unlike the figures for music, which occurs at virtually every worship service, these are percentages of congregations in which drama or dance may have occurred only once during the past year, so we cannot be sure that the two thirds of individuals who attend religious services at least once a year saw drama or dance. Still, conservatively assuming that 20 percent of American adults attend religious services weekly, we calculate that 14 percent of all Americans (70 percent of the one fifth who attend weekly) experienced drama at a worship service in the past year, and 6 percent experienced dance. Assume further, again conservatively, that *none* of the 20 percent of individuals who saw live dance and *none* of the 16 percent who saw a play were thinking of dance or drama in worship services when they reported these activities. The upshot here is that, though less than a majority, a healthy proportion of all live performance of drama and dance viewed by American adults occurs in congregations' worship services.

We might wonder, of course, whether music, drama, dance, painting, or sculpture heard or seen in a religious context is perceived or understood as "art." There is evidence, for example, that attendance at cultural events occurring at places of worship and other community venues such as schools, community centers, parks, restaurants, and public buildings is motivated differently than attendance at cultural events occurring in conventional arts venues such as theaters or museums. People who attend events in conventional arts venues are much more likely than attendees of events in community venues to say that they were motivated to attend because they wanted to learn more about an art form, experience the high quality of the art, or learn something about another time or culture (Walker 2003). If motivations for attending cultural and art events vary with venue, it seems likely that the meanings attributed to the activities—and even whether or not participants consider the activity to be "art" at all—also will vary both across venues and, within venues, across events of different sorts. Hearing a choral group in a church building may mean something different to listeners than hearing that same choral group in a concert hall; hearing that group sing during the church's worship service may mean something different still. It seems likely that individuals will be less likely to interpret a concrete instance of music, dance, or other expression as "art" when it occurs during worship than when it occurs elsewhere.

When the 1998 General Social Survey asked a representative sample of religious service attenders if they had "any experiences with the arts" at their place of worship during the previous year, 33 percent said yes. Respondents to this survey were told to think of "activities like viewing performances or exhibits, singing in a choir, or playing an instrument," so we cannot tell how many of those who answered yes to this question were thinking of experiences in worship as opposed to experiences in their congregation's building but outside the context of a worship service. This ambiguity notwithstanding, this result still means that 22 percent of all American adults (one third of the 66 percent who attended a religious service at least once in the past year) subjectively experience "the arts" at their place of worship.

What are we to make of this? On the one hand, at least one

kind of art—music—occurs at virtually every worship service, so the finding that only one third of religious service attenders report experiencing the arts at their place of worship (and not necessarily *in* worship) implies that much, perhaps most, of the arts activity occurring in worship is *not* subjectively understood as art by worshipers. On the other hand, if 22 percent of American adults are conscious of experiencing the arts at their place of worship, that still is more people than report attending a classical music performance (16 percent), approximately the same number as the 20 percent who report attending dance or the 24 percent who report attending drama, but less than the 39 percent who report attending a popular music concert (Marsden 1999, 2001). Even by this more subjective measure, congregations emerge as prominent settings for experiencing art.

The 1998 General Social Survey did not ask individuals about other venues at which they may have experienced the arts, so we cannot use that study to assess congregations' relative importance among places where people may experience the arts. Other surveys, however, ask individuals about multiple venues at which they attend or participate in artistic or cultural events. These surveys provide a glimpse of the place that congregations hold in the larger cultural arena both by producing events themselves and by providing physical space for artistic activities, whether or not those activities occur in worship or are otherwise produced by the congregation.

The 1997 Survey of Public Participation in the Arts, for example, asked individuals whether they had attended live performances of jazz, classical music, opera, musical plays, nonmusical plays, ballet, or other dance within the previous year. They asked a subset of those who attended an event about the type of place where the performance was held. Most of these events (64 percent) were held in venues devoted exclusively to artistic performance, such as concert halls, opera houses, and theaters. Although only 4 percent of respondents reported attending one of these performances in a religious facility, that is the same percentage who reported attending these events in a nightclub or coffeehouse, and only slightly fewer than reported attending these events in schools or colleges (6 percent each). Of the venues other than those dedicated to artistic performances, only parks or other open-air facilities were mentioned significantly more often (10 percent) than places of worship as sites where artistic consumption occurred.

Religious facilities are more common venues for classical music (12 percent of these events) and dance other than ballet (5 percent), whereas opera and ballet performances were least likely to be attended in places of worship. No respondents to this survey said that they had attended opera or ballet at a religious facility. In sum, although churches, synagogues, and so on clearly are not sites at which a large proportion of these types of artistic events are held, they hold their own among sites that are not dedicated exclusively to artistic performance, especially when it comes to classical music and dance other than ballet.[7]

Places of worship emerge as more prominent sites of artistic consumption when individuals are asked about their cultural and artistic activity in broader terms. In 1998 the Urban Institute asked random samples of individuals in five communities whether they attended "any cultural events or activities" in a variety of venues, including a "church, synagogue, or other place of worship" (Walker 2002, 2003; Walker and Scott-Melnyk 2002). Table 7.2 shows the results for each site as well as the average percentage across all five sites reporting participation at each venue. The number of people who report attending events is much larger here than in the Survey of Public Participation in the Arts, described earlier, probably because

Table 7.2 Cultural participation at various venues in five locations

Percent attending cultural events or activities in a:	Humboldt County (CA)	Kansas City metro area	Milpitas (CA)	Gilroy (CA)	Mayfair (CA)	Average across 5 sites
Park, open-air facility, or street	76	67	64	75	62	69
Elementary, middle, high school, or college	66	56	49	57	50	56
Concert hall, theater, or performing arts center	57	57	52	53	38	52
Church, synagogue, or other place of worship	39	54	49	48	56	49
Museum or art gallery	51	49	47	42	34	45
Nightclub, coffeehouse, or restaurant	46	41	43	44	38	43
Community center, senior center, grange hall, or fire hall	46	28	37	38	32	36
Public library or government or public building	32	29	41	36	34	34

Source: Cultural Participation Survey, Urban Institute, 1998.

asking broadly about "cultural events or activities" evokes more varied types of events than asking specifically about jazz, opera, ballet, and so on. Religious facilities also appear as relatively more common sites of cultural consumption in this survey. Between 39 and 56 percent of individuals in each location reported attending a cultural event at a place of worship. In terms of their importance relative to the seven other types of sites asked about in this survey, religious facilities range from the second most common venue for cultural events (in Mayfair, California) to the second least common venue (in Humboldt, California).[8]

A related survey of arts and cultural *organizations* in these same communities found that one third of all performing and visual arts groups had performed or exhibited in places of worship (Walker 2003). Performing in places of worship was more common than performing in commercial buildings (16 percent), about as common as performing in public buildings (36 percent), and less common than performing in open spaces (42 percent), community centers (47 percent), or schools (62 percent). Even though more arts *groups* perform in community centers than in places of worship, it seems that more *people* attend those performances in places of worship than in community centers. Overall, religious facilities are in the middle of the pack as places for experiencing live cultural events, falling behind parks, schools, and theaters, but outpacing museums, restaurants, community centers, and public buildings.

These studies have their limits and ambiguities, but they paint a broadly similar picture of the role of congregations in the larger arena of arts and culture. Evidence from still another survey adds to this picture. When a representative sample of adults in the United States was asked about a set of artistic activities in which they might have engaged in childhood, 41 percent report having sung in a choir or ensemble at church, which is more than the 26 percent who played in a band or orchestra but less than the 46 percent who took art classes, the 47 percent who sang in a choir or ensemble at school, or the 54 percent who performed in a school play (Wuthnow 2003a:60). Taking these surveys together, we would overstate the case to say that religious congregations are central to the live consumption of all types of art in the United States, but it would be fair to say that places of worship are significant sites of consumption even for arts other than music.

The evidence I have presented so far supports the idea that congregations are indeed a significant part of the larger cultural and artistic arena, but I have not yet provided evidence that their contributions to this arena are greater than their contributions to the social service or political arenas. We have seen that congregations devote much smaller proportions of their resources to social service and political activities than they do to cultural and artistic activities, and they involve many fewer people in social services and politics than in the arts, but it remains possible that even those small (from the congregation's perspective) contributions to social services and politics might constitute large chunks of the society's activity in those arenas. It also remains possible that, with or without the active involvement of a congregation's people, places of worship are as significant as physical sites for social service delivery as they are for cultural events.

Evidence that allows us to compare directly congregations' share of all the social services and political activities occurring in American society with their share of all the artistic activity occurring in the society is even harder to come by than evidence that provides a glimpse of congregations' relative importance in the artistic arena alone. Given the current state of knowledge, the claim that congregations' share of all artistic activity in the society is greater than their share of all political or social service activity remains a conjecture rather than established fact. Some indirect evidence, however, suggests that such a conjecture is not altogether fanciful.

Sidney Verba and his colleagues' (1995) analysis of political participation allows some comparison of congregations' relative importance in the artistic arena with their relative importance in the political arena. They find that more individuals are asked to be politically active in their congregations than in the workplace or in other nonpolitical organizations, but significantly fewer are asked to be politically active in congregations than in explicitly political organizations. Thirty-two percent of Americans are asked to vote or to take other political action (sign a petition, write a letter, or get in touch with a public official) through their association with a political organization, compared with 23 percent who are asked to do these things through congregations, 13 percent who are asked to do these things in the workplace, and 6 percent who are asked to do these things through other nonpolitical organizations (Verba et al. 1995:373). From this perspective, congregations are visible players in the political arena, but 40 percent more people receive political cues from specifically political associations than from congregations. As we saw earlier, by contrast, congregations are the single most important site for the consumption of live music.

Congregations seem to provide a larger share of the live political cues in the society than of, say, live drama or dance, but it is difficult to know how to aggregate congregational shares of various types of art to produce a measure of congregational presence in the arts in general that would be comparable to Verba and colleagues' measure of their presence in the world of political cues. It seems likely, however, that congregations' dominance of live music would more than compensate for relatively lower levels of their share in other artistic arenas.

Moreover, since, as we saw in Chapter 4, notifying people about opportunities for political action is the single most common kind of political activity in which congregations engage, and since producing and consuming music is the single most common kind of artistic activity in which congregations engage, comparing congregations' importance for this one specific kind of political activity with their importance for this one specific kind of artistic activity seems informative even in the absence of estimates about congregations' relative importance in the arts in general or in politics in general.[10]

Congregations are even less prominent in providing opportunities for exercising the kinds of civic skills that lead to more effective political participation. Here the workplace is much more significant than either congregations or other nonpolitical organizations. More than twice as many people attend meetings where decisions are made in their workplaces as in their congregations (46 percent versus 21 percent), more than twice as many plan such meetings in workplaces as in congregations (23 percent versus 11 percent), more than twice as many make a speech or presentation in workplaces as in congregations (26 percent versus 12 percent), and more than four times as many people write a letter in the workplace as in a congregation (38 percent versus 8 percent).[11]

Compare these indications of the relative importance of congregations in providing opportunities to exercise civic skills with the relative importance of congregations in providing opportunities to exercise at least one sort of artistic skill. Virtually all congregations sing together, which means that two thirds of all Americans have the opportunity to sing in congregations at least once a year. This is compared with 11 percent of individuals who say they have performed music, dance, or theater, 24 percent who play a musical instrument, 8 percent who sing music from musical plays, and 2 percent who sing opera music.

At least as far as singing is concerned, congregations provide a far larger share of the opportunities for exercising this artistic skill than they provide for exercising the civic skills studied by Verba and his colleagues.

The main point Verba and colleagues make about congregations is that the opportunities they provide to practice civic skills are particularly important to the relatively disadvantaged. There is some evidence that congregations' relative importance to arts exposure also varies across the social spectrum. In the Urban Institute survey of five communities, "65 percent of African Americans and 54 percent of Hispanics who attended events heard or saw music, dance, theater, or visual arts in a place of worship in the past year, compared with 46 percent of whites" (Walker 2003:5). Congregations are significant sites of exposure to the arts for every demographic group, but they are more significant to some groups than to others. If congregations' relative importance in providing exposure to art varies across social groups, it seems likely that their relative importance as sites offering opportunities to practice artistic skills also will vary across social groups.[12]

Overall, then, it seems that congregations play a larger role in the society's artistic arena than they play in the society's political arena. What about their role in the social services arena? The data here are even more limited than they are for politics. Indeed, I know of only one study in which an attempt was made to assess congregations' share of the social services arena as a whole, and that study was of only one community. Still, the results are suggestive. Robert Wuthnow and his colleagues surveyed individuals in the fifteen inner-city census tracts with the lowest median household incomes in the Lehigh Valley area of northeastern Pennsylvania. The research team identified the twenty-five service organizations "that provided nearly all the social services to low-income residents of the Lehigh

Valley" (Wuthnow et al. 2003:11). None of these organizations was a congregation. Respondents were then asked whether they had contacted each of these organizations for assistance and also whether they had contacted a congregation for assistance. Forty percent of the respondents who contacted any organization contacted a secular nonprofit organization, 36 percent the public welfare department, 28 percent a religious social service organization, and only 22 percent a congregation (Wuthnow et al. 2003; Wuthnow 2003b). Fewer than one fourth of Lehigh Valley respondents who contacted any agency for social services contacted a congregation. Given what we know about the small scale and emergency need focus of most congregational social service activity, it seems likely that congregations' share of all social service activity in this area would appear even smaller if we were able to assess it in terms of the number of contact hours spent with the needy or the value of the resources dispensed to the needy through these various sites.[13]

There are specific domains within the larger social services arena in which congregations' share is larger than their share of the arena as a whole. For example, one half of all emergency food providers active in Detroit in the winter of 1999 were congregations (Eisinger 2002:116). Congregations also are sometimes considered prominent within the child care arena, but their level of presence here does not approach their level of presence among emergency food providers. One four-state study found fewer than 20 percent of child care centers operated by congregations (Morris and Helburn 2000). Another national survey (cited in Bogle 2001:8) found fewer than 20 percent housed in a religious facility. Fewer than 1 percent of Head Start programs in the country are run by congregations. In Arizona—a state in which there is research on where Head Start programs are located, regardless of who runs them—only 6 percent are located in places of worship.[14]

Taking account of congregational presence in the one or two social service sub-arenas in which they are more prominent does not, however, change the basic picture. It seems unlikely, for example, that there is a sub-arena as important to the social services world as music is to the arts world, and in which congregations' share approaches their share of all live music performance in the society. Moreover, although congregations connect to both the social services and the cultural realms sometimes *as congregations* and sometimes as mere physical locations for activities that do not involve the congregations' people, the relative importance of these two modes of connecting is different in social services than it is in the arts. Congregations seem more important in the social services arena as providers of physical space than as providers, *qua* congregations, of social services. The opposite is true for the arts. There, mainly but not only because of the intimate connection between worship and the arts, congregations seem more significant as providers of arts experiences *qua* congregations than as mere venues for performances. It seems reasonable to weigh congregational participation in an activity more heavily when the congregation is involved as a congregation than when it is involved only by virtue of its physical space. All things considered, even though congregations are noticeably present in some social service sub-arenas (especially feeding the hungry), it is difficult to see how their share of all the social service activity occurring in American society could approach their share of all live artistic activity in the society.

So, if we were able to assess more directly and more comprehensively congregations' share of all the face-to-face activity across different arenas of American social life, I think we would find that they account for a larger share of all artistic activity than of either social services or political activity. Available evidence does not allow me to establish this proposition definitively. Rather, I offer it as a conjecture for future research to confirm or falsify.

No one will be surprised at the centrality of worship and religious education to congregational life.[15] Although it might be more surprising, the evidence at hand leaves little doubt that artistic activities are far more important to congregations than either politics or social services. If we ask what congregations mainly do, the answer is, in the first place, gather people for worship and religious education. But another answer is that, in their pursuit of worship and religious education, congregations generate as a by-product more artistic activity than either social services or political activity. Although many might wish it were otherwise, congregations facilitate art, and perhaps, on occasion, even beauty, more commonly and more intensively than they pursue either charity or justice. Moreover, it seems that they are more prominent sites of artistic activity than of either social service or political activity. Clarifying the relative importance of these various activities to congregations, and the relative importance of congregations to these various kinds of activities, yields, I hope, a more accurate picture of what congregations do and how they contribute to the world around them.

⟡ 8 ⟡

Beyond Congregations

Throughout this book I have been treating congregations as social units with enough coherence, unity of purpose, and autonomy to justify saying that they *do* things. The National Congregations Study itself treats congregations in this same way, assuming that each congregation is a more or less coherent and at least somewhat independent unit about which data can be gathered concerning "its" characteristics and activities. This approach has much to commend it, not least that congregations are indeed relatively coherent and relatively autonomous local collectivities, and highlighting their organizational unity and relative independence is the only way to answer very basic questions about the extent to which congregations engage in social services, politics, the arts, or other activities.

At the same time, conceptualizing congregations as coherent and autonomous organizations that act *as congregations* is complicated by at least two considerations. On the one hand, an activity attributed to a particular congregation might actually be something less than an activity of that congregation, as when it is initiated and carried out, as are many "congregational" activities, by a small subgroup of individuals within the congregation. On the other hand, an activity attributed to a congregation might be something more than an activity of that congregation, as when its source is a denomination, tradition, or movement within which a congregation is embedded or by which it is influenced. In neither case is it obvious that the congregation is appropriately treated as a coherent and autonomous actor in its own right, responding as a collectivity out of a shared sense of local needs. In the first instance its activity may reflect the interests of only a small subset of its people; in the second instance its activity may reflect a larger tradition of which it is a part. Recognizing these complications introduces certain conceptual and interpretive difficulties, but it also prompts provocative observations and questions about the nature of congregational structures and activities, the sources of those structures and activities, and the mechanisms by which they change.

Congregations as Aggregates of Individuals or Groups

A congregation is an aggregate of individuals or, perhaps more appositely, a group of small groups that may or may not cohere into a community or fellowship or organization with true collective identity and unity of purpose. A corollary of this social fact about congregations is that a congregation's ancillary activities may reflect the interests and energies of only a small number of individuals within the congregation. In Chapter 3 we saw that, in congregations with some social service programming, only ten individuals on average are involved as volunteers in those activities. In that chapter I also reported examples of congregations in which only a small number of people produce the congregation's social services or political activities: congregational social welfare projects that depend on the enthusiasm of very small groups, sometimes just one or two individuals; a Peace and Justice Committee that sponsors many activities despite its small numbers and its recognition that much of the congregation does not share its concerns; a professionally run tutoring program involving three hundred volunteers of whom only four or five are from the sponsoring congregation. Such examples could be multiplied almost endlessly.

Initiatives that actively involve only a handful of people still may be genuine initiatives of the congregation as a whole, perhaps because they are highly visible, officially supported through congregational vote, or symbolically central to a congregation's life. Still, we would do well to recall H. Paul Douglass's 1927 observation that the typical congregation is a group of groups. Douglass described one congregation as "a network of enterprises loosely knotted together rather than a closely woven fabric. Its unity is administrative rather than social." He called this congregation, which seemed to be less internally integrated than most, "an extreme expression of tendencies generally shown by the group of churches under examination" (Douglass 1927:203). In later work, Douglass and Edmund Brunner noted what this implies about the nature and significance of various congregational social service, political, and other ancillary activities: "Many activities listed as the church's activities are actually, in large measure, merely the activities of semi-independent constituencies" (Douglass and Brunner 1935:155). This observation applies as much today as it did earlier in the century.

From this perspective it becomes clear that not all activities that might be observed within a congregation or listed by a congregational leader will be "congregational activities" in quite the same way. Some activities, perhaps many, will exist only because of the inspiration, commitment, and energy of a small subgroup of individuals, and they will cease when those individuals lose interest or move on. Other activities will be truly congregation-sponsored and owned, and they will not depend in the same way on the interests and energies of a few people. We often do not know which activities are of which sort, but this uncertainty does not, in general, stop us from saying of both types of activities, "This congregation engages in activity X or sponsors program Y."

The aggregation-of-individuals or group-of-groups nature of congregations introduces interpretive difficulties regarding the nature of congregational action, but it may also point to a source of the astonishingly wide range of nonreligious activities taking place in congregations. Throughout this book I have emphasized the modal kinds of congregational social service and political activity, such as participating in food programs for the hungry or announcing opportunities for political action. But it also is worth noting the sheer range of activities that turn up in congregations. Scanning the long list of social service activities reported by NCS congregations, for example, we find congregations whose activities include reading to the mentally impaired, advocating environmental justice, protesting a Ku Klux Klan rally, developing a black history program, organizing a blood drive, participating in a diaper drive, helping to build a new library, providing hospice care, and convening support groups for parents of troubled children, people suffering from depression, individuals with eating disorders, Alzheimer's patients, abused women, and many other constituencies.

In addition to asking how much of any of this activity congregations do, we might also ask why such a variety of ancillary activity turns up in congregations. Perhaps the absence of coherence and unity of purpose across individuals and subgroups, the diffuseness of congregational goals, and congregations' character as a "network of enterprises loosely knotted

together" make them particularly open to individuals' enthusi-
asms and available as vehicles for various nonreligious activities. I made the point in earlier chapters that, although congregations do very little social service or political work, they
probably do relatively more such work than other kinds of organizations whose primary purpose, like that of congregations,
is something other than social services or politics. Perhaps this
is because congregations set very few hurdles in the way of
people who want to turn their interests and energies into a
"congregational" activity, and the barriers that do exist are low
even when only a few people are involved and even when
their interests are relatively idiosyncratic. R. Stephen Warner
(1994:63) put the point this way: in congregations "the burden
of proof rests with those who would exclude a potential activity
as illegitimate, and [congregations] will tend to absorb activities that are feasible given available resources"—and, I would
add, given the interest and energy of only a small group of
people.[1]

These considerations highlight an ambiguity in the phrase
"congregational program," but the ambiguity is potentially
productive. It calls attention to the ways in which congregations serve as sites in which individuals pursue their own interests and act on their own initiatives of various sorts. This seems
an accurate account of the sources of at least some types of
action within congregations, and it prompts additional questions. How much "congregational" action is truly action of the
collectivity as opposed to action of small numbers within the
collectivity? How much congregational action is fragile and
fleeting because it depends on the continuing commitment of a
few people rather than becoming an institutionalized part of
the congregation's work and identity? How much congregational social action is generated not by the objective needs of
communities but by the interests and passions of a few mem-

bers, which may or may not address the most urgent needs or reflect the interests and passions of a majority of members? Recognizing that congregations are aggregations of individuals and therefore, in a sense, less than coherent and unified collectivities is one way of moving beyond congregations as units of analysis toward looking more closely at the subgroups responsible for some activity—how much, we do not know—that passes as "congregational" activity.

Congregations as Instantiations of Larger Institutions

If some of what occurs in congregations is the result of subgroups of individuals pursuing their interests, other characteristics and actions of congregations have their source *outside* the congregation. This complicates the assumption that congregations are autonomous local actors, responding mainly to the needs of their constituents and their neighborhoods. They are, at least in part, instantiations of larger traditions, institutions, and movements. Like the complication introduced by recognizing the ways in which congregations are not quite coherent and unified groups, recognizing the ways in which congregations are not quite fully autonomous actors suggests another way to move beyond congregations as units of analysis.

Denominations are, of course, a particularly important "external" source of congregational structure and activity. This was most apparent in Chapter 5, in my examination of styles of worship. We saw there that denominations and religious traditions strongly shape congregations' worship practices. Here I would put the point more strongly. Saying that a congregation's worship is highly ceremonial, for example, might mean that the congregation faithfully enacts ritual elements prescribed by the denomination or religious tradition in which it is embedded, exercising little discretion or autonomy in the process, and reflecting its institutional connections more than the worship preferences of its people. From this perspective, the phrase "congregation's worship practices" seems to miss the institutional reality that many worship practices in many congregations are not initiated by congregations free to choose any worship style they please in response to the tastes and preferences of the gathered.

Denominations are important sources of worship practices for congregations, but congregations draw much more than worship practices from denominations. One analyst of Catholic churches in Chicago put the point sharply:

> Although not readily apparent to the ethnographer immersed in a rich congregational universe, Catholic parishes increasingly reconstitute archdiocesan organizations and reforms, and they are increasingly forced to work across parish boundaries on terms established by the archdiocese. In other words, the archdiocese both limits and facilitates parochial initiatives . . . To describe contemporary urban parishes without reference to [archdiocesan influences] is to analyze words without a grammar. (D'Agostino 2000:269–270)

Catholic churches are, of course, among the least autonomous of congregations, but they are not the only congregations whose denominational relations raise questions about the wisdom of treating congregations as relatively autonomous actors whose activities are generated mainly from within. When a denomination recommends that congregations have a certain set of standing committees, congregational structure is, in a sense, imported from "above." When congregations use denomination-produced hymnals, liturgies, or curricula, their worship and religious education practices are drawn from the larger institution in which they are embedded. When the denomination-supplied sets of envelopes used to organize members' weekly donations include envelopes for special collections in support of specific purposes or projects, a congregation's benevolence activity is a reflection of the denomination's priorities. When clergy bring to congregations ideas or projects learned in denomination-based seminaries or denomination-sponsored meetings, a congregation's activities again come to it from the larger institution. Many other specific points of denominational penetration of congregational life might be identified. The general theme here is that much congregational activity and structure come to the congregation from larger denominational institutions, and denominational sources of congregational activity are not limited to strongly centralized denominations or to the aspects of congregational life that are more centrally controlled. Denominations and religious traditions shape congregations via mechanisms other than literally centralized authority and control, and that shaping creates similarities across congregations whatever their local situations.[2]

Social movements are another important external source of congregational structure and activity. By "social movements" I mean organized efforts to create and diffuse particular kinds of activities or structures as widely as possible among congregations. Many of what we now consider standard and natural features of congregations became so because of such movements, which often cross denominational lines and also shape congregations unaffiliated with any denomination. Sunday schools, youth groups, choirs, and gospel choirs all became more or less standard features of American congregations in the nineteenth and twentieth centuries because successful social movements encouraged congregations to adopt these activities. Women's missionary societies—a congregational feature with less staying power than Sunday schools, youth groups, or choirs—also were created largely in response to a nationally organized women's foreign mission movement dedicated to establishing an auxiliary society in every local church.[3] Social movements also generate change in worship practices. In the eighteenth century, singing hymns to printed music became standard practice only after concerted effort by clergy to stamp out improvised singing in congregations (Becker 1982). Since then, a variety of liturgical reform movements have buffeted American congregations.

Congregations also draw activities from social movements that are not specifically religious. The civil rights and sanctuary movements come immediately to mind. A less well known example is the "National Negro Health Movement," which from 1915 to 1950 used African American churches "in a national strategy to bring modern public health practices to Blacks" (Thomas et al. 1994:576). Perhaps the movement manifest at the beginning of the twenty-first century in the more than one hundred organizations attempting to initiate community organizing projects within congregations will be successful enough that future observers will consider such projects a more or less standard piece of congregational infrastructure (Hart 2001). Furthermore, denominations and social movements are not the only external sources of congregational activity. A notable percentage of American congregations build or rehabilitate houses today because a national organization, Habitat for Humanity, provides a structure that facilitates such work.

In sum, much of what congregations are and much of what they do is part residue of past social movements, part interplay with contemporary social movements, and part instantiation of denominational practice. Whatever the particular mix, it seems clear that much congregational activity arises from external sources, and therefore treating congregations as autonomous collective actors that respond only to local challenges or the needs of the people in their pews or neighborhoods misapprehends the nature and source of at least some important kinds of congregational activity. These considerations should lead us to look more closely at the intersections between congregations, on the one hand, and the institutions and movements that shape them, on the other hand. When faced with the question, "Why do congregations do X?" we might look, in both the past and the present, for larger institutions and movements that promulgate X, and we might examine how it is that congregations welcomed or resisted that institution or movement. More generally, we might also ask about the relative importance at different times and places of denominations, social movements, and other external institutions as sources of congregational structure and activity.

Grappling with the conceptual complications highlighted in this chapter should not lead us to forget the many ways in which congregations indeed act as coherent, unified, and at least relatively autonomous local collectivities. Fully understanding religion's social organization certainly requires focusing on congregations as units of analysis and systematically examining what they do, how they do it, and why they do it. That is what I have tried to do in this book. At the same time, and somewhat ironically, we might also deepen our understanding of congregations by moving beyond them.

APPENDIX A

National Congregations Study Methodology

It may seem odd that, even though we have known for decades how to draw high-quality national samples of individuals, and even though there have been good national samples of some types of organizations at least since the 1980s, as of the late 1990s there was no high-quality national survey of congregations. There is, however, a straightforward reason why sampling congregations lagged behind sampling other types of organizations: there is no adequate sampling frame—no comprehensive list of American congregations—from which to select randomly a nationally representative sample of congregations. Some denominations have nearly comprehensive lists of associated congregations, but many do not, and, of course, no set of denominational lists will include congregations affiliated with no denomination. Telephone books also are problematic sampling frames for congregations. Yellow Page listings miss as many as 20 percent of congregations in some areas, and the subset of listed congregations is not a random one (Becker and Chaves 2000; cf. Kalleberg et al. 1990).[1] The absence of a comprehensive list of congregations has been a formidable obstacle in the road leading to a nationally representative sample of congregations and the basic knowledge that could be produced by surveying such a sample.

The National Congregations Study (NCS)—the survey on which this book is primarily based—overcame this obstacle by using a recent innovation in organizational sampling technology. The key insight is that organizations attached to a random sample of individuals constitute a random sample of organizations. It therefore is possible to generate a probability sample of organizations even in the absence of a comprehensive list of units in the organizational population. One simply starts with a random sample of individuals and asks them to name the organization(s) to which they are attached.[2]

The NCS is the first study implementing this strategy—called hypernetwork or multiplicity sampling—for congregations. The NCS is therefore methodologically innovative. Fully appreciating the substantive contributions developed in this book thus requires an understanding of certain technical features of these data. Still, this discussion of NCS methodology assumes no special expertise either in sampling or in survey research.[3]

Generating the NCS Sample

Generating a hypernetwork sample of organizations requires starting with a random sample of individuals. The NCS was conducted in conjunction with the 1998 General Social Survey (GSS)—an in-person interview with a representative sample of non-institutionalized English-speaking adults in the United States, conducted by the National Opinion Research Center at the University of Chicago. The 1998 GSS asked respondents who say they attend religious services at least once a year to report the name and location of their religious congregation. The congregations named by these respondents constitute the NCS congregational sample.

Pretesting indicated that, as Joe Spaeth and Diane O'Rourke (1996:43) suggest, it would not have been worthwhile to allow respondents to name more than one congregation, nor to ask for the congregation of a respondent's spouse if he or she attended one different from that of the respondent. Very few pretest respondents attended regularly at more than one place, and very few had a spouse who attended elsewhere. Moreover, when there was a spouse who attended a different congregation than did the respondent, there was a substantial drop-off in the quality of contact information that a respondent could provide about a spouse's congregation. Allowing multiple or spousal congregation nominations thus would have introduced considerable complexity in both data collection and sample properties without substantial gain in sample size.

The Probability-Proportional-to-Size Feature of the Sample

The probability that a congregation will appear in this sample is proportional to its size. Because congregations are nominated by individuals attached to them, larger congregations are more likely to appear in the sample than smaller congregations. Also, because the GSS sometimes interviews multiple people in the same neighborhood, some congregations are nominated by more than one GSS respondent. Weighted only to account for duplicate nominations, NCS data describe distributions of religious service attenders across congregations of different types. When the data are weighted inversely proportional to congregation size, univariate distributions represent distributions of congregations without respect to how many people are in them.[4] Both of these distributions often will be substantively interesting, and results are presented from both perspectives throughout this book. The key methodological point is that, although larger congregations are overrepresented in the NCS sample, they are overrepresented by a known degree, and that overrepresentation therefore can be undone with weights.

A contrived example may help clarify this feature of the NCS sample. Suppose that there are only two congregations in the universe, one with 1,000 regular attenders and the other with 100 regular attenders. Suppose further that the 1,000-person congregation runs a soup kitchen and the 100-person congregation does not. We might express this reality in one of two ways. We might say that 91 percent of the people are in a congregation with a soup kitchen (1,000/1,100), or we might say that 50 percent of the congregations run soup kitchens ($\frac{1}{2}$). It should be clear that both of these are meaningful numbers, and both are numbers we might want to know. NCS data can provide both sorts of numbers. Weighted only to take account of duplicate nominations, a percentage or mean from the NCS will be analogous to the 91 percent in this example. Weighted inversely proportional to congregation size, NCS univariate statistics are analogous to the 50 percent in this example. When the first number is larger than the second number, as in this example, bigger congregations are more likely to have this characteristic. When the second number is larger, smaller congregations are more likely to have the characteristic. When the two percentages are the same, the characteristic is unrelated to size.

All statistical models whose results are reported in this book are estimated using unweighted data, and diagnostic tests recommended by Christopher Winship and Larry Radbill (1994) are performed to check for misspecification related to the probability-proportional-to-size feature of the sample.

Collecting NCS Data

The GSS is a face-to-face interview conducted by experienced and well-trained interviewers who were instructed to glean from respondents as much locational information about their congregations as possible. NCS data were collected using the same interviewers who collected data from GSS respondents. Consequently, when turning to collection of the congregational data, the interviewer already was on site and was better able to locate the congregations named by GSS respondents, identify an informed leader to interview, and visit the congregation if telephone contact failed to yield a completed questionnaire. Using the same field staff also permitted recontacting GSS respondents in cases where additional locational information about congregations was needed. I attribute much of the success of NCS data collection, including its high response rate, to this administrative integration of the individual- and organization-level data collection efforts, and I strongly endorse Spaeth and O'Rourke's (1996:42–43) recommendation to conduct hypernetwork organizational studies in such an integrated fashion.

Once the congregational sample was generated, nominated congregations were located, and the NCS gathered congregational data using a one-hour interview with one key informant—a minister, priest, rabbi, or other staff person or leader—from each nominated congregation. Three quarters of NCS interviews were with clergy; 91 percent were with staff of some sort; 9 percent were with non-staff congregational leaders. Every effort was made to conduct these interviews by telephone, but we visited the congregation and conducted in-person interviews if telephone contact was difficult. Ninety-two percent of the interviews were completed by phone. The NCS response rate is 80 percent; complete data were collected from 1,236 congregations.[5]

NCS Measurement Strategy

The most important methodological issue confronted in constructing the NCS questionnaire involved the validity and reliability consequences of relying on a single key informant to report a congregation's characteristics. What congregational characteristics is it reasonable to expect a single organizational informant to report validly and reliably? What congregational characteristics is it best to avoid trying to measure by this method? Three general research findings guided questionnaire construction. First, social psychologists consistently find that people are biased reporters of the beliefs and attitudes of other individuals in that they systematically overestimate the extent to which other individuals share the informant's own views (Ross et al. 1977; Marks and Miller 1987). This "false consensus effect" persists even when people are given objective information about the attitudes and beliefs of the group about which they are asked to report (Krueger and Clement 1994). Also important for relating this research tradition to reporting about congregations, the bias is *stronger* when individuals are asked to report about groups or aggregates with which they identify or of which they are a part (Mullen et al. 1992). The false consensus bias is evident even when informants report about their friends' beliefs or attitudes (Marks and Miller 1987:76).

Second, organizational sociology has shown that organizations do not always have unified and cohesive goals, identities, missions, or cultures (Scott 1992:chap. 11). Different subsets of employees or members, different cliques, and people involved in different parts of the organization may have different, sometimes conflicting, goals, and different subsets of people within the same organization may see the organization's mission in different ways. There might, of course, be official and formal goals or missions, and a key informant would be in a position to report the content of such official goals, but the likelihood of variation inside organizations regarding goals, missions, and identities makes it problematic to seek a key informant's judgment about organizational goals or missions other than formal and official ones. Questions about organizational goals or missions assume the existence of clear goals, missions, or collective identities, and such an assumption may or may not be justified. In a situation in which goals are ambiguous or contested or variable, an informant's judgment about an organization's goals or mission is likely to represent the informant's interpretation of a complex reality rather than a more or less publicly available cultural fact about the congregation.

Third, in one of the few attempts to compare different methods of measuring characteristics of voluntary associations, J. Miller McPherson and Thomas Rotolo (1995) measured four different characteristics (size, sex composition, age composition, and educational composition) by three different methods (reports from a group official, reports from a randomly chosen respondent to a survey, and direct observation of a group meeting). They found very high correlations (between .8 and .9) among all three logged measures of size and sex composition, and only slightly smaller correlations between the leader report and direct observation for age and educational composition (.73 and .77, respectively). They conclude that for these four variables, "reports from an officer are just as reliable as direct-canvass measures and could reasonably be substituted for the latter" (McPherson and Rotolo 1995:1114).[6] Peter Marsden and Lisa Haueisen Rohrer (2001) find that key informant reports of organizational size and age are more reliable for single-site organizations (such as congregations) and when the key informant is in a leadership position.

This literature suggested several principles that guided NCS questionnaire construction and data collection strategy. From the false-consensus literature: key informants will not be very good at validly reporting the values, opinions, and beliefs of congregants. From the sociological literature on organizational goals: informants also will be unreliable reporters of a congregation's aggregate or overall goal or mission. On the positive side, from the research on key informant reporting: key informants, especially clergy, will be very good at reporting more or less directly observable features of the congregation and its people. Hence, the NCS questionnaire includes very few items, common in other key informant surveys of congregations, that asked the informant to report on congregants' goals, beliefs, values, or other aspects of their internal lives.[7] Nor does it include many items asking informants to describe, without tangible referents, general congregational goals or identities or missions.[8] Instead, almost all NCS items ask the informant—usually clergy and always a knowledgeable leader or staff person within the congregation—to report on more or less directly observable aspects of a congregation. Of course, restricting NCS questionnaire content largely to reports of more or less directly observable characteristics does not eliminate all threats to measurement validity and reliability. This restriction does, however, mitigate certain known threats to validity and reliability. In a context in which there were many more potential items to include than time to include them, this restriction seemed a sensible one, especially since the resulting question-naire still generates rich data on a wide range of subjects.

Appending Census Tract Data

After congregational data were collected, geographical infor-mation software was used to identify each congregation's census tract. Census tract data from the 1990 United States Census were then appended to each congregation's data re-cord. We were able to place all but one congregation in its cen-sus tract.

Public Availability of NCS Data

A public version of the NCS data set is available through two data archives: the American Religion Data Archive, based at Pennsylvania State University *(www.thearda.com)*, and the Inter-university Consortium for Political and Social Research (ICPSR), which is based at the University of Michigan *(www.icpsr.umich.edu)*. It is ICPSR Study no. 3471.

Users who would like to explore selected univariate statistics and bivariate cross-tabulations may do so on the NCS Web site: *//saint-denis.library.arizona.edu/natcong*.

APPENDIX B

Selected Summary Statistics from the National Congregations Study

	Statistics from attenders' perspective	Statistics from congregations' perspective
Age and tradition		
Median founding date	1924	1940
Median date worship began at present location	1957	1958
Percent with no denominational affiliation	10.7	19.1
Percent associated with each denomination or tradition:		
No denomination or tradition	9.7	17.9
Roman Catholic	28.8	6.2
Southern Baptist Convention	11.2	16.9
Three Black Baptist denominations	3.0	2.8
Other Baptist	4.0	5.7
United Methodist	9.2	12.0
Evangelical Lutheran Church of America	4.4	3.1
Lutheran Church–Missouri Synod	1.9	1.5
Presbyterian Church (USA)	3.0	2.3
Assemblies of God	1.5	1.9

	Statistics from attenders' perspective	Statistics from congregations' perspective
Other Pentecostal	1.9	2.3
Episcopal Church	2.5	3.2
United Church of Christ	2.0	1.9
Other mainstream Protestant	2.9	3.6
Other sectarian Protestant	3.9	6.4
Churches of God/Christ	1.9	2.7
Jewish	1.6	1.0
Non-Christian and non-Jewish	1.5	2.6
Other Christian	5.1	6.0

Governance and leadership

Clergy

Percent with a head clergyperson or leader	95.5	92.5
Percent where head clergy or leader is female	5.6	10.0
Percent with head clergyperson or leader of each ethnicity:		
White	82.2	74.6
Black	11.9	19.7
Hispanic	2.1	2.2
Asian/Pacific Islander	1.3	1.8
Other	2.5	1.8
Median year senior clergyperson took this position	1992	1994
Median age of senior clergyperson	51	49
Percent of head clergy with graduate degree	66.8	44.5
Percent of head clergy with high school diploma or less	4.3	11.1

Staff

Percent with no full-time staff	14.7	40.4
Percent with 1 full-time staff person	20.3	34.8
Percent with 2 full-time staff people	10.5	8.6
Percent with more than 2 full-time staff people	54.5	16.2
Median number of full-time staff	3	1

	Statistics from attenders' perspective	Statistics from congregations' perspective
Percent with no part-time staff	17.2	42.9
Percent with 1 part-time staff person	10.0	17.2
Percent with 2 part-time staff people	12.3	12.1
Percent with more than 2 part-time staff people	60.5	27.8
Median number of part-time staff	3	1
Percent with no paid staff	6.9	23.5
Lay leadership		
Median number of leaders	50	20
Median percent of leaders who are female	52	50
Percent with any committees or boards	93.3	86.5
Median number of committees meeting within the past year	6	3
Percent with one committee that is the most important governing body or coordinating committee	86.7	81.4
Median size of main committee	10	7
Median percent of main committee members who are female	43	40
Percent using any type of service offered by a denomination, other religious organization, or an outside consultant	44.0	31.1
Percent experiencing a conflict within the last two years for which a special meeting was called	26.5	27.7
Percent experiencing a conflict within the last two years that led some people to leave the congregation	26.4	26.7
Size and social composition		
Mean number of people associated in any way with the congregation's religious life	2,552	379
Median number of people associated in any way with the congregation's religious life	750	140

	Statistics from attenders' perspective	Statistics from congregations' perspective
Mean number of people regularly participating in the congregation's religious life	1,180	171
Median number of people regularly participating in the congregation's religious life	400	75
Mean number of adults regularly participating in the congregation's religious life	777	112
Median number of adults regularly participating in the congregation's religious life	275	50
Median percent of regular participants who are new to the congregation in the past year	10	10
Percent with more than half their people living within a ten-minute walk	10.3	6.8
Median percent of regular participants living within a ten-minute walk	10	10
Percent with more than half their people living within a ten-minute drive	57.2	53.2
Median percent of regular participants living within a ten-minute drive	60	60
Percent with more than 20% of their people living in households with income under $25,000/year	43.4	55.9
Median percent of regular participants with household income under $25,000/year	20	30
Percent with more than 20% of their people living in households with income higher than $100,000/year	11.6	3.9
Median percent of regular participants with household income higher than $100,000/year	5	0

	Statistics from attenders' perspective	Statistics from congregations' perspective
Percent with more than 50% of their people having a college degree	25.9	13.5
Median percent of regular participants with a college degree	30	15
Percent with more than 50% of their people having less than a high school diploma	3.3	6.8
Median percent of regular participants with less than a high school diploma	5	5
Median percent of regular participants over 60 years old	25	25
Median percent of regular participants under 35 years old	25	25
Median percent of regular participants owning their own businesses	6	5
Median percent of regular participants who are female	60	60
Percent of congregations more than 80% white and non-Hispanic	66.1	66.1
Percent of congregations more than 80% black	11.9	16.4
Percent of congregations more than 50% Hispanic	5	2
Median percent of regular participants living in households with two parents and at least one child	50	40
Median percent of regular participants living in households with one parent and at least one child	10	5
Recruitment and communication efforts		
Percent making any effort to recruit new participants	89.5	89.4
Percent doing each of the following within the past year:		
Placed an ad in the newspaper	50.3	44.7

	Statistics from attenders' perspective	Statistics from congregations' perspective
Encouraged people to invite a new person	86.8	86.9
Conducted or used a survey	32.1	25.3
Mailed or distributed a flyer	50.8	48.1
Followed up with visitors	74.2	79.4
Had a special recruitment committee	46.7	35.4
Percent using E-mail to communicate with members	30.9	21.8
Percent with a Web site	28.6	17.6
Worship services		
Percent with 1 service in typical week	14.3	26.9
Percent with 2 services in typical week	20.4	25.5
Percent with 3 services in typical week	23.6	31.9
Percent with more than 3 services in typical week	41.6	15.0
Median number of services in typical week	3	2
Median length of most recent main service	70 min.	75 min.
Median length of most recent sermon	20 min.	25 min.
Median number of minutes of music at most recent main service	20	20
Median number of socializing minutes before/after typical service	30	30
Median attendance at most recent main service	229	70
Median percent of regularly participating adults attending more than one service in the past week	5.2	22.2
Median number of people speaking at most recent main service	3	2
Median percent of speakers at most recent main service who are male	67	75

	Statistics from attenders' perspective	Statistics from congregations' perspective
Percent of most recent main services with each characteristic:		
Sermon or speech	97.1	94.8
Singing by congregation	98.1	96.3
Singing by choir	72.3	51.6
Singing by soloist	49.8	40.6
Time to greet one another	84.4	78.6
Silent prayer/meditation	80.7	73.7
Part of service specifically for children	48.3	47.4
Participation by teens	45.6	39.7
People saying "amen"	52.9	62.7
Applause	58.6	54.6
Laughing out loud	74.5	74.2
Written order of service	84.2	71.0
Overhead projector	14.8	12.1
People read or recite something together	75.1	63.0
Incense	7.2	3.6
Jump, shout, or dance spontaneously	13.1	19.2
Raise hands in praise	48.0	45.1
Communion	48.3	28.7
Use musical instrument(s):	91.2	84.2
Piano	68.2	69.4
Organ	70.4	52.7
Drums	25.0	20.1
Electric guitar	30.0	21.5
Percent with the following in any worship in past year:		
Dance by teens or adults	29.1	17.4
Skit or play by teens or adults	70.1	61.5
Hired singers or musicians	51.2	34.7
People told of opportunities for political activity	36.7	26.3
Time for people other than leaders to testify	71.9	78.0
Speak in tongues	18.7	23.6

	Statistics from attenders' perspective	Statistics from congregations' perspective
Percent with joint worship service in last year	66.2	65.0
Percent with joint worship in last year with other than Christian or Jewish congregation	4.6	3.7
Percent with joint worship in last year with congregation with different racial/ethnic makeup	30.7	27.9

Congregation-sponsored groups and services

Groups and classes

Percent with religious education classes	96.6	89.9
Median number of religious education classes meeting at least monthly	10	4
Percent with no choir	13.4	36.2
Percent with 1 choir	17.5	27.0
Percent with 2 choirs	19.8	14.7
Percent with 3 or more choirs	49.3	22.1
Percent with groups meeting once a month or more	88.7	73.5
Median number of monthly groups	4	2
Percent with additional groups besides the ones meeting once a month or more	50.2	29.4
Percent with a group in the past year focused on the following:		
Politics	12.5	6.6
Book discussion	42.1	30.2
Parenting	61.6	39.7
Building cleaning/maintenance	70.8	70.4
Physical healing	43.2	32.1
Voter registration	12.3	8.5
English as a second language	8.9	3.8
Environmental issues	13.6	7.7
Organize/encourage volunteer work	59.0	38.6
Discuss work problems/concerns	24.6	17.4
Practice gifts of spirit	19.6	12.7

	Statistics from attenders' perspective	Statistics from congregations' perspective
History/practice of own tradition	66.0	45.4
Prospective/new member class	79.4	55.9
Pray/meditate	80.7	66.9
Prepare a musical or theatrical performance	54.8	38.3
Attend a live performance elsewhere	52.2	42.7
Class to train new teachers	67.4	37.1
Discuss race relations	22.2	17.0
Discuss how to preserve your ethnic heritage	12.4	9.8
Discuss/learn about another religion	29.7	21.5
12-step or self-help groups	39.2	15.9
Lobbying	12.0	4.4
Managing personal finances	33.0	22.2
Organizing/participating in demonstration or march	21.4	9.2
Management of congregation's money	55.4	46.3
Overnight trip	62.5	45.5
Assess community needs	48.0	37.2
Percent ever distributing voter guides	26.6	17.2
Percent with an elementary or high school	23.6	5.9
Percent giving money to a college, university, or seminary	45.2	34.3
Social services		
Percent with social service, community development, or neighborhood organizing programs of any sort	75.2	56.6
Percent with 1 social service program	12.9	18.1
Percent with 2 social service programs	14.1	13.5
Percent with 3 social service programs	11.9	7.8
Percent with more than 3 social service programs	36.2	17.2
Median total number of social service programs	2	1

	Statistics from attenders' perspective	Statistics from congregations' perspective
Median amount spent on social service programs in the past year	$1,254	$0
Percent with anyone on paid staff spending more than 25% of their time on congregation's social service projects	12.9	6.2
Percent with anyone from the congregation doing volunteer work for congregation's social service projects	70.0	50.7
Median number of congregational volunteers working on congregation's social service projects	12	0
Percent collaborating with at least 1 additional group to provide social services	66.7	47.6
Percent collaborating with government to deliver services	15.5	11.1
Percent collaborating with any secular, nongovernmental group to deliver services	56.3	27.8
Percent collaborating with another congregation to deliver services	35.7	23.4
Percent collaborating with another noncongregational religious group to deliver services	29.6	15.5
Percent with outside funding support for social service programs	13.2	10.6
Percent with outside funding support from foundations, businesses, or United Way	6.6	4.4
Percent with outside funding support from local, state, or federal government	3.7	2.6
Percent aware of charitable choice legislation	30.6	23.5

	Statistics from attenders' perspective	Statistics from congregations' perspective
Percent with a policy against receiving government support	14.4	16.2
Percent who would apply for government money to support human services programs	48.1	38.8

Speakers

Percent having any visiting speakers in the past year	89.4	82.0
Median number of visiting speakers in past year	5	4
Percent having the following types of visiting speakers in the past year:		
Clergy from other congregations	71.0	65.4
Elected government officials	12.3	6.1
Academics or professors	37.7	19.7
Denominational representatives	61.7	50.9
Representatives of social service organizations	39.2	21.9
Missionaries	62.8	45.2
Someone running for office	6.3	4.3

Finances

Percent with a formal written budget	87.7	72.6
Median income in past year	$258,000	$60,000
Median income from individuals in past year	$230,000	$52,800
Percent receiving income in the past year from sale or rent of your building or property	37.8	23.4
Percent receiving income in the past year from denomination or religious group	10.1	11.5
Median budget for past year	$250,000	$55,597
Percent giving money to denomination in the past year	82.7	72.4

	Statistics from attenders' perspective	Statistics from congregations' perspective
Median amount given to denomination in past year	$12,350	$1,671
Percent giving money to other religious organizations or agencies in the past year	62.0	50.2
Percent with an endowment, savings account, or reserve fund	73.9	59.8
Median amount in endowment, savings, or reserve	$20,000	$1,000
Percent trying to obtain a permit or license from government in the past year	36.3	17.0
Percent of those applying who were refused a permit in the past year	1.5	1.0
Percent of all congregations refused a permit in past year	0.5	0.2
Building		
Percent owning their own building	94.9	86.4
Percent meeting in a church/temple/mosque	92.9	86.6
Percent meeting in a school	3.3	5.2
Percent meeting in building other than church, temple, mosque, or school	3.8	8.3
Percent where people come to view the building or art or stained glass	55.0	32.7
Percent whose building was used in past year by groups with no connection to the congregation	67.2	42.9
Median number of outside groups using congregation's building in past year	3	0
Percent whose building was used for rehearsals or performances by groups with no connection to the congregation	29.4	14.0
Percent whose building was used for art exhibits	11.0	4.7

	Statistics from attenders' perspective	Statistics from congregations' perspective
Doctrine and theology		
Percent with special rules regarding:		
Diet	15.0	7.2
Dancing	12.7	21.2
Prohibiting smoking tobacco	17.1	27.6
Joining other groups	19.2	20.3
Prohibiting alcohol use	24.0	43.5
How much money people give to the congregation	21.4	20.6
Whom single people date	16.3	19.4
Cohabitation	54.5	54.3
Homosexual behavior	57.4	58.7
Percent encouraging use of New International Version of the Bible	22.0	21.4
Percent considering Bible to be literal and inerrant	63.0	77.3
Percent saying their congregation would be considered *politically:*		
more on the conservative side	55.0	61.1
right in the middle	37.0	30.9
more on the liberal side	8.0	8.0
Percent saying their congregation would be considered *theologically:*		
more on the conservative side	52.5	59.3
right in the middle	37.5	29.4
more on the liberal side	10.0	11.3
Geography and neighborhood characteristics		
Percent in each region:		
Northeast	4.7	2.9
Middle Atlantic	14.7	9.8
East North Central	17.2	12.8
West North Central	7.3	6.5
South Atlantic	18.2	16.8
East South Central	8.0	19.8
West South Central	12.2	12.9
Mountain	6.0	8.9
Pacific	11.6	9.7

	Statistics from attenders' perspective	Statistics from congregations' perspective
Percent in census tracts with 50% or more adults with some college education	35.4	21.0
Percent in census tracts with at least 30% of individuals below the poverty line	10.1	13.0
Percent in census tracts with at least 5% of individuals immigrating in past 18 years	15.1	13.2
Percent in census tracts with at least 80% African Americans	5.0	3.9
Percent in census tracts with at least 5% unemployment	26.9	31.7
Percent in predominantly urban census tracts	61.0	44.3
Percent in predominantly rural census tracts	23.2	40.7

Notes: Means and medians in "attenders" column refer to the congregation attended by the average attender of religious services. Percentages give the percentage of religious service attenders in congregations with the stated characteristic.

Means and medians in "congregations" column refer to the average congregation. Percentages give the percentage of congregations with the stated characteristic.

Notes

1. What Do Congregations Do?

1. Compare the definition offered by Wind and Lewis (1994:1–3).

2. I am using "congregational religion" to refer to the local religious gatherings as I have defined them—not, as is common in the sociological and religious studies literature, to refer to the subset of congregations subject only to local control. This narrower, more technical, usage—by which congregational polity is often contrasted with presbyterial and episcopal polity—usually connotes such things as local control over clergy hiring, financial matters, and other aspects of congregational life; local ownership of buildings and property; lay leadership in many parts of the congregation's work; dependence on voluntary donations from local members for necessary material support; and so on. These two meanings of "congregational" should not be confused. When R. Stephen Warner (1994:73), for example, writes about "de facto congregationalism" in American religion, he is arguing, rightly, that congregations (in the broader sense of local religious gatherings) tend in the American context toward a congregational structure (in the narrower sense of local control). When I say that congregations are the predominant way in which American religion is socially organized, I mean only that the main social form of religion in the United States is the local gathering as I have defined it, whatever the structure of organizational control overlying these gatherings.

3. On contemporary rates of weekly attendance at religious services, see Hadaway et al. (1993, 1998); Chaves and Cavendish (1994); and the

Symposium on Surveys of U.S. Church Attendance in the February 1998 *American Sociological Review*. For trends over time in religious affiliation, compare United States Department of Commerce, Bureau of the Census (1958) with results from more recent surveys such as Davis and Smith (2000). Hout and Fischer (2002) provide a recent analysis of this trend. For trends over time in religious service attendance, see Presser and Stinson (1998), Putnam (2000: chap. 4), Chaves and Stephens (2003), and Hout and Fischer (2003). For international comparisons, see Inglehart and Baker (2000) and Greeley (2003).

4. For early- and mid-twentieth-century research on congregations, see, for example, Morse and Brunner (1923); Brunner (1923a, b); Douglass (1926, 1927); Mays and Nicholson (1933); Douglass and Brunner (1935); Wilson (1945); Fichter (1951); and Kloetzli (1961). More recent studies (or collections of studies) based on one or only a few congregations include Ammerman (1987, 1997a); Becker et al. (1993); Becker (1999); Eiesland (2000); Freedman (1993); Harris (1998); Livezey (2000b); Olson (1989); McRoberts (2003); Sider and Unruh (2001); Warner (1988); Warner and Wittner (1998); Wellman (1999); Wilkes (1994); Williams (1974); Wind and Lewis (1994); Wineburg (1994); and Zuckerman (1999). Recent studies based on surveys of larger numbers of congregations (sometimes complemented by case studies of a smaller number of congregations) within one denomination, within a particular ethnic group, within a selected set of denominations, or within a single or small number of locales include Ammerman (2002); Billingsley (1999); Chang et al. (1994); Cnaan (1997, 2000); Dudley and Roozen (2001); Grettenberger (2000); Hall (1996); Hoge and Roozen (1979); Hoge et al. (1996); Jackson et al. (1997); Leege and Welch (1989); Lincoln and Mamiya (1990); Miller (1997); Miller (1998); Pressley and Collier (1999); Roozen and Carroll (1989); Roozen and Hadaway (1993); Roozen et al. (1984); Printz (1998); Salamon and Teitelbaum (1984); Silverman (2000); Stone (2000); Thomas et al. (1994); Wineburg (1990–91); and Wood (1981).

5. The NCS is methodologically innovative. Readers who are familiar with certain key features of NCS methodology and data will more fully appreciate the substantive contributions developed in this book. Appendix A contains additional methodological detail about the NCS. I should note at the outset that, although the NCS includes Muslim, Buddhist, and Hindu congregations, these three groups combined, although growing, still make up less than 2 percent of the population of the United States (Sherkat 1999; Smith 2001). Consequently, there are too few such congregations in the NCS data to permit meaningful analysis of these subgroups.

6. See, for example, Hopewell (1987); Ammerman (1997a); Becker (1999); and Livezey (2000a).

7. Systematic analysis of collective worship (as in, for example, Ducey 1977 and Tamney 1984) is much less common in the sociological literature than analysis of congregational culture more broadly conceived.

8. A similar emphasis on processes by which specific practices are drawn from a larger repertoire of practices also can be found in the social movements literature. See, for example, Tilly (1993) and Tarrow (1994).

9. The renewed conversation about religion and the arts is evident, for example, in Wuthnow (2003a) and Arthurs and Wallach (2001).

2. Members, Money, and Leaders

1. Unless otherwise noted, all numerical facts reported in the text and tables are from the National Congregations Study.

2. This basic fact about how people are distributed across congregations underlines the importance of the probability-proportional-to-size feature of the NCS sample, described in detail in Appendix A. For some purposes we will want to know about characteristics of congregations without taking congregational size into account; for other purposes we will want to know about the opportunities and experiences to which people in congregations are exposed. NCS data permit analysis from both perspectives. The skewed nature of congregational size distributions implies that these two perspectives could present very different views of congregational life.

3. These umbrella organizations are not always referred to as "denominations" by their members. They may be called conventions, associations, or, simply, churches. Indeed, some groups explicitly deny, for theological reasons, that they constitute a "denomination," even though they establish extra-congregational organizational structures—publishing companies, regional clergy associations, seminaries, and the like—that characterize denominations as an organizational form. I use the generic term "denomination" as a label for these umbrella groups with which many congregations are affiliated.

4. The Catholic numbers are the same in both tables because all of the Catholic churches in the NCS sample are formally affiliated with one and only one "denomination": the Roman Catholic Church. For Catholics in this sample, denominational affiliation and religious tradition are coterminous.

5. The largest groups in the liberal-moderate category are, in size order beginning with the largest, the United Methodist Church, Evangeli-

cal Lutheran Church in America, Presbyterian Church (USA), Episcopal Church, and United Church of Christ. The largest groups in the conservative-evangelical category are the Southern Baptist Convention, nondenominational congregations, Lutheran Church–Missouri Synod, and Assemblies of God. No other group in either category is represented by more than fifteen congregations in the NCS sample. Note also that predominantly African American congregations are included in this categorization unless they are affiliated with one of the seven major traditionally African American denominations. About half of predominantly African American congregations are associated with one of these seven denominations, which account for about 5 percent of all congregations. See Steensland et al. (2000) for a detailed suggestion about how to categorize denominations into similarly conceptualized major traditions.

6. See Hout and Fischer (2003) for more evidence of strong generational differences in religious participation and belief.

7. All the empirical facts in this paragraph are from Hout et al. (2001).

8. Computed by Sylvia Ronsvalle using data from Ronsvalle and Ronsvalle (2000).

9. Ibid.

10. See, for example, Cormode (1992); Nemeth and Luidens (1994); *State of the UCC* (1997).

11. McMillan and Price (2003:13) note that the increase in average salary for clergy partly reflects a decreasing proportion of Catholic priests (who are, on average, paid less than clergy in other traditions) in the national clergy pool.

12. The Great Depression's debilitating effect on organized religion in the United States leaves a trace to this day in the age distribution of American congregations. In 1998 only 4 percent of religious attenders were in congregations founded in the 1930s, compared with 6 percent in congregations founded in the first decade of the twentieth century, 5 percent in congregations founded in the 1910s, 7 percent in congregations founded in the 1920s, 7 percent in congregations founded in the 1940s, 10 percent in congregations founded in the 1950s, 7 percent in congregations founded in each of the next three decades, and 5 percent in those founded in the 1990s.

13. Four percent of Phi Beta Kappa members who graduated from college in the late 1940s became clergy, a figure dropping to 2 percent for early 1970s college graduates and 1 percent for early 1980s college graduates (Bowen and Schuster 1986). Eight percent of American Rhodes scholars in 1904–1909 became clergy, but only 4 percent in 1955–1959 and 1 percent in 1975–1977 (author's calculations from *Register of Rhodes*

Scholars, 1903–1981). The GRE results are from Grandy and Greiner (1990).

14. See Ruger and Wheeler (1995:5) for clergy salary differences across religious traditions.

15. Rural congregations' disadvantage in the competition for clergy extends across centuries and continents. Consider Harline and Put's (2000:157–158) description of the situation in Flanders in the first decade of the seventeenth century: "Priests seemed plentiful enough . . . [but] most avoided the parish, at least the rural sort. Well-trained priests preferred a position with a sparkling prebend and little care—precisely what most rural parishes did not offer . . . Few were the university students groomed for the trials and undignified incomes of rural parishes . . . [A]s the archbishop put it in one letter, it was 'almost impossible' to find Dutch-speaking pastors for rural parishes unless they had been 'raised to it from their youngest days.'"

3. Social Services

1. Most of the recent social scientific literature on congregations' social services is based on case studies of small numbers of congregations (Harris 1995; Unruh 1999; Bartkowski and Regis 1999; McRoberts 2003); surveys of congregations in only one city, state, or religious denomination (Wineburg 1992; Williams et al. 1997; Printz 1998; Miller 1998; Ebaugh and Pipes 1998; Grettenberger 2000; Stone 2000; Silverman 2000; Cnaan 2000); surveys of congregations within a particular ethnic group or set of denominations (Lincoln and Mamiya 1990; Thomas et al. 1994; Billingsley 1999; Ammerman 2000; Dudley and Roozen 2001); surveys of a subset of older, urban congregations (Cnaan 1997); or a national sample of congregations with a very low response rate (Hodgkinson and Weitzman 1992).

2. See Ackerman and Burke (2001) for a summary of legislation containing charitable choice language.

3. See Austensen (2001) for a summary of activities in ten states as of fall 2001 and Orr (2001) for a summary of efforts in three California counties.

4. Some other congregational studies find social service activity in 90 percent or more of congregations (see, for example, Hodgkinson and Weitzman 1992; Printz 1998; Cnaan 1997, 2000; Stone 2000; Dudley and Roozen 2001). These studies report higher rates because they overrepresent larger, more established urban congregations—the congregations most likely to do social services—and because they measure social

service activity in a way more likely than the NCS to pick up the most informal and sporadic kinds of human aid given by congregations to their own members and to people who knock on their doors.

5. The NCS asked congregational informants, "Has your congregation participated in or supported social service, community development, or neighborhood organizing projects of any sort within the past 12 months?" Respondents were instructed to exclude any "projects that use or rent space in your building but have no other connection to your congregation." Respondents whose congregations participated in or supported such programs were asked to describe these programs in an open-ended way. There was no limit to the number of programs an informant could mention. The maximum number of programs mentioned by any congregation was twenty. Interviewers were instructed to probe for each mentioned program's purpose, and they recorded verbatim each program description offered by the respondent. These verbatim program descriptions were then used to code a set of variables, each one indicating a certain program characteristic. Some of these variables indicate program content (such as food, clothing, or health care). Others indicate a target group for the activity (such as children or the homeless or the elderly). These variables are not mutually exclusive; a single program might be characterized in several ways. For instance, a program described as a "soup kitchen for the homeless" would count both as a program aimed at the homeless and as a food program. Social service activities also occasionally were reported in response to another open-ended item asking informants to describe any groups of people from the congregation who meet for "religious, social, recreational, or other purposes." Social service activities offered in response to this item are included in the results reported in this chapter.

6. These numbers do not take into account the value of staff time, volunteer time, or donations to denominations. Compare the estimates in Biddle (1992). The total number of programs in which a congregation engages is highly correlated both with the total amount of money it spends on social services and with the total number of volunteers involved in any activity.

7. See Chapter 7 for additional discussion of results from clergy time-use studies.

8. See Mamiya (1994) and Shipps et al. (1994) for examples of very active congregations.

9. Corporations, for example, donate on average only 1 percent of their profits to charity (Galaskiewicz 1997).

10. These patterns are based on a regression equation in which the number of programs reported by each congregation is the dependent

variable. In addition to the variables emphasized in the text, this analysis also controls urban versus rural location, regional location, congregational founding date, the percentage of attenders living within a ten-minute walk, and the education level of the head clergyperson. Using alternative dependent variables—the logged number of programs, the logged amount of money congregations spend on social services, or the logged number of volunteers involved with a congregation's social service activities—does not substantially change the results. Neither does using negative binomial regression, the technically correct modeling approach with a dependent variable of this sort. See Chaves and Tsitsos (2001) for additional details on this analysis, and see Tsitsos (2003) for more detail on the differences in social service activity between predominantly African American and predominantly white congregations.

11. See Farnsley (2000) for a very similar pattern in one city.

12. We should not be too quick to assume, however, that congregations located in poor neighborhoods and having few middle-class members are therefore socially embedded in the local area. In the poor Boston neighborhood that McRoberts (2003) studied, even the storefront churches drew few members from the immediate area.

13. For examples of this sort of claim, see Carlson-Thies (1999:30); Sherman (1995:60–61); White House (2001:4–5); Frumkin (2002:117–118).

14. The "long-term and face-to-face" category in Table 3.1 includes programs such as job training, domestic abuse shelters, hospice care, substance abuse programs, Big Brothers and Big Sisters, any type of counseling, tutoring or mentoring, and educational programs such as teaching reading or English as a second language. Any program description implying that people from the congregation engaged in these kinds of face-to-face, intensive activities was counted as "long-term and face-to-face." If a congregation's involvement with programs of these sorts is limited to donating money, that program is not counted on this measure. The "short-term and fleeting" category includes programs that appear to involve only cursory interactions with needy people, or no interactions at all, such as providing cash, food, clothes, temporary shelter, or anything described as "emergency" or "temporary" aid. I would not want to overinterpret results based on these two indicators. Many of the verbatim program descriptions are very cryptic, and many did not contain enough information to code either of these variables, which is why the percentages they yield sum to a number smaller than the 57 percent of congregations that report some type of social service activity. Still, these measures represent a start on the task of assessing the extent to which congregations specialize in a more personal approach to social services.

15. See, for example, Roozen et al. (1984:93); Salamon and Teitelbaum (1984:63); Wineburg (1992:112); Caldwell et al. (1995:321); Printz (1998:table 1); Silverman (2000:table 5).

16. Nancy Ammerman surveyed three hundred congregations in nine communities and found that "nearly two-thirds (64 percent) reported little involvement in community programs or concerns [and] few if any programs that bring them into contact with people other than their own members" (Ammerman 1997a:64).

17. This study of churches within one Chicago neighborhood also illustrates a point made earlier: within poor neighborhoods, the congregations filled with middle-class people who commute from the suburbs perform more social services than the congregations peopled by the predominantly poor local residents.

18. A similar picture emerges from a study of the degree of contact between churches and individuals within two low-income public housing complexes in Indianapolis (Smith 2001).

19. In drawing on case studies here, I am selecting examples that illustrate the difficulty and rarity of congregation-based social services that are in fact distinctively holistic and personalistic. I do not mean to imply that there are no examples of congregations that genuinely integrate needy people or that genuinely involve their members in social services that focus on crosscutting needs in a personal way. Of course these exist, but we know from the National Congregations Study that they are rare. I am drawing on the case study literature to illustrate the most typical congregational approach to social services.

20. Monsma and Mounts (2001) found that "holistic" activities constituted a larger *proportion* of religious organizations' operations than of secular organizations' operations, but this is because religious organizations perform fewer of the standard job-oriented activities than secular organizations, not because they perform more of the values-oriented activities.

21. "Conservative congregations" are defined here as congregations associated with conservative denominations or congregations identified as theologically conservative by NCS informants in response to a question asking them to describe their congregations, theologically speaking, as "more on the conservative side," "right in the middle," or "more on the liberal side." Controlling for a host of other differences between conservative and nonconservative congregations does not change the pattern evident in Table 3.2.

22. Comprehensively assessing the relative effectiveness of religiously based social services requires attention to organizations other than congregations. A full discussion of this issue is beyond the scope of this book, but it is worth noting that there is no empirical basis for concluding that religious organizations are, in general, more effective than secular orga-

nizations at delivering social services. Nor is there any good theoretical reason to expect that they would be so. See Chaves (2002) for more detail on the effectiveness question, including a summary of the relevant empirical literature.

23. For each program mentioned, informants were asked whether the congregation administered the program by itself or "in collaboration with other groups or organizations." In the case of collaborative programs, respondents were asked to name the two most important collaborators. Responses were recorded verbatim. "Collaborator" was not further defined for respondents; any group mentioned in response to these questions is considered a collaborator. Each collaborator for each program was categorized according to its organizational type. This variable was then aggregated to create four congregation-level collaborator variables, one each indicating whether or not the congregation collaborated on any program with another congregation, a non-congregational religious organization, a government agency or office, or a nongovernmental secular organization. A program-level data set also was constructed from these same responses. This data set, where each record corresponds to one of the 3,728 programs mentioned by a congregation in the sample, was used to assess whether programs of certain types (rather than congregations of certain types) are associated with collaborators of certain types.

24. Other surveys also find high degrees of collaboration with secular organizations: Ammerman (2000) found that 44 percent of all congregational connections are with secular organizations. She found 58 percent cooperating with secular nonprofits and 29 percent cooperating with a government agency (Ammerman forthcoming). Lincoln and Mamiya (1990) found 71 percent of urban black churches collaborating with social agencies; Williams et al. (1997) found 60 percent of urban black churches collaborating. A 1990 survey of northern black churches found extensive collaboration on community health activities between congregations and secular organizations (Thomas et al. 1994:577).

25. Readers might note the dates of this and other examples of government funding of religious organizations. Government funding of religious and even congregation-based social services was the status quo long before the charitable choice movement or faith-based initiative emerged in the late 1990s.

26. The bivariate results in Table 3.4 are sustained by multivariate analysis. Using congregations (rather than programs) as the unit of analysis, a dependent variable coded 1 for all congregations having at least one holistic program is regressed on a variable indicating whether or not a congregation has at least one secular collaborator on any program, and again on whether or not a congregation has at least one government collaborator on any program. In both cases the analysis is limited to congre-

gations with at least one collaborator on at least one social service program, and many other variables are controlled. The results are clear. Controlling many things, we find that congregations with secular collaborators are significantly *more* likely to be engaged in longer-term, more personal, more face-to-face kinds of social service activities than are congregations without such collaborations. Congregations with government collaborators are no less likely than congregations without government collaborators to participate in or support those kinds of programs. See Chaves and Tsitsos (2001) for more details.

27. Wuthnow (2000:30) reaches a similar conclusion: "The effectiveness of church service work is heavily dependent on the presence of nonprofit service organizations with which [churches] can partner or otherwise cultivate close relationships." A 2000 study of fourteen socially active congregations in Hartford found that *all* have had government support of some sort (Dudley n.d.:13). See Caldwell et al. (1995:319); Williams et al. (1997:16); and Wineburg (2001) for additional supporting evidence and similar conclusions. This point also applies, not incidentally, to religious social services other than those based in congregations. After exhaustively reviewing the literature on religiously based social services, McCarthy and Castelli (1998:5) concluded that "most religion-sponsored social services have extensive and complex connections with other sectors of society, including government."

28. In his 1926 book Douglass at first classified 10.5 percent of the 1,044 urban churches in his sample as "socially adapted" (Douglass 1926:54). But, as he explained later, he considered this sample to be unrepresentative. When he focused only on the subsample of 418 congregations which he believed to be a more representative sample of urban congregations, he found only 4 percent to be "socially adapted" (Douglass 1926:271).

29. Adjusted for inflation, $150 in 1933 had about the same buying power as $1,880 in 1998. This is slightly more than the $1,500 we observe the average congregation spending today on social services, but recall that these surveys from the 1920s and 1930s are based on samples that overrepresented more active congregations.

30. Interestingly, Douglass and Brunner also worried about mixing social work with evangelism, and they questioned the efficacy of such a mix even from the evangelist's point of view: "In [a] cruder version of the evangelistic motive, social work is little more than a bait to get recipients of charity to allow themselves to be exposed to religious propaganda . . . In this field it is exceedingly difficult to do justice; but church people generally have undoubtedly lacked adequate sensitiveness to the viewpoints of the recipients of their social benefactions when these benefactions are closely bound up with religious aims . . . In view of the weakness of direct

religious teaching in securing direct character results even in Protestant Sunday schools, it would seem safe largely to trust to good works to speak for themselves" (Douglass and Brunner 1935:204). These sentences are as wise now as when they were composed.

31. It is important to draw this distinction between the two reasons for the declining percentage of social assistance occurring within religious organizations or institutions whenever one is assessing the nature of secularization. Whether the arena is social services, education, family life, science, or something else, secularization produced by religion's losing control of activities it once controlled is a qualitatively different phenomenon from secularization produced by the emergence of new activities, decisions, or organizations under secular auspices from their beginnings. See Chaves (1997) for elaboration of this point.

32. See the case studies in Douglass (1927) for more examples.

33. For an example, see Wallis (2001).

34. See, for example, Kramer (1981); Smith and Lipsky (1993); Grønbjerg (1993); and Salamon (1995a) for discussions of this more general question.

35. Dummy variables indicating each of the eight types of political activity measured in the NCS were regressed on a variable indicating whether or not the congregation received any government funding in support of its social service activities, and again on a variable indicating the percentage of the congregation's budget coming from government sources. These analyses include controls for congregations' denominational affiliation, self-described liberal or conservative theology, racial composition, percent of members with four-year college or higher degrees, percent with household income over $100,000 in 1998, percentage under age 35, percent over age 60, whether or not the congregation is located in the South, whether or not it is located in an urban area, size, founding date, and educational level of its head clergyperson. *All* of the sixteen government funding coefficients were either null (in nine equations) or significantly positive (in seven equations). Interestingly, a similar analysis based on longitudinal data from nonprofit organizations in Minneapolis–St. Paul yields similar results. For nonprofit organizations in general, as for congregations, government funding does not seem to decrease political activity. See Chaves et al. (2004) for more details.

4. Civic Engagement and Politics

1. See, for example, Hodgkinson and Weitzman (1992); Verba et al. (1995); Zald and McCarthy (1998); Skocpol and Fiorina (1999); Putnam (2000); Bane et al. (2000); and Dionne and Chen (2001).

2. For discussions of the extent to which voluntary associations might detract from as well as contribute to civil society, see, for example, Putnam (2000:chap. 22); Portes (1998); Foley and Edwards (1997); and Fiorina (1999).

3. For research on religious differences in civic participation, see, for example, Beyerlein and Hipp (2003); Wuthnow (1999); Hall (1998, 1999); Schwartz (1998); Hoge et al. (1998); and Wilson and Janoski (1995). Analysis of only one data set fails to find that moderate and liberal Protestants engage in more bridging kinds of civic activities; see Smith (1998:40–42); Regnerus et al. (1998:481–493). These exceptional findings appear to be an artifact of unusual measurement procedures.

4. Table 4.1 does not include congregations other than Christian churches and Jewish synagogues because, although the NCS contains data on other congregations, there are too few within any one tradition to report statistics based on these subsamples. There are only thirty congregations in the NCS that are neither Jewish nor Christian. This set of thirty congregations includes Muslim mosques and Buddhist temples, among other types of congregations. Reporting statistics for such a heterogeneous category seems unwise, and looking at each of these groups separately would, of course, reduce the case base even further. With only twenty synagogues in the NCS sample, perhaps I ought not include even Jews in this table. The 95 percent confidence intervals around the percentages of synagogues engaged in various activities are wide—as high as plus or minus 22 percentage points for percentages close to 50—but these confidence intervals are not so large as to render the Jewish percentages meaningless. For this reason I err on the side of inclusiveness, but I urge readers to recognize these wider-than-usual confidence intervals and interpret the numbers cautiously. By comparison, no percentage describing the activity level within the other three religious traditions represented in Table 4.1 has an associated 95 percent confidence interval wider than plus or minus 6 percentage points. Although I include synagogue numbers in the table for the reader's information, I call attention to them in the text only where it seems reasonable to draw a comparative conclusion even in the face of the wide confidence intervals produced by the small sample.

In this chapter I emphasize the percentages of people attached to congregations engaged in particular activities rather than the percentages of congregations engaged in them. When it comes to congregations' civic engagement, it seems more useful to know how many people are in congregations engaging in certain kinds of activities than it is to know how many congregations engage in those activities. For the purposes of this chapter, for example, it seems more relevant to point out that 39 percent of religious service attenders are in congregations that had as a visiting speaker a representative of a community social service agency than to point out that only 22 percent of congregations had such a speaker.

5. Protestant congregations are categorized in Table 4.1 as either "moderate and liberal" or "conservative and evangelical" based on their denominational affiliations. See note 5 in Chapter 2 for more detail about this categorization. I have included predominantly African American congregations in this analysis by classifying them within the relevant religious tradition. With a few exceptions that I will note, there are not, in general, race differences in the rate at which congregations engage in these civic activities.

6. Because I am emphasizing the fact that moderate and liberal Protestant congregations engage in more bridging civic activities, Table 4.1 also reports whether the percentage of liberal and moderate congregations engaged in each activity is statistically different from the percentage of all other congregations engaged in that activity in multivariate analyses. These analyses hold constant many other congregational and community characteristics. The specific control variables are listed in the note to Table 4.1. All of the multivariate analyses mentioned in this chapter contain this same set of controls. I will say more about these multivariate analyses later, but readers may focus solely on the simple percentages in Table 4.1 without fear of being substantively misled.

7. Table 4.1 reports findings from only a subset of the social service items available in the NCS. But the pattern I emphasize here is not dependent on the particular items chosen. There is *no* social service activity in which conservative Protestants are more likely to engage than moderate or liberal Protestants.

8. Consistent race differences are more evident on the education items than in any other arena. Controlling other things, predominantly African American congregations are significantly more likely than predominantly white congregations to engage in each of these education-related activities except sponsoring an elementary or high school. Beyond the education arena, predominantly black churches are significantly more likely than predominantly white churches to engage in only five of the activities listed in Table 4.1.

9. When denominational affiliation and other characteristics are held constant, congregations described by informants as theologically conservative are significantly different in the less engaged direction on thirteen of the activities listed in Table 4.1. On only one item are self-described conservative congregations significantly more likely to engage in a bridging activity: controlling for many characteristics, they are more likely to have had a group which attended a live musical or theatrical performance outside the congregation.

10. This section draws on Beyerlein and Chaves (2003). See that article for a more comprehensive bibliography on religion and politics and for additional detail regarding the analyses and results described in this chapter.

11. This literature is too vast to cite in its entirety. For representative examples, see Green et al. (1996); Guth et al. (1997); Harris (1999); Jelen (1992); Kohut et al. (2000); Leege and Kellstedt (1993); Manza and Brooks (1997); Olson and Carroll (1992); Olson (2000); Peterson (1992); Regnerus et al. (1999); Verba et al. (1995); Wald et al. (1988); and Wilcox (1996).

12. Rather than being based on nationally representative samples of congregations, research focusing on religious institutions and political activity has been based on case studies of religiously based political organizations (for example, Wilcox 1996); case studies of particular congregations (for example, Balmer 1993:chap. 8; Wood 1994; Park 1998); surveys of individuals within a relatively small number of congregations (for example, Jelen 1992; Wald et al. 1988); or congregations, clergy, or activists associated with a particular political or social movement (for example, McAdam 1982; Morris 1984; Smith 1996; Hart 2001).

13. Voter guide production and distribution is not unique to Christian right groups. The League of Women Voters, for example, distributes voter guides, as does Interfaith Alliance, an association of liberal and moderate Christians. When a congregational informant said that voter guides had been distributed, he or she also was asked who wrote or produced the guides. Responses to this open-ended question allowed NCS coders to determine whether the guides were produced by an organization associated with the religious right.

14. Another comparison point is offered by the Form 990 that some charities are required to file with the IRS. In 1998, only 1.5 percent of "public charities"—organizations with 501(c)(3) IRS status—reported lobbying expenditures on their Form 990. Looking at subtypes of these organizations, we find that 4.6 percent of environmental and animal-related organizations lobbied, as did 2.8 percent of health organizations, 1.1 percent of human service organizations, 0.8 percent of arts and cultural organizations, and 0.7 percent of mutual benefit associations (Boris and Krehely 2002:306). These numbers are much smaller than the survey-based numbers concerning nonprofits' political activity reported in the main text, probably because lobbying activity and expenditures are underreported to the IRS.

15. Note that this number is close, as it should be, to the comparable percentage from the NCS: 37 percent of individuals are in congregations in which people are told at worship services about opportunities for political activity.

16. Guth et al. (1997) have made a similar point concerning the political activities of white Protestant clergy.

17. The religious tradition differences evident in Table 4.3 are sustained when other important variables are controlled. Readers will not be substantively misled by focusing on the simple percentages in Table 4.3. See Beyerlein and Chaves (2003) for details on the multivariate analyses.

18. See, for example Hadden (1969); Quinley (1974).

19. Given the small number of synagogues in the sample, I refrain from attempting to characterize synagogue-based political activity beyond observing that synagogues seem at least as likely to be politically active as congregations within any Christian tradition.

20. Moreover, the liberal Protestant difference usually is not even much reduced by the presence of controls. In only four regression equations is the coefficient indicating that moderate and liberal Protestant congregations are more likely to engage in a public activity reduced by as much as 25 percent when all controls are added.

21. When the thirty items in Table 4.1 are separately regressed, with controls, on congregations' founding date, the coefficients associated with founding date indicate that more recent founding is associated with less bridging activity. In nine of these equations the coefficient is significant at least at the .10 level. The founding date coefficient is never significantly different from zero in the other direction. In no case, in other words, are younger congregations *more* likely than older congregations to engage in bridging activity.

5. Worship

1. From the social movements literature, see Tilly (1978, 1993) for analysis of changing repertoires of contentious collective action. From the culture literature, see Lamont (1992), Cerulo (1995), and Spillman (1997) for analysis of how social and institutional contexts influence which elements from available cultural repertoires are selected and deployed.

2. I know only whether or not each of these elements occurs in a worship service. The NCS did not collect data on the order in which these elements occur (or reoccur) in a service, so I am unable to use or develop strategies to analyze structure in sequences à la Cerulo (1995) or Abbott and Hrycak (1990).

3. I might add a third nearly universal practice to these two: collecting monetary contributions from the gathered. Unfortunately, the NCS did not ask whether or not an offering was taken at the most recent service.

4. This fact, especially the prominence of music and singing in congregational life, is part of what creates an intimate connection between congregations and the arts, a connection I explore in the next two chapters.

5. Some combinations of elements are more likely to occur simply because the specific elements themselves are more likely to occur. Any combination of elements that includes a sermon, for example, will be more likely to occur than a combination that does not include a sermon simply because virtually all worship services include a sermon or speech. But the likelihood of observing a particular combination of worship elements is not completely, or even strongly, determined simply by the relative frequency with which individual elements occur. In a loglinear analysis of each of the three-element combinations mentioned in the text, a model including two-way interactions fits the data massively better than a model that includes only the main effects. This means that the likelihood of observing these combinations in a worship service is not well predicted simply from knowing the frequency with which each element occurs.

6. See, for example, DiMaggio (1978), Bourdieu (1984), and Bryson (1996).

7. I refer here, of course, to the theory of "church" and "sect" in the sociology of religion. Early versions of this theory can be found in Troeltsch ([1911] 1981) and Niebuhr (1929). More recent formulations can be found in Stark and Bainbridge (1985), Iannaccone (1988), and Stark and Finke (2000).

8. Social scientists have used multidimensional spaces in a variety of ways (Péli and Nooteboom 1999:1132–33). In this chapter I draw most directly on the tools McPherson (1983b) has developed to locate organizations and cultural practices in two- (or more) dimensional spaces.

9. It is somewhat misleading to represent these two dimensions as orthogonal, but the correlation between the percent of adults in a congregation with B.A. degrees and the percent who are less than thirty-five years old is only $-.03$, so there is only a slight distortion in Figure 5.1.

10. For each pair of worship elements, I measure the social distance between them by the difference between the mean value on a social characteristic for one element in the pair and the mean value on that same social characteristic for the other element in the pair. In congregations using soloists in worship, for example, 23 percent of their adults, on average, have bachelor's degrees. In congregations with choirs, a relatively similar 26 percent of their adults have college degrees, but in congregations that speak in tongues, only 16 percent have college degrees. By this measure of social distance, the worship element "singing by soloist" is closer to "singing by choir" than to speaking in tongues. The former

distance is (26 − 23 =) 3; the latter distance is (23 − 16 =) 7. I operationalize the practice distance between elements with a simple correlation (multiplied by -1) measuring how often each pair of elements occurs jointly in the same congregation, and then I correlate the measure of social distance with the measure of practice distance. The correlation, for example, between the college degree distances among elements and the practice distances among elements is .35. This is the strongest correlation I have been able to find between a socio-demographic distance and a practice distance among worship elements. It remains strong even when distances on other dimensions are controlled. When I calculate the distances between each pair of points in Figure 5.1—the distance between worship elements in a social space defined by both education and age— the correlation between those distances and elements' distances in practice from each other is .37. Note that using this particular *two*-dimensional social distance increases the correlation with practice distance only slightly over the correlation using education as the single relevant dimension of social distance.

11. The correlations described in note 10 between the co-occurrence of pairs of worship elements in the same worship events and their proximity in social space can be construed as measures of the extent to which variation in congregations' worship practices is shaped by congregations' tendency toward social homogeneity. If congregations were no more socially homogeneous than the surrounding society, or if they were more socially homogeneous than the society but their social differences were unrelated to worship practices, these correlations would be zero.

12. See chap. 8 in Ducey (1977) for a description of how various individuals within congregations work together to produce worship services.

13. See Whitehouse (1995:203–217) for a comparison of some of these accounts.

14. Interestingly, enthusiasm correlates positively with the length of a worship service (.46) and with the proportion of attenders who attend more than one worship service in a week (.23). Ceremony, by contrast, correlates negatively with both of these measures of more intensive religious participation (−.06 with service length and −.29 with the proportion of attenders attending more than one service). More enthusiastic worship tends to go with more intensely gathered congregations.

15. I use the dimensions extracted from the factor analysis to investigate the connections between religious traditions and worship practices. These factors represent the ceremonial and enthusiasm dimensions of worship in a way that is somewhat more abstract than a representation based simply on counting how many of the relevant elements appear in a given worship service. The factor scales, however, have the advantage of

being constructed so as to be empirically independent of each other, meaning that a particular worship event's score on the enthusiasm dimension is unrelated to its score on the ceremony scale.

16. Religious traditions are placed in this space by calculating the mean and standard deviation on the ceremony and enthusiasm factors for congregations within each tradition. The midpoint of a tradition's box represents the mean value of its congregations on each of the two dimensions. I then draw one–standard deviation boxes around these means. That is, the height of each box represents the mean plus or minus .5 standard deviations on ceremony, and the width of each box represents the mean plus or minus .5 standard deviations on enthusiasm. Since the overall mean of each factor is zero, one can tell whether a tradition is above or below average on either of the two dimensions by noting where it falls relative to the zero line on each axis. More important, however, are traditions' positions relative to one another. I place only selected major traditions on this figure to avoid excessive clutter. No interpretations or conclusions depend on the particular subset of denominations and traditions represented in this figure.

17. This approach both follows and extends McPherson (1983b). The extension is that I place denominations in a *cultural practice* space rather than in a *socio-demographic* space. This enables a richer kind of ecological analysis, not least because it enables comparisons between denominations' positions in social space and their positions in cultural space.

18. Denominational differences remain strong and significant when congregations' scores on each of these two dimensions are regressed on denominational dummy variables while controlling for congregations' size; race, social class, and age composition; region; urban versus rural location; founding date; and whether or not the congregation is led by a clergyperson with a graduate degree. Most of the social and organizational variables also are significant in these models. Even when denominational dummy variables are included, a congregation's size, race and age composition, region, and founding date significantly predict the levels of both enthusiasm and ceremony in its worship. Social class composition predicts the level of enthusiasm but not ceremony, and urban versus rural location and whether or not the congregation is led by a clergyperson with a graduate degree predict the level of ceremony.

19. The Jehovah's Witness location reflects the pedagogical nature of Witness worship, with much Bible study and question-and-answer-style review of theological principles.

20. See Stark and Finke (2000) for a recent version of this sort of account.

21. See, for example, the research summarized and cited in Hannan and Freeman (1989) and Singh and Lumsden (1990). Sandell (2001) found that change over sixty years in average congregational size within Sweden's free church movement was consistent with the ecological assumptions that an individual congregation's initial size did not change over time, and that change over time in average congregational size was produced only by turnover within the population of congregations—by births and deaths in congregations of different sizes.

22. Although neither Baptist nor Pentecostal worship overlaps Catholic worship in Figure 5.2, the denominational boxes are drawn with a window of only one standard deviation around the ceremony and enthusiasm means. Baptist and Pentecostal worship overlaps Catholic worship nearer the tails of these distributions. There are Catholic worship services in which people speak in tongues.

23. Thanks to Laura Stephens for analyzing changes over time in the Presbyterian Directory for Worship. The strong impression of historical continuity in the directory created by this numerical analysis is confirmed by Hall's (1994) narrative history of the Directory for Worship. A nuance: change occurred in only eighteen years between 1788 and 2002, but in some of those years changes were made to several sections of the directory.

24. A study of conflict in twenty-four Chicago-area congregations found that almost 20 percent were about worship or ritual practices (Becker 1999:38). A national survey of clergy found that 11 percent of reported conflicts were about worship (McMillan 2002). Conflict over worship style is not new to American religion. In 1780 one Ezra Barker complained in a letter: "But they so suddenly exchanged old tunes for new ones and introduced them in the Publick Worship and the old ones being neglected it was but a few that could bear a part in the delightful part of Divine Worship. The old singers became uneasy and began to complain and not without cause . . . Some tunes were introduced soon which by some were thought not fit to be used in so Solemn Worship. Several have showed their dislike by going out" (Smith 1931:784–785).

25. This point recalls Stinchcombe's argument that "organizational types generally originate rapidly in a relatively short historical period, to grow and change slowly after that period," and so "the time at which this period of rapid growth took place is highly correlated with the present characteristics of organizations of the type." This is because "organizations which are founded at a particular time must construct their social systems with the social resources available" (Stinchcombe 1965:168). Something similar seems to apply to religious traditions and their worship practices. Stinchcombe's observation that organizations' structural

characteristics reflect early imprinting may apply with equal force to their cultural practices.

26. See note 18 for details.

27. Others have drawn on ecological language and imagery when studying religion, but not in the way I do here. Eiesland (2000), for example, uses ecological language to call attention to cooperation among religious organizations. Elsewhere, an ecological approach to studying religion is equated with explicit recognition of religious organizations' social and institutional contexts (Eiesland and Warner 1998:40), or used metaphorically to emphasize themes of organizational adaptability and resource dependence (Ammerman 1997a:346–347). I use "ecological" to refer to an analytical framework in which religious organizations' niches can be precisely identified and in which questions about organizational change and competition can be pursued via analysis of these niches and their relations to one another.

28. See, for example, Mohr and Duquenne (1997), Mohr (1998), and Breiger (2000) for other ways to analyze cultural practices.

6. The Arts

1. There is, however, a recent resurgence of scholarly interest in the connections between art and religion, much of it prompted by the Luce Foundation. See, for example, Brown (2000); Arthurs and Wallach (2001); Morgan and Promey (2001); Wuthnow (2003a); Marti (forthcoming:chap. 4).

2. Although she did not try to characterize the difference between art and religion, Joyce Carol Oates's (2000:30) description of the Golden Triangle area of East Texas clearly communicates the common assumption that the two now are fundamentally different: "There was no cultural life in the Golden Triangle, or the acknowledgment of its absence, unless churchgoing (among whites, predominantly Baptist) constituted culture."

3. These percentages are noticeably larger than those reported by Wuthnow (2003a:143), perhaps because the church members surveyed by Wuthnow concerning what goes on in their congregations are less likely to define certain practices as "drama" or "dance" than are the key informants, mainly clergy, who reported on worship elements for the NCS.

4. Providing exhibit space arguably exposes congregants to art, but providing rehearsal space to outside groups probably does not. Items like these that involve the mere use of a congregation's building by an outside group perhaps should not be included in a list of "bridging" arts activities.

I include them here nonetheless because they represent a type of openness to the world outside the congregation. Similarly, I included the presence of any outside group using or renting space in a congregation's building among the civic activities listed in Table 4.1

5. Bonding arts activities also occur outside worship, as when a group of members puts on a play or a show or a concert attended largely by other members of the congregation. Fifty-five percent of attenders are in congregations with this sort of group.

6. The rest of this chapter is based on Chaves and Marsden (2000).

7. On how social variables shape artistic consumption and production, see, for example, Marsden et al. (1982); Bourdieu (1984); Greeley (1996); DiMaggio and Ostrower (1990); Netzer (1992); DiMaggio (1996); Schmalzbauer (1999); Marsden (2001); and Wuthnow (2003a). DiMaggio (1996) found religious differences in museum attendance; Greeley (1996) found religious differences in musical tastes; Marsden et al. (1982), Marsden (2001), and Wuthnow (2003a) report religious differences in levels of artistic activity.

8. Promey (2001:192) makes this point about Protestants and images: "There are, in fact, no documented instances of American Protestantism in which images are entirely absent. Rather, over and over again, a larger visual-symbolic strategy emerges that dislodges certain kinds of images while granting other visual expressions greater authority."

9. The items in the bottom section of Table 6.1 are the same bridging items included in the "cultural activities" section of Table 4.1. The numbers here are slightly different from the numbers in that table because here I distinguish predominantly African American Protestant congregations from predominantly white Protestant congregations. I include synagogues in this table for the sake of comprehensiveness, but the numbers should be interpreted cautiously. As in Chapter 4, I mention Jewish numbers in the text only when comparison seems reasonably safe even in light of the wide confidence intervals around these percentages.

10. This same pattern emerges when an ideological rather than institutional indicator of the liberal-conservative split is used. Congregations endorsing biblical inerrancy are more similar to non-inerrantist congregations on nonbridging arts activities than on bridging arts activities. Congregations endorsing inerrancy are significantly less likely to engage in bridging forms of artistic activity.

11. This conclusion is based on two regression equations, one in which the dependent variable is a scale created by summing the items in the top section of Table 6.1, the other in which the dependent variable is a scale created by summing the items in the bottom section of Table 6.1. Each model specifies religious tradition with a set of four dummy vari-

ables indicating Catholic, moderate and liberal Protestant, Jewish, and other, with conservative and evangelical Protestants as the reference category. Each model includes controls for congregations' racial composition, geographic region, size, income and educational composition, founding date, urban versus rural location, social class composition of the congregation's neighborhood, and whether or not the congregation endorses biblical inerrancy. When the dependent variable is the nonbridging arts scale, the only statistically significant religious tradition effect is the negative coefficient associated with the Catholic dummy variable. When the dependent variable is the bridging arts scale, the coefficients associated with the Catholic, moderate and liberal Protestant, and Jewish dummy variables all are significant. Catholics do significantly less bridging arts activity than conservative Protestants; liberal Protestants and Jews do significantly more.

12. Similarly, Wuthnow found that Catholic parishioners are significantly less likely than Protestant churchgoers to report that their congregation has choirs, dramatic performances, or musical performances outside of worship (Wuthnow 2003a:143).

13. The relevant regression equation is described in note 11.

14. From this perspective, the cult classic *Why Catholics Can't Sing* (Day 1990), is mis-titled. Catholics *can* sing, they just do less of it in church.

15. This race difference in nonbridging arts activities—black congregations do more of this than white congregations—cuts across religious traditions, which is why I consider these to be differences in race-based cultural practice more than differences in religious tradition. In certain dimensions of worship style, as well as in other aspects of American life, race trumps religion as a social influence.

16. The R^2 for the bridging regression equation is .32 versus .20 for the nonbridging equation. It might also be that variation in nonbridging arts activities is structured by variables other than the ones included in these models rather than, as I say in the main text, that variation in those activities is less systematically structured than variation in the bridging arts activities.

17. Here I combine two observations offered by commentators on Chaves and Marsden (2000). The observation that liberal bridging arts activities may increase cultural inequality was offered by R. Stephen Warner; the observation that conservative avoidance of these activities may reflect an effort to substitute one sort of capital for another as the basis for cultural stratification was offered by Paul DiMaggio.

18. The extent to which music, dance, drama, and other artistic activities are experienced as art when they occur within congregations, either

as part of religious ritual or elsewhere, is a fascinating empirical question to which I return in the next chapter.

7. Culture in Congregations, Congregations in Culture

1. Even this figure overstates the number of people meeting in small groups for purposes other than worship, religious education, or administration, since many of the groups mentioned in response to an NCS question about groups that meet at least monthly were for Bible study or other religious education. The median participation level of fifteen people includes these religious education groups, which means that fewer than fifteen people, on average, participate in groups that meet at least monthly for purposes other than worship, religious education, or administration. The NCS asked how many people participated in *any* groups mentioned in response to this item, so I am not able to distinguish participation levels in groups of different sorts. Separate items asked about participation specifically in worship services, social service activities, religious education classes, and choirs.

2. See Warner (1997) for an exploration of this aspect of religious ritual.

3. There is reason to think that the arts are prominent in individual as well as in collective religious practice. Forty-three percent of people who pray listen to music or sing when they pray, 23 percent look at an art object, and 20 percent read poetry or literature. Fifty-six percent do at least one of these when they pray, compared with 40 percent who, when praying, read the Bible and 32 percent who, when praying, read a devotional guide (Wuthnow 2003a:88).

4. Author's calculations from the 1998 General Social Survey (Davis and Smith 2000).

5. Ninety-five percent of the two thirds of the population that attended religious services in the past year is 64 percent of the total population, 90 percent of the two thirds who are attenders is 60 percent of the population, and so on.

6. Unless otherwise noted, here and throughout this chapter all figures concerning Americans' participation in arts events are from either Marsden (1999) or National Endowment for the Arts (1998).

7. Most of the figures in this paragraph are reported in National Endowment for the Arts (1998). Some were calculated by the author directly from the survey data.

8. The site-specific numbers in Table 7.2 were provided to the author by the Urban Institute. The averages are from Walker (2002:4) and may

differ slightly from the arithmetic mean of the site-specific numbers reported in this table.

9. The last three figures are from table 13.1 of Verba et al. (1995:373). The first figure is the author's calculation based on pieces of data provided elsewhere in that book.

10. Another potential complication here is that I am limiting my attention to live artistic activities, whereas Verba et al. (1995) did not limit their attention to face-to-face political invitations. It might be that congregations provide a larger share of *face-to-face* political cues than of *all* political cues, whatever the manner of their delivery.

11. These numbers are calculated by multiplying the proportions in table 11.2 from Verba et al. (1995:312) by the proportions of people who have jobs and are church members. The latter figures are given below the table.

12. Comparisons involving education and income would be more directly relevant here than comparisons involving race and ethnicity. The Urban Institute data, however, were not yet publicly available as of the time of writing this book, and the ethnicity comparison is the only one reported so far in published material. The NEA data are publicly available, but unfortunately they are not suitable for pursuing this question.

13. The Lehigh Valley study also found that people with *less* acute financial needs are more likely than people with greater need to seek help from congregations.

14. The national Head Start figure is the author's calculation from the 2002 Head Start *Program Information Report* data. These data are available from Xtria in McLean, Virginia. The Arizona figure is the author's calculation from data described in Nagle (2001).

15. *Almost* no one will be surprised at this. Hodgkinson and Weitzman (1992:105) conclude that "almost as many congregations offered programs in human services as offered religious services and religious education." This conclusion is repeated uncritically in Glenn (2000:10).

8. Beyond Congregations

1. This is a version of a more general process noted by organizational sociologists (Cohen et al. 1972). In organizations with vague goals, unclear technologies, and a fluid set of participants, the problems that are pursued will be determined more by the particular and perhaps idiosyncratic concerns of the most interested individuals rather than by a rational process in which programs are developed in response to well-understood preexisting problems. Lines of action are pursued more because people

inside the organization want to pursue them than because they are the most appropriate responses to organizational or community problems.

2. This account of denominational sources of congregational structure and activity recalls DiMaggio's and Powell's (1983) argument about the coercive, mimetic, and normative sources of isomorphism among organizations within an institutional field.

3. See Boylan (1988) on Sunday schools; Coble (2001) on youth groups; Hood (1846) on choirs; Harris (1992) on gospel choirs; and Hill (1985) on women's mission societies.

Appendix A

1. Independent Sector's 1992 study represents the one major effort to draw a nationally representative sample of congregations using telephone books as the sampling frame. This is a laudable effort, and there is much useful information in the Independent Sector data (Hodgkinson and Weitzman 1992). At the same time, the combination of a telephone book sampling frame and low response rate (19 percent) makes this sample substantially biased toward large congregations.

2. This procedure was described in McPherson (1982), and it has been used to sample both employing organizations (Kalleberg et al. 1996; Bridges and Villemez 1994; Parcel et al. 1991) and voluntary associations (McPherson 1983a).

3. Readers who want more methodological detail than is provided here will find it in Chaves et al. (1999).

4. Weighting inversely proportional to congregational size means that a weight of 1/1,000 is applied to a 1,000-person congregation, a weight of 1/100 is applied to a 100-person congregation, and so on. These weights undo the overrepresentation of large congregations in this sample, and applying them enables description of the congregational population that treats each congregation, whatever its size, as one unit in that population.

5. The 80 percent response rate for the NCS is calculated using the conservative "RR3" method recommended by the American Association for Public Opinion Research (1998:18–19). This rate includes in the denominator the number of congregations of unknown sample eligibility that we estimate would have been eligible for sample inclusion if we had complete information. If we assume that *all* congregations of unknown eligibility would be eligible for sample inclusion, and therefore include all of the (126) eligibility-unknown congregations in the denominator of the response rate, the NCS response rate still would be 77 percent. (This is

the "minimum response rate" as defined by the American Association for Public Opinion Research.) Our cooperation rate—the percentage of congregations contacted that participated in the NCS—was 85 percent.

6. Half of the GSS respondents who named a congregation were also asked, "About how many members does this congregation have?" When both the GSS respondent's size report and the NCS informant's size report are logged, the two reports are correlated at about .7. Logging is appropriate because a constant, say, 10 percent discrepancy between two reports implies a much larger discrepancy in absolute value among bigger congregations (where one report might say 1,000 people and another 1,100 people) than among smaller congregations (where one report might say 100 people and another 110 people). Logging the size estimates treats the percentage difference between the two estimates as more important than the absolute value difference.

7. We did not, for example, include items of this sort: "How true is it that members/participants of your congregation are very excited and enthusiastic about the congregation's future?" or "How true is it that your congregation feels like one large, close-knit family?"

8. We did not, for example, include items of this sort: "How important is it to your congregation's sense of mission that you provide a close, family-like atmosphere?" or "How important is it to your congregation's sense of mission that you help the poor and those in need?"

References

Abbott, Andrew, and Alexandra Hrycak. 1990. "Measuring Resemblance in Sequence Data: An Optimal Matching Analysis of Musicians' Careers." *American Journal of Sociology* 96:144–185.

Ackerman, David M., and Vee Burke. 2001. *Public Aid and Faith-Based Organizations (Charitable Choice): An Overview*. Washington, DC: Congressional Research Service Report RS20809.

Ahlstrom, Sydney E. 1972. *A Religious History of the American People*. New Haven, CT: Yale University Press.

American Association for Public Opinion Research. 1998. *Standard Definitions: Final Dispositions of Case Codes and Outcome Rates for RDD Telephone Surveys and In-Person Household Surveys*. Ann Arbor: American Association for Public Opinion Research.

American Sociological Review. 1998. Symposium. 63, no. 1 (February):111–145.

Ammerman, Nancy. 1987. *Bible Believers: Fundamentalists in the Modern World*. New Brunswick, NJ: Rutgers University Press.

———. 1997a. *Congregation and Community*. New Brunswick, NJ: Rutgers University Press.

———. 1997b. "Organized Religion in a Voluntaristic Society." *Sociology of Religion* 58:203–215.

———. 2000. "Congregations and their Partners in Social Service Delivery: Methods and Findings from the Organizing Religious Work Project." Paper presented at the Association for Research on Nonprofit Organizations and Voluntary Action meetings, November, New Orleans.

———. 2002. "Connecting Mainline Protestant Churches with Public Life." In *The Quiet Hand of God: Faith-Based Activism and the Public Role of Mainline Protestantism*, edited by Robert Wuthnow and John H. Evans, 129–158. Berkeley: University of California Press.

———. Forthcoming. *Pillars of Faith: American Congregations and their Partners, Building Traditions, Building Communities*. Berkeley: University of California Press.

Anderson, Scott, John Orr, and Carol Silverman. 2000. *Can We Make Welfare Reform Work? The California Religious Community Capacity Study*. Sacramento: California Council of Churches.

Arthurs, Alberta, and Glenn Wallach, eds. 2001. *Crossroads: Art and Religion in American Life*. New York: New Press.

Austensen, Blake. 2001. "A Look at Faith-Based Programs." In *The Welfare Peer Technical Assistance Network*. Conference report, October, Indianapolis.

Balmer, Randall. 1993. *Mine Eyes Have Seen the Glory*. Expanded edition. New York: Oxford University Press.

Bane, Mary Jo, Brent Coffin, and Ronald Thiemann, eds. 2000. *Who Will Provide? The Changing Role of Religion in American Social Welfare*. Boulder: Westview Press.

Bankston, Carl L. III, and Min Zhou. 2000. "De Facto Congregationalism and Socioeconomic Mobility in Laotian and Vietnamese Immigrant Communities: A Study of Religious Institutions and Economic Change." *Review of Religious Research* 41:453–470.

Bartkowski, John P., and Helen A. Regis. 1999. *Religious Organizations, Anti-poverty Relief, and Charitable Choice: A Feasibility Study of Faith-Based Welfare Reform in Mississippi*. Arlington, VA: Pricewaterhouse-Coopers Endowment.

———. 2003. *Charitable Choices: Religion, Race, and Poverty in the Post-welfare Era*. New York: New York University Press.

Baum, Joel A. C., and Stephen J. Mezias. 1992. "Localized Competition and Organizational Failure in the Manhattan Hotel Industry, 1898–1990. *Administrative Science Quarterly* 37:580–604.

Becker, Laura L. 1982. "Ministers vs. Laymen: The Singing Controversy in Puritan New England, 1720–1740." *New England Quarterly* 55:79–96.

Becker, Penny Edgell. 1999. *Congregations in Conflict: Cultural Models of Local Religious Life*. New York: Cambridge University Press.

Becker, Penny Edgell, and Mark Chaves. 2000. "How Good Are Telephone Listings for Sampling Congregations?" Department of Sociology, University of Arizona.

Becker, Penny Edgell, Stephen J. Ellingson, Richard W. Flory, Wendy Griswold, Fred Kniss, and Timothy Nelson. 1993. "Straining at the Tie That Binds: Congregational Conflict in the 1980s." *Review of Religious Research* 34:193–209.

Benedict, Ruth. 1934. *Patterns of Culture.* London: Routledge and Kegan Paul.

Berezin, Mabel. 1994. "Cultural Form and Political Meaning: State-Subsidized Theater, Ideology, and the Language of Style in Fascist Italy." *American Journal of Sociology* 99:1237–86.

Berry, Jeffrey M. 2003. *A Voice for Nonprofits.* Washington, DC: Brookings Institution Press.

Beyerlein, Kraig, and Mark Chaves. 2003. "The Political Activities of Religious Congregations in the United States." *Journal for the Scientific Study of Religion* 42:229–246.

Beyerlein, Kraig, and John R. Hipp. 2003. "Civic Activism among U.S. Religious Traditions: What They Do and Why They Do It." Paper presented at the Society for the Scientific Study of Religion meetings, October, Norfolk, VA.

Biddle, Jeff E. 1992. "Religious Organizations." In *Who Benefits from the Nonprofit Sector?* edited by Charles T. Clotfelter, 92–133. Chicago: University of Chicago Press.

Billingsley, Andrew. 1999. *Mighty Like a River: The Black Church and Social Reform.* New York: Oxford University Press.

Bogle, Mary M. 2001. "The Involvement of Religious Congregations in Early Child Care and Education in the U.S." Washington, DC: Brookings Institution.

Boris, Elizabeth T., and Jeff Krehely. 2002. "Civic Participation and Advocacy." In *The State of Nonprofit America*, edited by Lester Salamon, 299–330. Washington, DC: Brookings Institution Press.

Bourdieu, Pierre. 1984. *Distinction: A Social Critique of the Judgement of Taste*, translated by Richard Nice. Cambridge, MA: Harvard University Press.

Bowen, Howard R., and Jack H. Schuster. 1986. *American Professors: A National Resource Imperiled.* New York: Oxford University Press.

Boylan, Anne M. 1988. *Sunday School: The Formation of an American Institution, 1790–1880.* New Haven: Yale University Press.

Breiger, Ronald L. 2000. "A Tool Kit for Practice Theory." *Poetics* 27:91–115.

———. 2002. "Relation of Denominations' Similarity on Practices to Switching Behavior." Memorandum, July 28. Department of Sociology, University of Arizona, Tucson.

Bridges, William P., and Wayne J. Villemez. 1994. *The Employment Rela-*

tionship: Causes and Consequences of Modern Personnel Administration.
New York: Plenum.

Brody, Evelyn. 1997. "Charitable Endowments and the Democratization
of Dynasty." *Arizona Law Review* 39:873–948.

Brown, Frank Burch. 2000. *Good Taste, Bad Taste, and Christian Taste: Aesthetics in Religious Life.* New York: Oxford University Press.

Bruce, Steve. 1990. *Pray TV: Televangelism in America.* London:
Routledge.

Brunette-Hill, Sandi, and Roger Finke. 1999. "A Time for Every Purpose: Updating and Extending Blizzard's Survey on Clergy Time
Allocation." *Review of Religious Research* 41:47–63.

Brunner, Edmund deS. 1923a. *Church Life in the Rural South: A Study of
the Opportunity of Protestantism Based upon Data from Seventy
Counties.* New York: Negro Universities Press.

———, ed. 1923b. *Churches of Distinction in Town and Country.* New
York: George H. Doran Company.

Burke, Vee. 2001. "Comparison of Proposed Charitable Choice Act of
2001 with Current Charitable Choice Law." Order Code RL31030.
Washington, DC: Congressional Research Service, Library of Congress.

Burns, Jeffrey M. 1994. "¿Qué es esto? The Transformation of St. Peter's Parish, San Francisco, 1913–1990." In *American Congregations.*
Volume 1. *Portraits of Twelve Religious Communities,* edited by James
P. Wind and James W. Lewis, 396–463. Chicago: University of Chicago Press.

Bush, George W. 2001a. "Agency Responsibilities with Respect to
Faith-Based and Community Initiatives." Executive Order 13198.
Federal Register 66 (January 31):8495–98.

———. 2001b. "Establishment of White House Office of Faith-Based
and Community Initiatives." Executive Order 13199. *Federal Register* 66 (January 31):8499–8500.

Byrnes, Timothy A. 1991. *Catholic Bishops in American Politics.* Princeton:
Princeton University Press.

Byrnes, Timothy A., and Mary C. Segers, eds. 1992. *The Catholic Church
and the Politics of Abortion.* Boulder: Westview Press.

Bryson, Bethany. 1996. "'Anything but Heavy Metal': Symbolic
Exclusion and Musical Dislikes." *American Sociological Review*
61:884–899.

Caldwell, Cleopatra Howard, Linda M. Chatters, Andrew Billingsley,
and Robert Joseph Taylor. 1995. "Church-Based Support Programs
for Elderly Black Adults: Congregational and Clergy Characteristics." In *Aging, Spirituality, and Religion: A Handbook,* edited by

Melvin A. Kimble, Susan H. McFadden, James W. Ellor, and James J. Seeber, 306–324. Minneapolis: Fortress Press.

Calvin, John. [1537] 1954. "Articles Concerning the Organization of the Church and of Worship at Geneva." In *Calvin: Theological Treatises*, translated and edited by J. K. S. Reid, 48–55. Volume 22 of *The Library of Christian Classics*. Philadelphia: Westminster Press.

Carlson-Thies, Stanley. 1999. "Faith-Based Institutions Cooperating with Public Welfare: The Promise of the Charitable Choice Provision." In *Welfare Reform and Faith-Based Organizations*, edited by D. Davis and B. Hankins, 29–60. Waco, TX: J. M. Dawson Institute of Church-State Studies.

Carroll, Glenn R. 1985. "Concentration and Specialization: Dynamics of Niche Width in Populations of Organizations." *American Journal of Sociology* 90:1262–83.

Carroll, Jackson W., and Becky R. McMillan. 2002. "Pulpit and Pew: Preliminary Statistical Tables." Duke University Divinity School.

Cerulo, Karen A. 1995. *Identity Designs: The Sights and Sounds of a Nation.* New Brunswick, NJ: Rutgers University Press.

Chang, Patricia M. Y., David R. Williams, Ezra E. H. Griffith, and John Young. 1994. "Church-Agency Relationships in the Black Community." *Nonprofit and Voluntary Sector Quarterly* 23:91–105.

Chaves, Mark. 1997. "Secularization: A Luhmannian Reflection." *Soziale Systeme* 3:439–449.

——. 2002. "Religious Organizations: Data Resources and Research Opportunities." *American Behavioral Scientist* 45:1523–49.

Chaves, Mark, and James C. Cavendish. 1994. "More Evidence on U.S. Catholic Church Attendance." *Journal for the Scientific Study of Religion* 33:376–381.

Chaves, Mark, Helen Giesel, and William Tsitsos. 2002. "Religious Variations in Public Presence: Evidence from the National Congregations Study." In *The Quiet Hand of God: Faith-Based Activism and the Public Role of Mainline Protestantism*, edited by Robert Wuthnow and John H. Evans, 108–128. Berkeley: University of California Press.

Chaves, Mark, Mary Ellen Konieczny, Kraig Beyerlein, and Emily Barman. 1999. "The National Congregations Study: Background, Methods, and Selected Results." *Journal for the Scientific Study of Religion* 38:458–476.

Chaves, Mark, and Peter V. Marsden. 2000. "Congregations and Cultural Capital: Religious Variations in Arts Activity." Paper presented at the American Sociological Association meetings, August, Washington, DC.

Chaves, Mark, and Laura Stephens. 2003. "Church Attendance in the United States." In *Handbook of the Sociology of Religion*, edited by Michele Dillon, 85–95. New York: Cambridge University Press.

Chaves, Mark, Laura Stephens, and Joseph Galaskiewicz. 2004. "Does Government Funding Suppress Nonprofits' Political Activity?" *American Sociological Review* 69:forthcoming.

Chaves, Mark, and William Tsitsos. 2001. "Congregations and Social Services: What They Do, How They Do It, and with Whom." *Nonprofit and Voluntary Sector Quarterly* 30:660–683.

Chwe, Michael Suk-Young. 2001. *Rational Ritual: Culture, Coordination, and Common Knowledge*. Princeton: Princeton University Press.

Cnaan, Ram A. 1997. *Social and Community Involvement of Religious Congregations Housed in Historic Religious Properties: Findings from a Six-City Study*. Philadelphia: University of Pennsylvania School of Social Work.

———. 2000. *Keeping Faith in the City: How 401 Urban Religious Congregations Serve Their Neediest Neighbors*. Philadelphia: Center for Research on Religion and Urban Civil Society.

Cnaan, Ram A., with Robert J. Wineburg and Stephanie C. Boddie. 1999. *The Newer Deal: Social Work and Religion in Partnership*. New York: Columbia University Press.

Coble, Christopher Lee. 2001. "Where Have All the Young People Gone? The Christian Endeavor Movement and the Training of Protestant Youth, 1881–1918." Ph.D. dissertation, Harvard University.

Cohen, Michael D., James G. March, and Johan P. Olsen. 1972. "A Garbage Can Model of Organizational Choice." *Administrative Science Quarterly* 17:1–25.

Cormode, D. Scott. 1992. "A Financial History of Presbyterian Congregations since World War II." In *The Organizational Revolution: Presbyterians and American Denominationalism*, edited by Milton J. Coalter, John M. Mulder, and Louis B. Weeks, 171–198. Louisville: Westminster/John Knox Press.

Coughlin, Bernard J. 1965. *Church and State in Social Welfare*. New York: Columbia University Press.

D'Agostino, Peter R. 2000. "Catholic Planning for a Multicultural Metropolis, 1982–1996." In *Public Religion and Urban Transformation: Faith in the City*, edited by Lowell W. Livezey, 269–291. New York: New York University Press.

Davis, James Allan, and Tom W. Smith. 2000. *General Social Surveys, 1972–2000*. Chicago: National Opinion Research Center.

Day, Thomas. 1990. *Why Catholics Can't Sing: The Culture of Catholicism and the Triumph of Bad Taste.* New York: Crossroad.

Department of Health and Human Services. 2001a. "Fiscal Year (FY) 2001 Funding Opportunities." *Federal Register* 66 (March 20):15733–35.

———. 2001b. "Changes to a Fiscal Year (FY) 2001 Funding Opportunities Notice." *Federal Register* 66 (May 24):28757–58.

DiMaggio, Paul. 1978. "Social Class and Arts Consumption: The Origins and Consequences of Class Differences in Exposure to the Arts in America." *Theory and Society* 5:141–161.

———. 1985. "The World of Foods." Review of *Food in the Social Order: Studies of Food and Festivities in Three American Communities*, edited by Mary Douglas. *Contemporary Society* 14:555–557.

———. 1996. "Are Art-Museum Visitors Different from Other People? The Relationship between Attendance and Social and Political Attitudes in the United States." *Poetics* 24:161–180.

DiMaggio, Paul, Wendy Cadge, Lynn Robinson, and Brian Steensland. 2001. "The Role of Religion in Public Conflicts over the Arts in the Philadelphia Area, 1965–1997." In *Crossroads: Art and Religion in American Life*, edited by Alberta Arthurs and Glenn Wallach, 103–137. New York: New Press.

DiMaggio, Paul, and Francie Ostrower. 1990. "Participation in the Arts by Black and White Americans." *Social Forces* 68:753–778.

DiMaggio, Paul, and Walter W. Powell. 1983. "The Iron Cage Revisited: Institutional Isomorphism and Collective Rationality in Organizational Fields." *American Sociological Review* 48:147–160.

DiMaggio, Paul, and Michael Useem. 1978. "Social Class and Arts Consumption: The Origins and Consequences of Class Differences in Exposure to the Arts in America." *Theory and Society* 5:141–161.

Dionne, E. J. Jr., and Ming Hsu Chen, eds. 2001. *Sacred Places, Civic Purposes: Should Government Help Faith-Based Charity?* Washington, DC: Brookings Institution Press.

Douglas, Mary. 1999. *Implicit Meanings: Selected Essays in Anthropology.* 2d ed. London: Routledge.

Douglass, H. Paul. 1926. *1,000 City Churches.* New York: George H. Doran Company.

———. 1927. *The Church in the Changing City.* New York: George H. Doran Company.

Douglass, H. Paul, and Edmund deS. Brunner. 1935. *The Protestant Church as a Social Institution.* New York: Harper and Brothers.

Ducey, Michael H. 1977. *Sunday Morning: Aspects of Urban Ritual.* New York: Free Press.

Dudley, Carl S. N.d. "Welfare, Faith-Based Ministries, and Charitable Choice." Hartford Institute for Religion Research, Hartford Seminary, Hartford, CT.

Dudley, Carl S., and David A. Roozen. 2001. *Faith Communities Today: A Report on Religion in the United States Today.* Hartford, CT: Hartford Seminary.

Ebaugh, Helen Rose, and Janet Saltzman Chafetz. 2000a. "Structural Adaptations in Immigrant Congregations." *Sociology of Religion* 61:135–153.

———. 2000b. *Religion and the New Immigrants: Continuities and Adaptations in Immigrant Congregations.* Walnut Creek, CA: AltaMira Press.

Ebaugh, Helen Rose, and Paula Pipes. 1998. "Immigrant Congregations as Social Service Providers: Are They Safety Nets for Welfare Reform?" Paper presented at the annual meetings of the Association for the Sociology of Religion, August, San Francisco.

Eisinger, Peter. 2002. "Organizational Capacity and Organizational Effectiveness among Street-Level Food Assistance Programs." *Nonprofit and Voluntary Sector Quarterly* 31:115–130.

Eiesland, Nancy L. 2000. *A Particular Place: Urban Restructuring and Religious Ecology in a Southern Exurb.* New Brunswick, NJ: Rutgers University Press.

Eiesland, Nancy, and R. Stephen Warner. 1998. "Ecology: Seeing the Congregation in Context." In *Studying Congregations: A New Handbook*, edited by Nancy T. Ammerman, Jackson W. Carroll, Carl S. Dudley, and William McKinney, 40–77. Nashville: Abingdon Press.

Farnsley, Arthur Emery II. 2000. "Congregations, Local Knowledge, and Devolution." *Review of Religious Research* 42:96–110.

———. 2001. "Can Faith-Based Organizations Compete?" *Nonprofit and Voluntary Sector Quarterly* 30:99–111.

Fichter, Joseph H. 1951. *Dynamics of a City Church.* Chicago: University of Chicago Press.

Finke, Roger, and Rodney Stark. 1992. *The Churching of America, 1776–1990: Winners and Losers in Our Religious Economy.* New Brunswick, NJ: Rutgers University Press.

Fiorina, Morris P. 1999. "Extreme Voices: A Dark Side of Civic Engagement." In *Civic Engagement in American Democracy*, edited by Theda Skocpol and Morris Fiorina, 395–425. Washington, DC: Brookings Institution Press and New York: Russell Sage.

Flynt, Wayne. 1994. "'A Special Feeling of Closeness': Mt. Hebron Baptist Church, Leeds, Alabama." In *American Congregations.* Volume 1. *Portraits of Twelve Religious Communities*, edited by James P. Wind and James W. Lewis, 103–158. Chicago: University of Chicago Press.

Foley, Michael W., and Bob Edwards. 1997. "Escape from Politics? Social Theory and the Social Capital Debate." *American Behavioral Scientist* 40:550–561.

Freedman, Samuel G. 1993. *Upon This Rock: The Miracles of a Black Church.* New York: HarperCollins.

Frumkin, Peter. 2002. *On Being Nonprofit: A Conceptual and Policy Primer.* Cambridge, MA: Harvard University Press.

Frumkin, Peter, and Alice Andre-Clark. 2000. "When Missions, Markets, and Politics Collide: Values and Strategy in the Nonprofit Human Services." *Nonprofit and Voluntary Sector Quarterly* 29 (supplement):141–163.

Galaskiewicz, Joseph. 1997. "An Urban Grants Economy Revisited: Corporate Charitable Contributions in the Twin Cities, 1979–81, 1987–89." *Administrative Science Quarterly* 42:445–471.

Galaskiewicz, Joseph, Myron Dowell, and Wolfgang Bielefeld. 1997. "Testing Theories of Organizational Growth." Paper presented at the American Sociological Association meetings, August, Toronto.

Gallup, George Jr., and D. Michael Lindsay. 1999. *Surveying the Religious Landscape: Trends in U.S. Beliefs.* Harrisburg, PA: Morehouse Publishing.

Gans, Herbert J. 1999. *Popular Culture and High Culture: An Analysis and Evaluation of Taste.* New York: Basic Books.

Geertz, Clifford. 1973. "Religion as a Cultural System." In *The Interpretation of Cultures*, 87–125. New York: Basic Books.

Gellner, Ernest. 1969. "A Pendulum Swing Theory of Islam." In *Sociology of Religion: Selected Readings*, edited by Roland Robertson, 127–138. Baltimore: Penguin Books.

Glenn, Charles L. 2000. *The Ambiguous Embrace: Government and Faith-Based Schools and Social Agencies.* Princeton: Princeton University Press.

Goodstein, Laurie. 1998. "Church Debate over Voter Guides." *New York Times*, October 29:A21.

Grandy, Jerilee, and Mark Greiner. 1990. "Academic Preparation of Master of Divinity Candidates." Part of the series *Ministry Research Notes: An ETS Occasional Report.* Princeton: Educational Testing Service.

Greeley, Andrew M. 1989. *Religious Change in America.* Cambridge, MA: Harvard University Press.

———. 1996. "Catholics, Fine Arts, and the Liturgical Imagination." *America* 174, no. 17 (May 18):9–14.

———. 2003. *Religion in Europe at the End of the Second Millenium: A So-ciological Profile.* New Brunswick, NJ: Transaction Publishers.

Green, John C., James L. Guth, Corwin E. Smidt, and Lyman A. Kellstedt, eds. 1996. *Religion and the Culture Wars.* Lanham, MD: Rowman and Littlefield.

Green, John C., M. J. Rozell, and Clyde Wilcox, eds. 2000. *Prayers in the Precincts: The Christian Right in the 1998 Elections.* Washington, DC: Georgetown University Press.

Grettenberger, Susan. 2000. *Churches as a Community Resource and Source of Funding for Human Services.* Washington, DC: Aspen Insti-tute.

Grønbjerg, Kirsten A. 1993. *Understanding Nonprofit Funding: Managing Revenues in Social Services and Community Development Organizations.* San Francisco: Jossey-Bass.

Guide to Charitable Choice: The Rules of Section 104 of the 1996 Federal Wel-fare Law Governing State Cooperation with Faith-Based Social-Service Providers. 1997. Washington, DC: Center for Public Justice and Annandale, VA: Christian Legal Society, Center for Law and Reli-gious Freedom.

Guth, James L., John C. Green, Corwin E. Smidt, Lyman A. Kellstedt, and Margaret M. Poloma. 1997. *The Bully Pulpit.* Lawrence: Uni-versity of Kansas Press.

Hadaway, C. Kirk, Penny Long Marler, and Mark Chaves. 1993. "What the Polls Don't Show: A Closer Look at U.S. Church Attendance." *American Sociological Review* 58:741–752.

———. 1998. "Overreporting Church Attendance in America: Evidence That Demands the Same Verdict." *American Sociological Review* 63:137–145.

Hadden, Jeffrey K. 1969. *The Gathering Storm in the Churches.* Garden City, NY: Doubleday.

Hall, Peter Dobkin. 1996. "Founded on the Rock, Built upon Shifting Sands: Churches, Voluntary Associations, and Nonprofit Organiza-tions in Public Life, 1850–1990." Paper presented at the 1996 Asso-ciation for Research on Nonprofit and Voluntary Associations meetings, November, New York.

———. 1998. "Religion and the Organizational Revolution in the United States." In *Sacred Companies: Organizational Aspects of Reli-gion and Religious Aspects of Organizations,* edited by N. J. Demerath III, Peter Dobkin Hall, Terry Schmitt, and Rhys H. Williams, 99–115. New York: Oxford University Press.

———. 1999. "Vital Signs: Organizational Population Trends and Civic Engagement in New Haven, Connecticut, 1850–1998." In *Civic En-*

gagement in American Democracy, edited by Theda Skocpol and Morris P. Fiorina, 211–248. Washington, DC: Brookings Institution Press and New York: Russell Sage Foundation.

Hall, Stanley R. 1994. "American Presbyterians and the Directory for Worship, 1645–1989." *American Presbyterians* 72:71–85.

Hannan, Michael T., and John Freeman. 1989. *Organizational Ecology*. Cambridge, MA: Harvard University Press.

Harline, Craig, and Eddy Put. 2000. *A Bishop's Tale: Mathias Hovius among His Flock in Seventeenth-Century Flanders*. New Haven: Yale University Press.

Harris, Fredrick C. 1999. *Something Within: Religion in African-American Political Activism*. New York: Oxford University Press.

———. 2001. "Black Churches and Civic Traditions: Outreach, Activism, and the Politics of Public Funding of Faith-Based Ministries." In *Can Charitable Choice Work? Covering Religion's Impact on Urban Affairs and Social Services*, edited by Andrew Walsh, 140–156. Hartford, CT: Leonard E. Greenberg Center for the Study of Religion in Public Life, Trinity College.

Harris, Margaret. 1995. "Quiet Care: Welfare Work and Religious Congregations." *Journal of Social Policy*:53–71.

———. 1998. *Organizing God's Work: Challenges for Churches and Synagogues*. New York: St. Martin's Press.

Harris, Michael W. 1992. *The Rise of Gospel Blues: The Music of Thomas Andrew Dorsey in the Urban Church*. New York: Oxford University Press.

Hart, Stephen. 2001. *Cultural Dilemmas of Progressive Politics: Styles of Engagement among Grassroots Activists*. Chicago: University of Chicago Press.

Hauser, Arnold. 1999. *The Social History of Art*. 3d edition. New York: Routledge.

Hill, Patricia R. 1985. *The World Their Household: The American Woman's Foreign Mission Movement and Cultural Transformation, 1870–1920*. Ann Arbor: University of Michigan Press.

Hodgkinson, Virginia A., and Murray S. Weitzman. 1992. *From Belief to Commitment: The Community Service Activities and Finances of Religious Congregations in the United States*. 1993 edition. Washington, DC: Independent Sector.

Hofferth, Sandra L., and John F. Sandberg. 2001. "Changes in American Children's Time, 1981–1997." In *Children at the Millenium: Where Have We Come From, Where Are We Going? Advances in Life Course Research*, edited by Timothy Owens and Sandra Hofferth, 193–229. New York: Elsevier Science.

Hoge, Dean R., and David A. Roozen. 1979. *Understanding Church Growth and Decline: 1950–1978.* New York: Pilgrim Press.

Hoge, Dean R., Charles Zech, Patrick McNamara, and Michael J. Donahue. 1996. *Money Matters: Personal Giving in American Churches.* Louisville: Westminster John Knox Press.

———. 1998. "The Value of Volunteers as Resources for Congregations." *Journal for the Scientific Study of Religion* 37:470–480.

Hopewell, James F. 1987. *Congregation: Stories and Structures.* Philadelphia: Fortress Press.

Holifield, E. Brooks. 1994. "Towards a History of American Congregations." In *American Congregations.* Volume 2. *New Perspectives in the Study of Congregations,* edited by James P. Wind and James W. Lewis, 23–53. Chicago: University of Chicago Press.

Hood, George. 1846. *A History of Music in New England.* Boston: Wilkins, Carter, and Company.

Hout, Michael, and Claude S. Fischer. 2002. "Why More Americans Have No Religious Preference: Politics and Generations." *American Sociological Review* 67:165–190.

———. 2003. "Religious Diversity in America, 1940–2000." Paper presented at the meetings of the Society for the Scientific Study of Religion, October, Norfolk, VA.

Hout, Michael, Andrew Greeley, and Melissa J. Wilde. 2001. "The Demographic Imperative in Religious Change in the United States." *American Journal of Sociology* 107:468–500.

Hutchison, William R. 1976. *The Modernist Impulse in American Protestantism.* Cambridge, MA: Harvard University Press.

Iannaccone, Laurence R. 1988. "A Formal Model of Church and Sect." *American Journal of Sociology* 94:S241–S268.

Inglehart, Ronald, and Wayne E. Baker. 2000. "Modernization, Cultural Change, and the Persistence of Traditional Values." *American Sociological Review* 65:19–51.

Jackson, Maxie C., John H. Schweitzer, Marvin T. Cato, and Reynard N. Blake. 1997. "Faith-Based Institutions' Community and Economic Development Programs Serving Black Communities in Michigan." Paper presented at the Association for Research on Nonprofit and Voluntary Associations meetings, December, Indianapolis.

Jaffe, Frederick S., Barbara L. Lindheim, and Philip R. Lee. 1981. *Abortion Politics.* New York: McGraw-Hill.

Jelen, Ted G. 1992. "Political Christianity: A Contextual Analysis." *American Journal of Political Science* 36:692–714.

Kalleberg, Arne L., David Knoke, Peter V. Marsden, and Joe L. Spaeth.

1996. *Organizations in America: Analyzing Their Structures and Human Resource Practices.* Thousand Oaks, CA: Sage Publications.

Kalleberg, Arne L., Peter V. Marsden, Howard E. Aldrich, and James W. Cassell. 1990. "Comparing Organizational Sampling Frames." *Administrative Science Quarterly* 35:658–688.

Kloetzli, Walter. 1961. *The City Church: Death or Renewal.* Philadelphia: Muhlenberg Press.

Kohut, Andrew, John C. Green, Scott Ketter, and Robert C. Toth. 2000. *The Diminishing Divide: Religion's Changing Role in American Politics.* Washington, DC: Brookings Institution.

Kramer, Ralph M. 1981. *Voluntary Agencies in the Welfare State.* Berkeley: University of California Press.

Krueger, Joachim, and Russell W. Clement. 1994. "The Truly False Consensus Effect: An Ineradicable and Egocentric Bias in Social Perception." *Journal of Personality and Social Psychology* 67:596–610.

Lamont, Michèle. 1992. *Money, Morals, and Manners: The Culture of the French and American Upper-Middle Class.* Chicago: University of Chicago Press.

Laudarji, Isaac B., and Lowell W. Livezey. 2000. "The Churches and the Poor in a 'Ghetto Underclass' Neighborhood." In *Public Religion and Urban Transformation: Faith in the City,* edited by Lowell W. Livezey, 83–105. New York: New York University Press.

Leege, David C., and Lyman A. Kellstedt. 1993. *Rediscovering the Religious Factor in American Politics.* Armonk, NY: M. E. Sharpe.

Leege, David C., and Michael R. Welch. 1989. "Catholics in Context: Theoretical and Methodological Issues in Studying American Catholic Parishioners." *Review of Religious Research* 31:132–148.

Lichterman, Paul. 2004. *Elusive Togetherness: Religious Groups and Civic Engagement in America.* Princeton, NJ: Princeton University Press.

Lieberson, Stanley. 2000. *A Matter of Taste: How Names, Fashions, and Culture Change.* New Haven: Yale University Press.

Lincoln, C. Eric, and Lawrence H. Mamiya. 1990. *The Black Church in the African American Experience.* Durham: Duke University Press.

Lindner, Eileen W., ed. 2001. *Yearbook of American and Canadian Churches, 2001.* Nashville: Abingdon Press.

Livezey, Lowell W. 2000a. "The New Context of Urban Religion." In *Public Religion and Urban Transformation: Faith in the City,* edited by Lowell W. Livezey, 3–25. New York: New York University Press.

———, ed. 2000b. *Public Religion and Urban Transformation: Faith in the City.* New York: New York University Press.

Lynd, Robert S., and Helen Merrell Lynd. 1929. *Middletown: A Study in Modern American Culture.* New York: Harcourt Brace Jovanovich.

———. 1937. *Middletown in Transition: A Study in Cultural Conflicts.* New York: Harcourt Brace Jovanovich.

Mamiya, Lawrence H. 1994. "A Social History of the Bethel African Methodist Episcopal Church in Baltimore: The House of God and the Struggle for Freedom." In *American Congregations.* Volume 1. *Portraits of Twelve Religious Communities,* edited by James P. Wind and James W. Lewis, 221–292. Chicago: University of Chicago Press.

Manza, Jeff, and Clem Brooks. 1997. "The Religious Factor in U.S. Presidential Elections, 1960–1992." *American Journal of Sociology* 103:38–81.

Mark, Noah. 1998. "Birds of a Feather Sing Together." *Social Forces* 77:453–485.

Marks, Gary, and Norman Miller. 1987. "Ten Years of Research on the False-Consensus Effect: An Empirical and Theoretical Review." *Psychological Bulletin* 102:72–90.

Marsden, Peter V. 1999. "Religion, Cultural Participation, and Cultural Attitudes: Survey Data on the United States, 1998." Report to the Henry Luce Foundation, Department of Sociology, Harvard University.

———. 2001. "Religious Americans and the Arts in the 1990s." In *Crossroads: Art and Religion in American Life,* edited by Alberta Arthurs and Glenn Wallach, 71–102. New York: New Press.

Marsden, Peter V., John Shelton Reed, Michael D. Kennedy, and Kandi M. Stinson. 1982. "American Regional Cultures and Differences in Leisure Time Activities." *Social Forces* 60:1023–49.

Marsden, Peter V., and Lisa Haueisen Rohrer. 2001. "Organizational and Informant Differences in the Reliability of Survey Reports on Organization Size and Age." Paper presented at the American Sociological Association meetings, August, Los Angeles.

Marti, Gerardo. Forthcoming. *A Mosaic of Believers: Diversity and Religious Innovation in a Multi-ethnic Church.* Bloomington: Indiana University Press.

Marty, Martin E. 1991. *Modern American Religion.* Vol. 2. *The Noise of Conflict, 1919–1941.* Chicago: University of Chicago Press.

———. 1994. "Public and Private: Congregation as Meeting Place." In *American Congregations.* Vol. 2. *New Perspectives in the Study of Congregations,* edited by James P. Wind and James W. Lewis, 133–166. Chicago: University of Chicago Press.

Mays, Benjamin Elijah, and Joseph William Nicholson. 1933. *The Negro's Church.* New York: Russell and Russell.

McAdam, Doug. 1982. *Political Process and the Development of Black Insurgency.* Chicago: University of Chicago Press.

McAdam, Doug, Sidney Tarrow, and Charles Tilly. 2001. *Dynamics of Contention.* New York: Cambridge University Press.

McCarthy, John D. 1987. "Pro-life and Pro-choice Mobilization: Infra-structure Deficits and New Technologies." In *Social Movements in an Organizational Society,* edited by Mayer N. Zald and John D. Mc-Carthy, 49–66. New Brunswick, NJ: Transaction.

McCarthy, John, and Jim Castelli. 1998. *Religion-Sponsored Social Service Providers: The Not-So-Independent Sector.* Washington, DC: Aspen Institute.

McMillan, Becky. 2002. "Finding the Invisible Conflict: Perceptions from the Pulpit and Pew." Paper presented at the annual meetings of the Society for the Scientific Study of Religion, November, Salt Lake City.

McMillan, Becky R., and Matthew J. Price. 2003. *How Much Should We Pay the Pastor? A Fresh Look at Clergy Salaries in the Twenty-First Century.* Pulpit and Pew Research Report, Duke University Divinity School.

McPherson, J. Miller. 1982. "Hypernetwork Sampling: Duality and Differentiation among Voluntary Organizations." *Social Networks* 3:225–249.

———. 1983a. "The Size of Voluntary Associations." *Social Forces* 64:1044–64.

———. 1983b. "An Ecology of Affiliation." *American Sociological Review* 48:519–532.

McPherson, J. Miller, and James R. Ranger-Moore. 1991. "Evolution on a Dancing Landscape: Organizations and Networks in Dynamic Blau Space." *Social Forces* 70:19–42.

McPherson, J. Miller, and Thomas Rotolo. 1995. "Measuring the Composition of Voluntary Groups: A Multitrait-Multimethod Analysis." *Social Forces* 73:1097–1115.

McPherson, J. Miller, and Lynn Smith-Lovin. 1987. "Homophily in Voluntary Organizations: Status Distance and the Composition of Face-to-Face Groups." *American Sociological Review* 52:370–379.

McRoberts, Omar M. 2003. *Streets of Glory: Church and Community in a Black Urban Neighborhood.* Chicago: University of Chicago Press.

Miller, Donald E. 1997. *Reinventing American Protestantism: Christianity in the New Millenium.* Berkeley: University of California Press.

Miller, Paul. 1998. "Hunger, Welfare Reform, and Non-profits: Food Banks and Churches." Department of Sociology, University of Montana, Missoula.

Ministry Needs and Resources in the Twenty-First Century. 2000. Chicago: Division for Ministry, Evangelical Lutheran Church in America.

Mohr, John W. 1998. "Measuring Meaning Structures." *Annual Review of Sociology* 24:345–370.

Mohr, John W., and Vincent Duquenne. 1997. "The Duality of Culture and Practice: Poverty Relief in New York City, 1888–1917." *Theory and Society* 26:305–356.

Monsma, Stephen V. 1996. *When Sacred and Secular Mix: Religious Nonprofit Organizations and Public Money.* Lanham, MD: Rowman and Littlefield.

Monsma, Stephen V., and Carolyn M. Mounts. 2001. "Welfare-to-Work: The Comparative Role of Government, For-Profit, Non-Profit, and Faith-Based Agencies in Four Cities." Paper presented at the annual meetings of the Association for Research on Nonprofit Organizations and Voluntary Action, December, Miami.

Morgan, David, and Sally M. Promey. 2001. *The Visual Culture of American Religions.* Berkeley: University of California Press.

Morris, Aldon. 1984. *The Origins of the Civil Rights Movement.* New York: Free Press.

Morris, John R., and Suzanne W. Helburn. 2000. "Child Care Center Quality Differences: The Role of Profit Status, Client Preferences, and Trust." *Nonprofit and Voluntary Sector Quarterly* 29:377–399.

Morse, H. N., and Edmund deS. Brunner. 1923. *The Town and Country Church in the United States as Illustrated by Data from One Hundred Seventy-Nine Counties and by Intensive Studies of Twenty-Five.* New York: George H. Doran Company.

Mullen, Brian, John F. Dovidio, Craig Johnson, and Carolyn Copper. 1992. "In-Group–Out-Group Differences in Social Projection." *Journal of Experimental Social Psychology* 28:422–440.

Nagle, Ami. 2001. "Arizona Head Start Facility Capacity Study." Phoenix: Arizona Head Start Association.

National Endowment for the Arts. 1998. *1997 Survey of Public Participation in the Arts.* Research Division Report 39. Washington, DC: National Endowment for the Arts.

Nemeth, Roger J., and Donald A. Luidens. 1994. "Congregational vs. Denominational Giving: An Analysis of Giving Patterns in the Presbyterian Church in the United States and the Reformed Church in America." *Review of Religious Research* 36:111–122.

Netting, F. Ellen. 1982. "Secular and Religious Funding of Church-Related Agencies." *Social Service Review* (December):586–604.

Netzer, Dick. 1992. "Arts and Culture." In *Who Benefits from the Nonprofit Sector?* edited by Charles T. Clotfelter, 174–206. Chicago: University of Chicago Press.

Niebuhr, Gustav. 1996. "Public Supports Political Voice for Churches." *New York Times*, June 25:A1, C18.

Niebuhr, H. Richard. 1929. *The Social Sources of Denominationalism.* New York: Henry Holt.

Oates, Joyce Carol. 2000. "Pilgrim's Progress." *New York Review of Books* 47 (November 2):30–32.

Olasky, Marvin. 1992. *The Tragedy of American Compassion.* Washington, DC: Regnery Gateway.

Olson, Daniel V. A. 1989. "Church Friendships: Boon or Barrier to Church Growth?" *Journal for the Scientific Study of Religion* 28:432–447.

Olson, Daniel V. A., and Jackson W. Carroll. 1992. "Religiously Based Politics: Religious Elites and the Public." *Social Forces* 70:765–786.

Olson, Laura R. 2000. *Filled with Spirit and Power: Protestant Clergy in Politics.* Albany: State University of New York Press.

Orr, John. 2001. *Religion and Welfare Reform in Southern California: Is Charitable Choice Succeeding?* Los Angeles: Center for Religion and Civic Culture, University of Southern California.

Papaioannou, George. 1994. "The History of the Greek Orthodox Cathedral of the Annunciation." In *American Congregations.* Volume 1. *Portraits of Twelve Religious Communities,* edited by James P. Wind and James W. Lewis, 520–571. Chicago: University of Chicago Press.

Parcel, Toby L., Robert L. Kaufman, and Leeann Jolly. 1991. "Going Up the Ladder: Multiplicity Sampling to Create Linked Macro-to-Micro Organizational Samples." *Sociological Methodology* 20:43–79.

Park, Kristin. 1998. "The Religious Construction of Sanctuary Provision in Two Congregations." *Sociological Spectrum* 18:393–421.

Patillo-McCoy, Mary. 1998. "Church Culture as a Strategy of Action in the Black Community." *American Sociological Review* 63:767–784.

Péli, Gábor, and Bart Nooteboom. 1999. "Market Partitioning and the Geometry of the Resource Space." *American Journal of Sociology* 104:1132–53.

Peterson, Richard A. 1994. "Cultural Studies through the Production Perspective: Progress and Prospects." In *The Sociology of Culture: Emerging Theoretical Perspectives,* edited by Diana Crane, 163–189. Cambridge, MA: Blackwell.

Peterson, Steven. 1992. "Church Participation and Political Participation: The Spillover Effect." *American Politics Quarterly* 20:123–139.

Popielarz, Pamela A., and J. Miller McPherson. 1995. "On the Edge or In Between: Niche Position, Niche Overlap, and the Duration of Voluntary Association Memberships." *American Journal of Sociology* 101:698–720.

Portes, Alejandro. 1998. "Social Capital: Its Origins and Applications in Modern Sociology." *Annual Review of Sociology* 24:1–24.

Presser, Stanley, and Linda Stinson. 1998. "Data Collection Mode and Social Desirability Bias in Self-Reported Religious Attendance." *American Sociological Review* 63:137–145.

Pressley, Calvin O., and Walter V. Collier. 1999. "Financing Historic Black Churches." In *Financing American Religion*, edited by Mark Chaves and Sharon Miller, 21–28. Walnut Creek, CA: AltaMira Press.

Price, Matthew J. 2000. "Place, Race, and History: The Social Mission of Downtown Churches." In *Public Religion and Urban Transformation: Faith in the City*, edited by Lowell W. Livezey, 57–81. New York: New York University Press.

Printz, Tobi Jennifer. 1998. "Faith-Based Service Providers in the Nation's Capital: Can They Do More?" No. 2 in *Charting Civil Society*, a series by the Center on Nonprofits and Philanthropy. Washington, DC: Urban Institute.

Promey, Sally M. 2001. "Pictorial Ambivalence and American Protestantism." In *Crossroads: Art and Religion in American Life*, edited by Alberta Arthurs and Glenn Wallach, 189–231. New York: New Press.

Putnam, Robert D. 2000. *Bowling Alone: The Collapse and Revival of American Community*. New York: Simon and Schuster.

Quinley, Harold E. 1974. *The Prophetic Clergy: Social Activism among Protestant Ministers*. New York: Wiley.

Rappaport, Roy A. 1999. *Ritual and Religion in the Making of Humanity*. New York: Cambridge University Press.

Register of Rhodes Scholars, 1903–1981. 1981. Oxford: Alden Press.

Regnerus, Mark D., David Sikkink, and Christian Smith. 1999. "Voting with the Christian Right: Contextual and Individual Patterns of Electoral Influence." *Social Forces* 77:1375–1401.

Regnerus, Mark D., Christian Smith, and David Sikkink. 1998. "Who Gives to the Poor?" *Journal for the Scientific Study of Religion* 37:481–493.

Reid, Elizabeth J. 1999. "Nonprofit Advocacy and Political Participation." In *Nonprofits and Government: Collaboration and Conflict*, edited by Elizabeth T. Boris and C. Eugene Steuerle, 291–325. Washington, DC: Urban Institute Press.

Ronsvalle, John, and Sylvia Ronsvalle. 2000. *The State of Church Giving through 1998*. Champaign, IL: empty tomb.

Roof, Wade Clark, and William McKinney. 1987. *American Mainline Religion: Its Changing Shape and Future*. New Brunswick, NJ: Rutgers University Press.

Roozen, David A., and Jackson W. Carroll. 1989. "Methodological Issues in Denominational Surveys of Congregations." *Review of Religious Research* 31:115–131.

Roozen, David A., and C. Kirk Hadaway. 1993. *Church and Denominational Growth*. Nashville: Abingdon Press.

Roozen, David A., William McKinney, and Jackson W. Carroll. 1984. *Varieties of Religious Presence*. New York: Pilgrim Press.

Ross, Lee, David Greene, and Pamela House. 1977. "The 'False Consensus Effect': An Egocentric Bias in Social Perception and Attribution Processes." *Journal of Experimental Social Psychology* 13:279–301.

Ruger, Anthony, and Barbara G. Wheeler. 1995. *Manna from Heaven? Theological and Rabbinical Student Debt*. Auburn Studies, no. 3. New York: Auburn Theological Seminary.

Sager, Rebecca, Laura S. Stephens, and Mary Nell Trautner. 2001. "Serving Up God? The Manifestations of Religion in Faith-Based Social Service Organizations." Paper presented at the annual meetings of the American Sociological Association, August, Anaheim.

Salamon, Lester M. 1995a. *Partners in Public Service: Government-Nonprofit Relations in the Modern Welfare State*. Baltimore: Johns Hopkins University Press.

———. 1995b. "Explaining Nonprofit Advocacy: An Exploratory Analysis." Draft paper prepared for delivery at the Independent Sector Spring Research Forum.

Salamon, Lester M., and Fred Teitelbaum. 1984. "Religious Congregations as Social Service Agencies: How Extensive Are They?" *Foundation News* (September–October):62–65.

Sandell, Rickard. 2001. "Organizational Growth and Ecological Constraints: The Growth of Social Movements in Sweden, 1881 to 1940." *American Sociological Review* 66:672–693.

Schmalzbauer, John. 1999. "Bach, Rock, and the Rock of Ages: Religion and Musical Taste in America." Paper presented at the annual meetings of the Association for the Sociology of Religion, August, Chicago.

Schwartz, David. 1998. "Secularization, Religion, and Isomorphism: A Study of Large Nonprofit Hospital Trustees." In *Sacred Companies: Organizational Aspects of Religion and Religious Aspects of Organizations*, edited by N. J. Demerath III, Peter Dobkin Hall, Terry Schmitt, and Rhys H. Williams, 323–339. New York: Oxford University Press.

Scott, W. Richard. 1992. *Organizations: Rational, Natural, and Open Systems*. 3d edition. Englewood Cliffs, NJ: Prentice Hall.

Shaw, Stephen J. 1994. "An Oak among Churches: St. Boniface Parish,

Chicago, 1864–1990." In *American Congregations.* Volume 1. *Portraits of Twelve Religious Communities,* edited by James P. Wind and James W. Lewis, 349–395. Chicago: University of Chicago Press.

Sherkat, Darren E. 1999. "Tracking the 'Other': Dynamics and Composition of 'Other' Religions in the General Social Survey, 1973–1996." *Journal for the Scientific Study of Religion* 38:551–560.

Sherman, Amy L. 1995. "Cross Purposes: Will Conservative Welfare Reform Corrupt Religious Charities?" *Policy Review* (fall 1995):58–63.

———. 2000. *The Growing Impact of Charitable Choice: A Catalogue of New Collaborations between Government and Faith-Based Organizations in Nine States.* Washington, DC: Center for Public Justice.

Shipps, Jan, Cheryll L. May, and Dean L. May. 1994. "Sugar House Ward: A Latter-day Saint Congregation." In *American Congregations.* Volume 1. *Portraits of Twelve Religious Communities,* edited by James P. Wind and James W. Lewis, 293–348. Chicago: University of Chicago Press.

Sider, Ronald J., and Heidi Rolland Unruh. 2001. "Evangelism and Church-State Partnerships." *Journal of Church and State* 43:267–295.

Silverman, Carol. 2000. "Faith-Based Communities and Welfare Reform: California Religious Community Capacity Study: Quantitative Findings and Conclusions." In *Can We Make Welfare Reform Work? California Religious Community Capacity Study,* 66–84. Sacramento: California Council of Churches.

Singh, Jitendra V., and Charles J. Lumsden. 1990. "Theory and Research in Organizational Ecology." *Annual Review of Sociology* 16:161–195.

Skocpol, Theda, and Morris Fiorina, eds. 1999. *Civic Engagement in American Democracy.* Washington, DC: Brookings Institution Press and New York: Russell Sage.

Smith, Christian. 1996. *Resisting Reagan: The U.S. Central America Peace Movement.* Chicago: University of Chicago Press.

———. 1998. *American Evangelicalism: Embattled and Thriving.* Chicago: University of Chicago Press.

Smith, David Horton. 1997. "The Rest of the Nonprofit Sector: Grassroots Associations as the Dark Matter Ignored in Prevailing 'Flat Earth' Maps of the Sector." *Nonprofit and Voluntary Sector Quarterly* 26:114–131.

Smith, Frances Grace. 1931. "The American Revolution Hits Church Music." *New England Quarterly* 4:783–788.

Smith, R. Drew. 2001. "Churches and the Urban Poor: Interaction and Social Distance." *Sociology of Religion* 62:301–313.

Smith, Steven Rathgeb, and Michael Lipsky. 1993. *Nonprofits for Hire: The Welfare State in the Age of Contracting.* Cambridge, MA: Harvard University Press.

Smith, Steven Rathgeb, and Michael Sosin. 2001. "The Varieties of Faith-Related Agencies." *Public Administration Review* 61:651–670.

Smith-Lovin, Lynn, and William Douglass. 1992. "An Affect-Control Analysis of Two Religious Groups." *Social Perspectives on Emotion* 1:217–247.

Spaeth, Joe L., and Diane P. O'Rourke. 1996. "Design of the National Organizations Study." In *Organizations in America: Analyzing Their Structures and Human Resource Practices,* by Arne L. Kalleberg, David Knoke, Peter V. Marsden, and Joe L. Spaeth, 23–39. Thousand Oaks, CA: Sage Publications.

Spillman, Lyn. 1997. *Nation and Commemoration: Creating National Identities in the United States and Australia.* New York: Cambridge University Press.

Stark, Rodney, and William Sims Bainbridge. 1985. *The Future of Religion: Secularization, Revival, and Cult Formation.* Berkeley: University of California Press.

Stark, Rodney, and Roger Finke. 2000. *Acts of Faith: Explaining the Human Side of Religion.* Berkeley: University of California Press.

State of the UCC, 1997. 1997. Cleveland: United Church Board for Homeland Ministries.

Steensland, Brian, Jerry Z. Park, Mark D. Regnerus, Lynn D. Robinson, W. Bradford Wilcox, and Robert D. Woodberry. 2000. "The Measure of American Religion: Toward Improving the State-of-the-Art." *Social Forces* 79:291–319.

Stewart, Donald M., Pearl Rock Kane, and Lisa Scruggs. 2002. "Education and Training." In *The State of Nonprofit America,* edited by Lester M. Salamon, 107–148. Washington, DC: Brookings Institution Press.

Stinchcombe, Arthur L. 1965. "Social Structure and Organizations." In *Handbook of Organizations,* edited by James G. March, 142–193. New York: Rand McNally.

Stone, Melissa M. 2000. "Scope and Scale: An Assessment of Human Service Delivery by Congregations in Minnesota." Paper presented at the Association for Research on Nonprofit Organizations and Voluntary Action meetings, November, New Orleans.

Stout, Harry S., and Catherine Brekus. 1994. "A New England Congregation: Center Church, New Haven, 1638–1989." In *American Congregations.* Volume 1. *Portraits of Twelve Religious Communities,* edited by James P. Wind and James W. Lewis, 14–102. Chicago: University of Chicago Press.

Swidler, Ann. 1986. "Culture in Action: Symbols and Strategies." *American Sociological Review* 51:273–286.

———. 2001. *Talk of Love: How Culture Matters.* Chicago: University of Chicago Press.

Tamney, Joseph B. 1984. "A Quantitative Analysis of Religious Ritual in Middletown: A Research Note." *Sociological Analysis* 45:57–64.

Tarrow, Sidney. 1994. *Power in Movement: Social Movements, Collective Action, and Politics.* New York: Cambridge University Press.

Thomas, Stephen B., Sandra Crouse Quinn, Andrew Billingsley, and Cleopatra Caldwell. 1994. "The Characteristics of Northern Black Churches with Community Health Outreach Programs." *American Journal of Public Health* 84:575–579.

Tilly, Charles. 1978. *From Mobilization to Revolution.* Reading, MA: Addison-Wesley.

———. 1993. "Contentious Repertoires in Great Britain, 1758–1834." *Social Science History* 17:253–280.

———. 1998. *Durable Inequality.* Berkeley: University of California Press.

Treadwell, David O. 2000. "Faith-Based Social Services Don't Need Feds' Money—or Meddling." *Arizona Daily Star,* November 4:E6.

Troeltsch, Ernst. [1911] 1981. *The Social Teaching of the Christian Churches.* Chicago: University of Chicago Press.

Tsitsos, William. 2003. "Race Differences in Congregational Social Activity." *Journal for the Scientific Study of Religion* 42:205–215.

United States Department of Commerce, Bureau of the Census. 1958. "Religion Reported by the Civilian Population of the United States: March 1957." *Current Population Reports: Population Characteristics.* Series P-20, no. 79. Released February 2.

Unruh, Heidi R. 1999. "Saving Souls, Saving Society: The Role of Evangelism in Church-Based Social Ministries." Paper presented at the Religious Research Association meetings, October, Boston.

Verba, Sidney, Kay Lehman Schlozman, and Henry E. Brady. 1995. *Voice and Equality: Civic Voluntarism in American Politics.* Cambridge, MA: Harvard University Press.

Wacker, Grant. 2001. *Heaven Below: Early Pentecostals and American Culture.* Cambridge, MA: Harvard University Press.

Wald, Kenneth D., Dennis E. Owen, and Samuel S. Hill. 1988. "Churches as Political Communities." *American Political Science Review* 82:531–548.

Walker, Chris. 2002. *Arts and Culture: Community Connections.* Washington, DC: Urban Institute.

———. 2003. "Participation in Arts and Culture: The Importance of Community Venues." Washington, DC: Urban Institute.

Walker, Chris, and Stephanie Scott-Melnyk. 2002. *Reggae to Rachmaninoff: How and Why People Participate in Arts and Culture.* Washington, DC: Urban Institute.

Wallis, Jim. 2001. *New York Times,* op-ed, February 3.

Warner, R. Stephen. 1988. *New Wine in Old Wineskins: Evangelicals and Liberals in a Small-Town Church.* Berkeley: University of California Press.

———. 1994. "The Place of the Congregation in the Contemporary American Religious Configuration." In *American Congregations.* Volume 2. *New Perspectives in the Study of Congregations,* edited by James P. Wind and James W. Lewis, 54–99. Chicago: University of Chicago Press.

———. 1997. "Religion, Boundaries, and Bridges." *Sociology of Religion* 58:217–238.

Warner, R. Stephen, and Judith G. Wittner, eds. 1998. *Gatherings in Diaspora: Religious Communities and the New Immigration.* Philadelphia: Temple University Press.

Warren, Mark R. 2001. *Dry Bones Rattling: Community Building to Revitalize American Democracy.* Princeton: Princeton University Press.

Weber, Max. [1920] 1978. *Economy and Society.* Berkeley: University of California Press.

———. [1922] 1991. *The Sociology of Religion.* Boston: Beacon Press.

Wedam, Elfriede. 2000. "Catholic Spirituality in a New Urban Church." In *Public Religion and Urban Transformation: Faith in the City,* edited by Lowell W. Livezey, 213–237. New York: New York University Press.

Wellman, James K. Jr. 1999. *The Gold Coast Church and the Ghetto: Christ and Culture in Mainline Protestantism.* Urbana: University of Illinois Press.

White House. 2001. *Rallying the Armies of Compassion.* White House press release, downloaded from *www.whitehouse.gov/news/reports,* February 24.

Whitehouse, Harvey. 1995. *Inside the Cult: Religious Innovation and Transmission in Papua New Guinea.* New York: Oxford University Press.

Wilcox, Clyde. 1996. *Onward Christian Soldiers? The Religious Right in American Politics.* Boulder: Westview Press.

Wilkes, Paul. 1994. *And They Shall Be My People: An American Rabbi and His Congregation.* New York: Ballantine.

Williams, David R., Ezra E. H. Griffith, John Young, Chiquita Collins, and Juallyne Dodson. 1997. "African-American Churches in New Haven: Correlates of Performance." Department of Sociology, University of Michigan.

Williams, Melvin D. 1974. *Community in a Black Pentecostal Church: An Anthropological Study.* Prospect Heights, IL: Waveland Press.

Wilson, Charles Lee. 1945. "A Social Picture of a Congregation." *American Sociological Review* 10:418–422.

Wilson, John, and Thomas Janoski. 1995. "The Contribution of Religion to Volunteer Work." *Sociology of Religion* 56:137–152.

Wind, James P., and James W. Lewis, eds. 1994. *American Congregations.* Volume 1. *Portraits of Twelve Religious Communities.* Chicago: University of Chicago Press.

Wineburg, Robert J. 1990–91. "A Community Study of the Ways Religious Congregations Support Individuals and the Local Human Services Network." *Journal of Applied Social Sciences* 15:51–74.

———. 1992. "Local Human Services Provision by Religious Congregations: A Community Analysis." *Nonprofit and Voluntary Sector Quarterly* 21:107–117.

———. 1994. "A Longitudinal Case Study of Religious Congregations in Local Human Services." *Nonprofit and Voluntary Sector Quarterly* 23:159–169.

———. 2001. *A Limited Partnership: The Politics of Religion, Welfare, and Social Service.* New York: Columbia University Press.

Winship, Christopher, and Larry Radbill. 1994. "Sampling Weights and Regression Analysis." *Sociological Methods and Research* 23:230–257.

Winston, Diane H. 1999. *Red-Hot and Righteous: The Urban Religion of the Salvation Army.* Cambridge, MA: Harvard University Press.

Wood, James R. 1981. *Leadership in Voluntary Organizations: The Controversy over Social Action in Protestant Churches.* New Brunswick, NJ: Rutgers University Press.

Wood, Richard L. 1994. "Faith in Action: Religious Resources for Political Success in Three Congregations." *Sociology of Religion* 55:397–417.

———. 2002. *Faith in Action: Religion, Race, and Democratic Organizing in America.* Chicago: University of Chicago Press.

Workforce Development Branch. 2000. *Faith-Based Initiative Solicitation for Proposal.* Program Development and Management Division, Employment Development Department, State of California.

Wuthnow, Robert. 1987. *Meaning and Moral Order: Explorations in Cultural Analysis.* Berkeley: University of California Press.

———. 1988. *The Restructuring of American Religion: Society and Faith since World War II.* Princeton: Princeton University Press.

———. 1989. *Communities of Discourse: Ideology and Social Structure in the Reformation, the Enlightenment, and European Socialism.* Cambridge, MA: Harvard University Press.

———. 1991. *Acts of Compassion: Caring for Others and Helping Ourselves.* Princeton: Princeton University Press.

———. 1994. *Producing the Sacred: An Essay on Public Religion.* Urbana: University of Illinois Press.

———. 1999. "Mobilizing Civic Engagement." In *Civic Engagement in American Democracy*, edited by Theda Skocpol and Morris Fiorina, 331–363. Washington, DC: Brookings Institution Press and New York: Russell Sage.

———. 2000. *Linkages between Churches and Faith-Based Nonprofits.* Washington, DC: Aspen Institute.

———. 2003a. *All in Sync: How Music and Art Are Revitalizing American Religion.* Berkeley: University of California Press.

———. 2003b. Personal communication, April 15.

Wuthnow, Robert, and John H. Evans. 2002. Introduction to *The Quiet Hand of God: Faith-Based Activism and the Public Role of Mainline Protestantism*, edited by Robert Wuthnow and John H. Evans, 1–24. Berkeley: University of California Pres.

Wuthnow, Robert, Conrad Hackett, and Becky Yang Hsu. 2003. "The Effectiveness and Trustworthiness of Faith-Based and Other Service Organizations: A Study of Recipients' Perceptions." Paper presented at The Role of Faith-Based Organizations in the Social Welfare System research forum co-sponsored by Independent Sector and Roundtable on Religion and Social Welfare, March, Washington, DC.

Yang, Fenggang, and Helen Rose Ebaugh. 2001. "Transformations in New Immigrant Religions and Their Global Implications." *American Sociological Review* 66:269–288.

Zald, Mayer N., and John D. McCarthy. 1998. "Religious Groups as Crucibles of Social Movements." In *Sacred Companies: Organizational Aspects of Religion and Religious Aspects of Organizations*, edited by N. J. Demerath III, Peter Dobkin Hall, Terry Schmitt, and Rhys H. Williams, 24–49. New York: Oxford University Press.

Zuckerman, Phil. 1999. *Strife in the Sanctuary: Religious Schism in a Jewish Community.* Walnut Creek, CA: AltaMira Press.

Index